Your Towns and Cities in th

Halifax
in the Great War

Your Towns and Cities in the Great War

Halifax
in the Great War

David Millichope

Pen & Sword
MILITARY

First published in Great Britain in 2015 by
PEN & SWORD MILITARY
an imprint of
Pen and Sword Books Ltd
47 Church Street
Barnsley
South Yorkshire S70 2AS

ISBN 978 1 78383 121 0

Printed and bound in England
by CPI Group (UK) Ltd, Croydon, CR0 4YY

Typeset in Times New Roman by Chic Graphics

Pen & Sword Books Ltd incorporates the imprints of
Pen & Sword Archaeology, Atlas, Aviation, Battleground, Discovery,
Family History, History, Maritime, Military, Naval, Politics, Railways,
Select, Social History, Transport, True Crime, Claymore Press,
Frontline Books, Leo Cooper, Praetorian Press, Remember When,
Seaforth Publishing and Wharncliffe.

For a complete list of Pen and Sword titles please contact
Pen and Sword Books Limited
47 Church Street, Barnsley, South Yorkshire, S70 2AS, England
E-mail: enquiries@pen-and-sword.co.uk
Website: www.pen-and-sword.co.uk

Contents

Acknowledgements

This book has had the benefit of research and written articles done by members of the Halifax Great War Heritage Society. Particularly helpful has been the information gathered from the group's work on a project indexing the war-related content of the local newspapers. I am also grateful for the numerous conversations I have had with them to gain those important pieces of information and valuable insights, which were so necessary for the topics included in this book. These have included Rob Hamilton, Elaine Beach, John Sunderland, Graham Bradshaw, Alan Rhodes, Rosemary Jones, Trish Morley, Richard Spendlove, Carla Spendlove and Ann Wilkinson.

I am particularly indebted to David Glover and Rob Hamilton for separately undertaking the onerous but invaluable task of reading through the entire manuscript to check for errors, making suggestions for improvements and adding supplementary information.

Thanks are also due to several other people who undertook to read through sections of the book to provide me with comments and suggestions: George Drake, Aimeé-Fox-Godden, Peter Rhodes, and Jeff Wilkinson.

Particular thanks are due to Stephen Gee who provided so many of the photographs for the book and replied so promptly and comprehensively to all of my requests.

A book of this sort requires the help and co-operation of many individuals and organisations and I am grateful to the following: Pauline Lancaster and all of the staff at the Calderdale Central library for their encouragement, support and advice willingly given at all times. I am particularly grateful for the access we were granted to the hard copies of the *Halifax Courier* and *Halifax Guardian* and the flexible working arrangements that made the task of research so much easier, Richard MacFarlane, Franne Wills, Dr Janette Martin, Angela Clare and Jeff Wilkinson of the Calderdale Museums Service, John Spencer of the Duke of Wellington's West Riding Regiment Museum, John Patchett, Dan Sudro and staff at the West Yorkshire Archives (Calderdale), The National Archives, Andrew Wilkinson for information on Herman van Dyk's diary, David Nortcliffe for information on St John Ambulance Brigade, George Bentley's family for photos and recollections of 'Little Khaki George' and Sheila Shepherd (Librarian) at Rishworth School.

I am also indebted to Dr John Hargreaves for undertaking to review the book for the Transactions of the Halifax Antiquarian Society.

I would also like to acknowledge three locally based websites I used extensively: *Malcolm Bull's Calderdale Companion*, *The John Holdsworth Family* and *Weaver to Web* (Calderdale Library and Information Service website). All reasonable efforts have been taken to establish the copyright status of images used and they are acknowledged with each item. In the case of *Punch* cartoons, I have used those created by artists who died more than 70 years ago and sourced them from either Project Gutenberg (http://www.gutenberg. org/) or the Internet Archive (https://archive.org/index.php). If any copyright holders feel that they have not been correctly acknowledged could they please contact the author at millichope42@gmail.com.

Finally, I must thank my wife, Pat, who has patiently held the home together while I disappeared for the best part of nine months.

Introduction

While writing this book I was very aware of the difficulty of what is meant by 'Halifax'. Today Halifax is a part of the Metropolitan Borough of Calderdale. This was formed in 1974 by the merger of the existing county borough of Halifax, the boroughs of Brighouse and Todmorden, the urban districts of Elland, Hebden Royd, Ripponden, Sowerby Bridge, Queensbury (part) and Shelf (part), and Hepton Rural District.

In terms of population size, Halifax is by far the largest of these districts, and arguably has always been the district's focus. In 1914-19, the provincial newspapers that served these areas and had the largest circulation, were based in Halifax. They were the *Halifax Courier* and the *Halifax Guardian*. Both these newspapers contained news from all the outlying towns, villages and districts but focused on Halifax itself. I have therefore taken my cue from this practice by calling this book *Halifax in the Great War*. Nevertheless, it recognises the relationship that Halifax had with these outlying districts. There are references to people and events from all of the Calderdale districts but no attempt has been made to make this book a proportional view of every district. It remains essentially the story of Halifax in the Great War.

It needs to be said that this publication has the benefit of a project undertaken by the Halifax Great War Heritage Society. This sought to index the war-related content of the local newspapers, particularly the *Halifax Courier* and, to a lesser extent, the *Halifax Guardian* and the *Brighouse Echo* – a formidable task given the huge amount of newsprint. Although local newspapers can be regarded as primary sources, care needs to be taken in their interpretation. We need to ask ourselves whose voices we are listening to. In the case of the *Halifax Courier*, two of them had to be the paper's wartime editors, John Denison and his son William Ernest Denison, both self-proclaimed Liberals.

However, in addition to this, most provincial newspapers tended to reflect what the community, as a whole, was thinking, so we can be fairly sure that this was the case with the Halifax papers. Local newspapers depended on sales and this was not just to a local elite. Most people who bought them would have been members of the working-class.

Whatever interpretation we put on the content of the local newspapers, one thing is clear: once war had been declared the local communities were broadly speaking staunchly supportive of the war effort. This should come as no surprise because studies such as those of Adrian Gregory of Cambridge University and Catriona Pennell of Exeter University have shown that, in this respect, Britain was indeed very united in its support of the war. There were, of course, many exceptions to this and resistance to a war can take many forms. Some of these will be dealt with in the chapters that follow. It is also difficult to put precise figures on dissent because the Defence of the Realm Act (DORA) prohibited 'reports likely to cause disaffection to His Majesty or to interfere with the success of His Majesty's forces'. This effectively imposed censorship on newspapers and it can be argued that we are not hearing a balanced view of the war from them. Censorship was rarely policed at local level for the simple reason that it was not feasible to keep a detailed eye on every provincial newspaper. However, there is documentary evidence in The National Archives of correspondence between the editor of the *Halifax Courier* and the Press Bureau so we must assume that the newspaper was at least trying to abide by guidelines issued by the Press Bureau. This was not just about the more obvious, such as omitting details of where regiments were operating, but also about the degree of content or even whether an item should be run at all. It should come as no surprise that the views of people who, in various ways, opposed the war received rather less news coverage than those who supported it. We must also be mindful that censorship policy was rarely static. What was considered acceptable at the beginning of the war might well have been moderated later in the war.

Despite all this, it must be said that local newspapers were surprisingly 'up front' in their content. Reporting of events was often verbatim, even if we allow for the tendency to be selective. We also need to be aware that there was less of the sensationalist interpretation that can be such a feature of modern day newspapers. A lot of newspaper content was straight reporting and often it is the minutiae that can be very valuable to a researcher. There was a major exception to this: reporting from the battlefronts. This was heavily censored at source. What the local newspapers were given to comment on was, therefore, already a heavily massaged message.

Both the *Halifax Courier* and the *Halifax Guardian* had daily as well as Saturday editions. For simplicity, I have made no distinction between weekday and Saturday editions and have used the titles *Halifax Courier* and *Halifax Guardian* for both.

For the sake of clarity I have taken some liberties with certain conventions. I do not use the term British Expeditionary Force (BEF) when referring to the Western Front. I simply refer to the BEF as the British Army. I do not use the full title of the Duke of Wellington's (West Riding) Regiment. This is simply the West Riding Regiment. When referring to the 1/4 and 2/4 Battalions of the West Riding Regiment I have used instead 4th Battalion West Riding Regiment and Reserve 4th Battalion West Riding Regiment. I believe this will create a clearer distinction for the general reader.

When using quotations from diaries, letters and the local newspapers I have sometimes made minor corrections to grammar and spelling to make the meaning more clear. In some cases I have also given the full version of an abbreviation. If it has been necessary to add extra information to make more sense of the quotation, I have enclosed this in square brackets. Anything in the normal curved brackets was already part of the quotation.

Where monetary values are used I have often included their modern day value (for 2014). This can be notoriously difficult because various factors can be used to indicate what yesterday's money means in today's terms. My personal choice has been to use an index that is relative to peoples earning power and for this I have used the Measuring Worth website, which can be found at http://www.measuringworth.com/. This gave me a factor increase of 150. If you have a personal favourite which is either more or less than this, then I am sure you can do the necessary maths to adjust my value.

This is the story of Halifax in the Great War and it has been necessary to be selective both in what was included and in how much detail. There is a lot of research material available that simply could not be included. The newspapers alone carry more information than could ever be represented here. It should also be borne in mind that, although the subject matter and its sources are treated seriously, this is essentially a story and not an academic survey. Content selection has, therefore, been subjective. Readers may sometimes wonder why I dwell in detail on some topics and give scant or even no attention to others. It became a personal selection that had a lot to do with keeping the text flowing as a narrative. To do otherwise would be to create a textbook for reference only.

The book has been written partly with a local readership in mind so I have included details that are relevant to that audience, such as the names of local people and map locations. Occasionally I have included an explanation of how something has changed since the Great War years. However, the book could equally be used as a case history for a more general reader seeking to understand how a local community fitted into the wider picture, so I ask the general reader to tolerate the local details.

This is by no means an exhaustive bibliography, but some of the local secondary sources on which I have drawn are:

Lee J. A. *Todmorden and the Great War* (Waddington and Sons, 1920)

Crawford, M. *Going to War: People of the Calder Valley and the First Weeks of the Great War* (Hebden Bridge Local History Society, 2013)

Hargeaves J. A. *Halifax* (Carnegie Publishing, 2003)

The Transactions of the Halifax Antiquarian Society (Printed by Smith-Settle)

Bruce C. D. *History of The Duke of Wellington's Regiment (1st and 2nd Battalions)* (Originally published by the Medici Society, 1927. Reprinted by The Naval and Military Press, 2002)

Bales P. G. *History of the 1/4 Battalion, Duke of Wellington's (West Riding) Regiment 1914-19* (Originally published by Edward Mortimer, 1920. Reprinted by The Naval and Military Press, 2002)

Fisher J. J. *History of Duke of Wellington's West Riding Regiment During the First Three Years of the Great War* (1918)

Wyrall E. *The Story of the 62nd (West Riding) Division 1914-19* (Originally published 1924. Reprinted by The Naval and Military Press, 2003)

The book takes a fairly broad sweep of the issues facing Halifax in the Great War and generally speaking follows a chronological path from 1914 to 1919. If I have been successful you should be able to feel how each year of the war brings new surprises and challenges that alter everybody's perceptions of what they are involved in. It begins as an unwanted guest and develops into a nightmare whose proportions no one had fully anticipated.

Each of the issues dealt with in this book could easily be a specialist topic in its own right and I became increasingly aware of the extent of available primary and secondary sources for which I had insufficient time to fully explore. There is nothing like research to uncover the extent of your own ignorance. As I have discovered myself, this book cannot be the final word on Halifax in the Great War. No book can. Even at a local level the subject matter covers a vast field and I hope to explore more of this in the years ahead. I hope I have done justice to the topic areas and would welcome any constructive comment, whether from local or national historians.

Finally, this is a book about how Halifax and its communities experienced the war. It is not a potted history of the war, neither is it a detailed and complete account of the local battalions. However, it is the war that drove Halifax's experience, so it is necessary to provide the context. Often it is the way in which the war was presented to the local communities of Halifax that becomes important, because this shaped how they chose to react. Equally, some of the Halifax responses to the war tell us much about how the country as a whole probably responded. This played a part influencing how the war was conducted at the higher levels. We therefore experience both a top-down bottom-up process. Some might say this is exactly what is meant by total war.

CHAPTER 1

1914
A Very British Way
of Going to War

Good intentions

On 11 July 1914, the Halifax newspapers carried a report which, from the distance of the twenty-first century has a strangely surreal feel to it. Chronologically it fell between the assassination of the heir to the Austro-Hungarian throne, Franz Ferdinand on 28 June, and Britain's entry into the war on 4 August. Oblivious to the sinister wheels that were turning on mainland Europe, a distinguished group of local dignitaries had assembled in Halifax Town Hall to propose the setting up of a Civic Council for Promoting International Friendships. The great and good of Halifax clearly had Germany in mind, although this remained largely unsaid. The *Halifax Courier* claimed that the meeting was 'representative of almost every class politically, religiously and socially', and the delegates wished that the movement would be taken up by other towns throughout the UK.

The account gives us a number of clues as to the mood of the people of Halifax in the immediate weeks before the British declaration of war. The mayor's keynote speech addressed a problem that had been on many people's minds off and on since the turn of the century.

> The present state of things was most deplorable and perilous [...]
> from Halifax alone the contribution that was sent towards the
> upkeep of the Army and Navy was something like £160,000 a year.

This was a direct reference to a need for armaments coupled with a
general unease about Germany, a sense that war was a possibility.
Despite this the mood was buoyant and there was an expectation that
something could and should be done to avoid it. Businessmen pointed
out that war would be disastrous for trade. Plans were proposed to
create links with Germany by exchange visits.

> It was proposed that Halifax the 42nd town in the list of English
> towns in order of population should link up with the 42nd town
> on the German list [...] to put the ordinary man in Halifax into
> touch with the larger world outside [...]

Alderman F. Whitley-Thompson was moved to point out that:

> [...] having in the past years travelled a great deal among
> continental nations I can affirm that the more that different
> nations see of each other the less likely are misunderstandings
> to arise.

Despite the uneasy peace that seemed to trouble the local dignitaries,
there was at this time no sense of any impending catastrophe. At the
beginning of the year Lloyd George himself had declared that relations
with Germany had never been so good. The recent assassination of
Franz Ferdinand had not filled the local newspapers with any anxieties
and there was little discussion over possible escalation into a general
European war. The prospect of an immediate war with Germany was
most emphatically not on most people's agenda in the summer of 1914.
One act of the International Friendships meeting was a letter written
by the two Halifax MPs (J. H. Whitley and James Parker) to Sir Edward
Grey, the foreign secretary. It makes an interesting crossover between
local and national affairs. Sir Edward Grey replied:

> I have received your letter in regards to the Halifax scheme. I
> fear I cannot give official approval to an organisation which is

naturally to be quite independent and to which the government will have no responsibility, but the object in view is one with which I have every sympathy and I have no hesitation in saying that **I see nothing in the scheme that conflicts in any way with the foreign policy of the government** [author's emphasis].

Less than four weeks after Sir Edward Grey's supportive words, Halifax had to cheer off its soldiers to war. It had clearly come as something of a surprise to everyone.

A smouldering crisis
We are more familiar with Britain's entry into World War Two. Nobody was particularly surprised when Neville Chamberlain made his historic radio announcement on 3 September 1939 that 'this country is at war with Germany'. The signs had been there for years and Britain had nearly gone to war in 1938, only to pull back with the signing of the Munich agreement. In 1914 there had been some expectation that war would come some day, but 1914 did not seem to be the likely year. Looking for the causes of a war often needs to ask an obvious question: were there people who wanted a war? There had already been war threatening crises in places such as Morocco and the Balkans, but diplomacy had always brought everyone back from the brink. War had been avoided then because of the simple truth that nobody at that time really wanted a war. Unfortunately for Europe, a mood shift in some German quarters was to upset this balance. One school of thought is clear on this issue. The chief of the German general staff, Helmuth von Moltke, and certain other notable key personnel, had decided they were prepared to go to war. Its motives were rooted in a fear of growing Russian modernisation which one day, it was expected, would threaten Germany's dominance of mainland Europe. Put simply, this German war faction wanted a war to defeat Russia sooner rather than later. Delay, and Russia would become too powerful.

As a plan it had a reasonable chance of success, but Germany's diplomatic performance from start to finish was so cack-handed that her bid for power involved creating too many enemies too quickly. Her chief ally and partner in crime, the Austro-Hungarian Habsburg Empire, also had a war party. In its case, it had the destruction of Serbia in mind. Of course, what it planned for was a short and 'small war' in the Balkans. What it certainly did not want was involvement in a general European war. However, Germany made sure that this was what Austria-Hungary got. The latter nation was not aware that Germany wanted to extend the war and so naively marched off to what proved to be its own nemesis.

The Great War, as it became known, was not inevitable, but the presence of war parties amongst the two nations of Austria-Hungary and Germany made it so. Austria-Hungary lit the fuse and Germany poured flammable liquid all over it. None of this was apparent to anyone, including the British public. It is not surprising to find a lack of interest or alarm as the European crisis unfolded. It was only in the last few days of peace, as war declaration followed war declaration and the armies marched off to war, that the British public caught up with the horrible reality of what was happening. We can see this vividly in the pages of the Halifax local newspapers during the summer months.

On 29 June 1914, the *Halifax Courier* reported the murder in Sarajevo of Franz Ferdinand, the heir to the Austro-Hungarian throne, and his wife. Under almost comic opera circumstances, Gavrilo Princip, a Bosnian-Serb, had managed to fatally shoot the royal couple. This was treated by the Halifax public exactly as it was: an assassination of a prince in a faraway land characterised by places with unpronounceable names. There was little clue that this would become anything more than that. The region was a politically unstable part of Europe that had endured a seemingly endless power struggle between several smaller emerging states and three old empires – Austria-Hungary, Russia and Ottoman Turkey. It was something that commanded little or no interest in Britain and seemed to have as much relevance as a Hans Christian Andersen fairy tale. Almost as if to justify the article's interest value, the *Halifax Courier* informed its readers that the Halifax Madrigal Society had performed in front of the ill-fated royal couple only last year at Windsor Castle.

In the immediate aftermath of the assassination, nobody in Halifax waited with bated breath and nobody really cared. Meanwhile, if you wanted more interesting news in the *Halifax Courier* you could always turn to the next page and read about a 'Midsummer Night's Ramble' or 'Ecclesiastical Table Talk'.

The lull before the storm

The big story of the week was the death of the politician Joseph Chamberlain. He had served in Gladstone's ministries and had been secretary of state for the colonies during the recently fought Boer War. It reminds us that the formative years of the politicians, about to be challenged by the new century's most serious crisis, were rooted in the nineteenth century. Other news included a report of an English rugby football team who had just beaten an Australian team by a margin of 101 to nil. How things have changed. The reporter was in splendid patronising form. 'Of course the match was so one sided that it needs little comment except the ground which was on the hard side.'

In the same issue, the Halifax Women's Suffrage Society pointed out

[…] They regretted very much that certain misguided advocates of women's suffrage had seen fit to damage the cause and their own reputation by methods which for a single moment they could not support […]

This was a clear reference to the militant suffragettes, and was a timely reminder that the actions of the suffragettes were generally unpopular and were not the only forces working for female enfranchisement.

The bank holiday crisis weekend

By the bank holiday weekend of 1 August, it was apparent that something dreadful was happening in Europe. The unfolding crisis had suddenly become newsworthy. Like the rest of the country, Halifax was preparing for the bank holiday weekend. If political thoughts were anywhere, they were on Ireland. A Home Rule Bill was being passed through parliament and Northern Ireland Protestant Unionists had been organising a private army for some time to resist it. Indeed, some members of the British Army were inclined to support it. Civil war threatened. Serious though it was, Northern Ireland was not mainland Britain and it was easy to get into holiday mood and push the Irish Question to the back of your mind.

Other things were also happening in Europe that looked troublesome. The long forgotten assassination of the heir to the Austrian throne had suddenly resurfaced and turned ugly. Austria had declared war on Serbia and Russia had started mobilising her forces to support her. A local war in the Balkans now seemed unstoppable. That still did not intrude into Halifax holiday thoughts too much. Who cared about Serbia? To those more familiar with European politics there was one very sinister development. Germany had declared martial law in response to Russia's mobilisation. Most of that would go over the heads of the average man or woman in the streets of Halifax but, brushing aside the diplomatic niceties, the stark reality was that Germany and Russia were on the brink of war with each other. Some people were alarmed. The *Halifax Courier* reported extraordinary measures at the Bank of England where investors had been converting paper money into gold. The bank declared an unprecedented four-day bank holiday. The Foreign Office , on the other hand, was playing down the severity of events. The *Halifax Courier* carried its advice, which was:

> The Foreign Office wish it to be known that there is no reason to believe at the present that British subjects travelling or residing on the Continent are in any danger, though they may be put to considerable inconvenience […] ordinary train services […] may be entirely suspended.

Elsewhere in the paper the Press Association had said, 'There has been no marked development in the European situation to affect this country.'

All of this spoke volumes for how quickly events had been unfolding. The truth was that everyone had been caught with their pants down. It is remarkable how in one week the mood of the country turned from 'What's it got to do with us?' into 'We must win this war at all costs.' It was as true of Halifax as anywhere else. On 1 August, the editor of the *Halifax Courier* was writing:

> It is lamentable to see efforts being made in this country to embroil us should there be a general war […] Are we to be rushed by jingoes into active interference? Let our countrymen beware!

By 8 August he had done a complete U-turn:

[…] the unscrupulous action of the Germans, their complete disregard of the neutrality of Belgium and Luxemburg to which they were parties has developed the situation terribly […] For us it is a life and death struggle with Germany.

Why did the week turn on its head in such a dramatic way, and how did Britain's position change from non-intervention into 'a life and death struggle with Germany'? If the weekend crisis is seen as some sort of tragic accident, in which Europe's leaders were somehow 'sleepwalking into war', it does not add up. The timescale was far too sharp to explain war by absent mindedness. Instead, events need to be seen as the product of a cynically executed plan by men who sought war; a flawed plan as it turned out.

The war party in Germany needed and wanted a war with Russia. This, they understood, also meant war with Russia's ally, France. The plan was to first quickly knock out France and then turn and defeat Russia. Timing was everything. It had two essential requirements: a backdoor into France and speed of operation. It is indicative of the dysfunctional way in which German foreign policy was conducted at the time, that the invasion of Belgium was chosen as Germany's backdoor strategy. Whatever diplomatic space remained for keeping Germany's opposition divided was lost by this one crass act. She created a ready-made crusade that in the long-run pitted Germany against a substantial proportion of the world's economic might. In the immediate short term, it neutralised most of Britain's non-intervention supporters. Even many of the British anti-war factions were incensed by what the Germans had done to Belgium. Democracies do not go to war easily, but three days after Leach and Warburton of Gibbet Street were still advertising holiday trips to Belgium in the *Halifax Courier*, Britain had declared war on Germany. There were more than one or two continental British holidaymakers who were embarrassed by the suddenness of it all.

The *Halifax Courier* of 8 August 1914 was full of stories:

Sir George Armytage (chairman of the Lancashire and Yorkshire Railway Company) and Lady Armytage are believed to be stranded in Germany, and considerable anxiety as to their safety is felt by the family and friends […] Sir George and Lady

HOLIDAYS—Personally Conducted Tours to
BELGIUM AND THE ARDENNES,
via Hull and Zebrugge,
leaving Halifax and district every Saturday until Sept. 26
EIGHT DAYS, at an inclusive sum of £5 5s.
Full programmes free from
LEACH & WARBURTON, 350, Gibbet-st., Halifax.
Telephone 788.

Halifax Courier *1 August 1914. Advertisement for Belgian holidays.*

> Armytage left England last Wednesday for Homburg [...]
> Nothing has been heard from them since their departure.
> Attempts have been made to get in touch with them by Telegraph
> but no reply has been received. They subsequently arrived safely
> back in Yorkshire.

An unnamed 'Halifax gentleman' was in Germany at the time and
experienced reactions firsthand.

> I heard that things were getting worse and I got my passport [...]
> Events progressed rapidly... About 6 p.m. news came that the
> mobilisation order had been given at Berlin. The whole town
> was in a fever of excitement [...] Banks were bombarded by
> panic stricken people [...] Food stores were packed out [...] I
> have never seen anything like it [...] One girl wept because her
> father had to join his regiment [...] There were fearful scenes
> on the streets – women crying, men excited or drunk, partings
> and so on [...] I took the 8.10 train to Basel [...] In the train were
> soldiers with guns and full equipment, going to their regiments.

Similarly, the 15 August 1914 edition of the *Halifax Courier* carried
other firsthand reports:

> Mr. Louis Thurley [...] Sowerby Bridge [...] Employed in [a]
> shipping office [...] in Antwerp [...] When the rupture occurred
> with Germany [...] Scenes in the streets were indescribable [...]

The efforts of the police were unable to prevent ugly demonstrations being made against the Germans and all German property. The homes and shops of these foreigners were attacked, particularly the cafes, and ruined.

A woman adventurer by the name of Mrs Harry Humphries had to interrupt her world tour and suddenly appeared at the home of her father in Sowerby Bridge. She had been on the continent for over a year and had come straight from Germany. The *Halifax Courier* reported:

After two or three days came the declaration of war. Just before leaving Germany, Mrs Humphries had many opportunities of seeing how the people behaved after war had been declared. She says that when Germans are getting ready for war they have a privilege of taking a last drink together in a cafe or restaurant [...] I found the men very noisy, singing battle songs day and night. The streets were black with people, and all the cafes and restaurants were full to overflowing with excited and gesticulating Germans [...] In Cologne I stayed in a hotel right in the Main Street [...] All night long soldiers were marching to arms [...] I saw hundreds of cavalry pass in the middle of the night, their long spears glittering in the dark, and all were singing and shouting [...] I tell you it was a sight I shall not forget – it was bloodcurdling! [...] The Germans blame the Russians for starting to interfere with Serbia and Austria [...] During the last few days she spent in France, Belgium, Germany, and Holland she says the people were excited to the verge of panic, and nothing but militarism was evident [...] The intensity of feeling was evident everywhere.

Responses to the outbreak of war

By the following weekend of 8 August, the *Halifax Courier* was full of the war. There had been precious little time to assess the rapidly changing situation, but it is clear from the newspaper's contents that events had quickly overtaken the thoughts of many of the paper's contributors as the week unfolded.

The Albion Street Adult School was still talking in terms of a limited war. They asked 'the townspeople of Halifax to unite in a strenuous effort to support Sir Edward Grey in his efforts for peace and for limiting the area of conflict of the war'.

Rev'd John Naylor of Square Church Brotherhood was one step ahead, but was urging neutrality:

> The shadow of a war of unparalleled magnitude is flowing across the continent of Europe [...] which will dwarf into comparative insignificance the armies of Napoleon [...] ought we to fight? This question the rev. gentleman answered in the negative.

James Parker, one of Halifax's two MPs, still held out hope that something could be done to stop the war:

> I have done all I could by working with all of those who desired to keep England out of the war. We have failed. War is declared. We will still work for peace and mediation at the first available opportunity.

The local branch secretary of the recently formed Neutrality League, E.W. Collinson, a local Quaker, inserted a huge one-page advert in the *Halifax Guardian* and the *Halifax Evening Courier* and organised a mass-distribution of leaflets to Halifax households. The war had nothing to do with Britain and she should stay out. The league linked the message to the unwelcome spectre of a victorious and dominant Russia. It was assisted by about fifty members of Square Church PSA Brotherhood, who met to divide Halifax into districts for the purpose of distributing 30,000 handbills. Despite protests from some of the attendees that 'it was already too late', the distribution went ahead.

The MP for Elland, Charles Trevelyan, a minister in Asquith's Liberal government, was very clear that it was all a dreadful mistake. He profoundly disagreed with the policy and actions of the Foreign Secretary and had marked his views by immediately resigning from the government. By way of explanation to his Elland constituents, he requested that the *Halifax Courier* print a letter setting out his views:

> [...] neither the original quarrel nor the remoter conflicts arising out of it ought to have been regarded as involving ourselves [...] it is not worth the life of a single British soldier.

BRITONS, DO YOUR DUTY

and keep your country out of a WICKED and STUPID WAR.

Small but powerful cliques are trying to rush you into it; you must

DESTROY THE PLOT TO-DAY or it will be TOO LATE.

Ask yourselves:
WHY SHOULD WE GO TO WAR?

THE WAR PARTY say...

All these reasons are false.

THE WAR PARTY DOES NOT TELL THE TRUTH.
The Facts are these:-

It is your duty to save your country from this disaster.

ACT TO-DAY OR IT
MAY BE TOO LATE.

THERE ARE A THOUSAND THINGS YOU CAN DO IF YOU REALLY LOVE YOUR COUNTRY.

Distribute the leaflets of the NEUTRALITY LEAGUE.

WE WANT HUNDREDS OF HELPERS!

Write or call on the Local Secretary:

E. W. COLLINSON. ST. JOHN'S PLACE. HALIFAX.

Full page advertisement placed by the Neutrality League, an organisation founded by long-time proponent of peace Sir Norman Angell. Halifax Courier 4 August 1914.

He deplored the tendency to regard Germany as the natural enemy, something he believed was the product of elitist influence. He also reinforced the point made by the Neutrality League:

[…] Russia will be victorious, with its savage recuperative forces of countless populations to brood over our stricken western civilisation.

It was a letter full of popular appeal for the working-classes and at the same time Trevelyan positioned himself as a patriot:

As the war proceeds more and more of the workers [will be] drawn into the fighting ranks and the breadwinners [will] disappear […] Blunder or no blunder the war is here […] and our simple common duty is to help to save our dear country.

Charles Trevelyan was to remain an outspoken and controversial figure throughout the war and later became a founder member of the Union of Democratic Control (UDC). This was a body that resisted Britain's subsequent move towards its increasingly militarist and authoritarian methods of conducting the war. After the war the UDC became more overtly pacifist and fifteen of its members served in the 1924 Labour government.

Local politician F. Whitley-Thomson pointed out what he believed was the 'falsity of Mr Trevelyan's position' – Germany's active encouragement of Austria's invasion of Serbia, her reluctance to come to the conference table and 'the cavalier way in which she pounced on Belgium'. He feared the prospect of Germany acquiring the port of Antwerp, which had been likened by many to a 'gun pointing at Britain's head'.

Rev'd Edward Kiek represented a viewpoint that most closely matched where the majority of people eventually positioned themselves:

I have been asked by friends in Halifax to use what little influence I possess on behalf of peace. It is, however, sufficiently clear that the peace of Europe has been endangered not by any action of ours but by the wanton violation of Belgian neutrality perpetrated by the armed forces of Germany […] I was strenuously opposed to any armed intervention on the part of Britain […] but Germany has […] made it clear that neither treaty rights nor moral obligations will be allowed to stand in the way of her military plans […] can anyone view with equanimity the acquirement by military Germany of what is practically the domination of Europe.

It was a viewpoint generated by fear and sustained by moral indignation, and persisted for the duration of the war. There was never anything in Germany's subsequent actions that dissuaded them that they had got it wrong.

There was, of course, a small if significant element that could never reconcile itself to the view that there was any point to the war. Local suffragette Lavena Saltonstall, who was by 1914 heavily involved in education, wrote from Oxford:

> [...] men with whom we have studied and fraternised for the last four or five years are being hauled up to take their part in the defence of England, and incidentally to fight with other men who year by year have come over from Europe to share our studies and recreations.

After 8 August it became increasingly difficult for views such as this to be expressed. The Defence of the Realm Act (DORA) and the self-censorship of Britain's newspapers rarely afforded much room to question whether the war was worthwhile.

War enthusiasm?

It has been an article of faith for some time now that the communities of the United Kingdom went off to war with a jingoistic enthusiasm. Adrian Gregory in his book *The Last Great War* has provided much evidence that the extent of war enthusiasm has been overstated and should be replaced by a more complex view of the responses. The Halifax MP, James Parker of the Independent Labour Party (ILP), was in London when war was declared. His eye witness account appears to conform to the traditional view that London did in fact exhibit the classic jingoistic response:

> London is back in Mafficking mood and the blood lust has gripped its people [...] I wish I could blot from my memory the scenes of the last three days [...] I confess I was appalled with the light hearted recklessness of my fellow men and women. Judging by the demonstrations of the crowd it might have been a picnic the nation was entering upon instead of the greatest crisis of a century – shouting, singing, cheering mobs beside themselves with blood lust and war intoxication [...] Inside the House of Commons there was a recklessness and enthusiasm for war that was horrible to witness. [...] The Tories cheered wildly. They wanted a fight with Germany [...]

James Parker, as an ILP Member of Parliament, held strongly anti-war views and may have unwittingly exaggerated the jingoism. Maybe what he witnessed on the streets was a drunken holiday crowd getting swept along by events. Nevertheless, an element of Jingoism existed. But was London typical? James Parker hoped the provincial towns were 'meeting the crisis in a far more serious mood'. Significantly, the local Halifax newspapers did not report any scenes approaching those of London.

The *Halifax Guardian* of 5 August reported that crowds had gathered on the previous evening and had become more animated:

> [...] the tension upon the public spirit was great, and yet it was discreetly held within bounds. It was more of an emotional excitement [...] a resignation and brave submission to the inevitable.

The editorial in the *Halifax Courier* of 8 August noted 'regret that the war is necessary is universal, for friendly feeling was slowly growing with Germany'.

William Henry Stott of West Vale recorded in his diary on 5 August, '11 o' clock last night war was declared against Germany, the greatest excitement prevails.' Excitement does not, of course, equate to jingoism and in Halifax at least it was a mixture of disbelief, alarm and emotional support for the soldiers about to march off for an uncertain future. These events were as likely to include weeping mothers as enthusiastic well-wishers.

What is this war going to be like?
The perceptions of the Halifax general public to the outbreak of war in 1914 must have been a bewildering mix of contradictions. War had taken everyone by surprise and events were moving quickly. Whilst adjusting to yesterday's news, there was always something new that entered the mix. As troops were mobilised, what did people think they were getting involved in? Certainly misconceptions and half-truths must have mingled with what factual information was available.

It is often said we go to war based on our recollections of the last war. In the case of the Halifax public the last wars were the various empire 'small wars', of which the Boer War was the most recent, although memories of Kitchener in the Sudan would not have been far away. Generally speaking there had been an element of empire romanticism about these wars, re-inforced no doubt, by the remoteness of the action and a feeling that British innate superiority would always win through. Most of the opposition were after all ethnic natives. It is true the South African Boers, who were of European stock, had been something of a shock, but even they had insufficient resources to ultimately defeat the British Empire. This somewhat rose-tinted view of warfare may well have been reinforced by the vivid imagery of childhood stories and contemporary adventure novels.

Germany was of course different. She was closer and infinitely more threatening. The myth that the British people wanted to go to war, and indeed saw it with a high degree of enthusiasm, has now been largely discredited. The *Halifax Courier* soberly expressed a general feeling that this was going to be a war of many casualties. Local MP James Parker also clearly understood this. The tone of the newspaper suggested that Halifax was battening down the hatches for a reasonably long haul and was expecting to have to cope with many types of social distress caused by the war. The *Halifax Guardian* (4 August 1914) declared on the eve of war:

> For ourselves, however, we think it difficult indeed to rebut the main arguments of Sir Edward Grey. War is hateful, atrocious, bloody. It means on the present scale at any rate, an intensity of suffering which nobody for the time being can actually imagine. There will be heavy financial losses, but that is small to the enormous toll that will be paid in human life. Households will be destroyed and whole countrysides devastated. And for what? The rectification in the end, perhaps, of a few Continental boundary lines […] but on the other hand there is honour and also obligation. The [Neutrality] League's manifesto does not suggest Germany is the aggressor, but seems to incline to lay the blame on Russia and France. To us this is not so. The torch has been lit by the Kaiser.

Mobilisation

Halifax, more than most places, had experience of what going to war meant, because it was a garrison town. The Halifax Barracks on Gibbet Street was the home depot of the Duke of Wellington's West Riding Regiment.

The 1st and 2nd battalions of the West Riding Regiment consisted of regular soldiers. They were the full-time professional soldiers who enlisted for a set number of years and could be sent on active service anywhere. In August 1914, the 1st battalion was on empire duty in India and the 2nd battalion was stationed in Dublin.

After completing their service, regular soldiers were required to serve a period of five years in the reserve when they could be called back into the army.

The 3rd battalion of the West Riding Regiment initially consisted of special reservists. These completed six months full-time training then returned to civilian life without serving in the army. They made up part of the national reserve but differed from the other reservists, who were ex-regular soldiers.

The 4th, 5th, 6th and 7th battalions consisted of Territorials. They were part time soldiers who attended for training once a week and a more extensive fortnight camp once a year. In peacetime they remained as civilians who lived at home. In times of national emergency they could be called-up for military duties but had signed-up for home duties only. Of these the only one that was based in Halifax and made up mainly of local men was the 4th Battalion. The other three were based respectively in Huddersfield (5th Battalion), Skipton (6th Battalion) and Milnsbridge (7th Battalion).

The war with Germany was going to involve a radically different mobilisation experience to the Boer war of 1899-1902. The 1st Battalion (regulars) West Riding Regiment remained in India throughout the war. They therefore played no part in the European theatre except for soldiers who were transferred from there. In Dublin, the 2nd Battalion West Riding Regiment received their orders to mobilise on the night of 3/4 August. In his book *Going to War*, Mike Crawford relates the feelings of their commander, Lieutenant Colonel Gibbs:

> The news was at once passed round being received with cheers by the youngsters […] although I can't help thinking some of us older soldiers […] received it with somewhat mingled feelings.

Many reservists reported to the Halifax Barracks before setting off to Dublin to join the battalion. On 13 August, 2nd Battalion West Riding Regiment left Dublin for France (Havre) on the ship HMS *Gloucester*.

Reservists recalled to the Halifax Barracks on Gibbet Street leave to join the 2nd Battalion West Riding Regiment on 7 August 1914. Stephen Gee Collection.

On 22 August it crossed the Belgian border as part of 13 Brigade (5th Division) and encamped around St Ghislain, not far from Mons. It was in action the next day. Halifax's war had started in earnest.

Over the bank holiday weekend the 4th Battalion West Riding Regiment were away on their annual training at Marske (North Yorkshire). Not surprisingly there was a sense of anticipation as they all became aware of the deepening European crisis. The German ultimatum to Belgium had been presented and rejected on 2 August. Germany had declared war on France the following day. In the early hours of Tuesday 4 August, the Territorials were ordered to return to their respective homes in and around Halifax, but to remain in a state of readiness. Despite arriving in the early hours they were met at Halifax Station by a cheering crowd of several hundreds.

The *Halifax Guardian* of 5 August continued the story of the previous day:

> Early in the evening the order arrived for mobilisation of all forces. The men of the 4th Battalion (Territorials) Duke of Wellington's Regiment […] began to make their appearance in

the thoroughfares in their Khaki uniforms […] making their way to the Drill Hall […] the public thoroughfares became more animated […] encouragement to the 'boys' or in any event a look of admiration and hope […]

They were billeted overnight in the Council Secondary School between Prescott Street and Oxford Road.

A busy day of mobilisations was on 5 August. The *Halifax Guardian* reported the departure of the 4th Battalion West Riding Regiment to their training destinations:

Inside the Drill Hall was a scene of greatest activity, but there was such a precision and regularity observed in all the work […] stores were all packed and taken to the station on lurries [sic] and flat carts […] mid-day there was a general inspection by the Commanding Officer […] assembled in the grounds of the Secondary School […] bugle sounded the 'fall in' […] the men marched out into Prescott Street, along Portland Place and thence down Horton Street to the Station […] immense crowds lined the footpaths and carriageways, the whole distance […]

4th Battalion West Riding Regiment (Territorials) marching down Horton Street as they leave on 5 August 1914 for the East Coast and eventually moving on to Doncaster. Stephen Gee Collection.

given a most enthusiastic send off with rousing cheers [...] for
the moment the war and its terrible consequences were forgotten
in the more genial feature of wishing God speed and good luck
to the departing Territorials.

The commander was Lieutenant-Colonel Atkinson and they were
believed to be going to Doncaster before being drafted to the East Coast
(Hull and Grimsby). Here they would be brought up to full strength.
Territorials were not obliged to serve abroad but when asked the
majority opted for foreign service.

It was not just infantry. Men of the Royal Army Medical Corps
reported to Wakefield. The 'D' company of the Queen's Own Yorkshire
Dragoons, who had been recruited from Halifax, Bradford and
Huddersfield, joined the headquarters in Huddersfield. At 9.00 am 160
Artillerymen reported to Arden Road Barracks, the headquarters of the
Halifax Battery of the West Riding Royal Field Artillery (RFA). They
were expected to be sent to Bradford.

Over by Christmas?

It is one of those givens of the Great War that everyone in Britain and
on the continent thought it was all going to be 'Over by Christmas'.
This phrase was virtually absent from the pages of the *Halifax Courier*.
Where it occurs at all, it is found only in the letters of soldiers or
soldiers' wives. In reality most British people's ideas of the war's
duration were very variable, with many newspaper references
preparing everyone for a relatively long haul. So why did this phrase
become so much a part of Great War mythology?

The kaiser had famously said that the German Army would be
'home before the leaves have fallen'. The strategic calculation for
Germany was simple: provoke a war and knock out France quickly,
then turn on Russia. Speed was essential. Germany had to have a short
war, otherwise she would lose. This may have gained a degree of
currency and might have been reinforced by the tendency of all soldiers
going off to war to say they would soon have the job done: over by
Christmas in fact. It served to reassure the families back home and at
the same time was a coping mechanism for the soldiers themselves. It
is also possible that recruiting sergeants were not above using the
phrase in an effort to encourage enlistment.

The local Halifax papers were full of the belief that 'Germany had bitten off more than she could chew' or 'her resources would be quickly overwhelmed'. The prevailing belief was that if the Allies could survive the initial onslaught, Germany would then be overwhelmed by their combined might. The tone of the Halifax newspapers was based on this belief. Germany's defeat was inevitable and imminent, maybe not next week, maybe not next month, but quite possibly within a year or less. Victory was assured and just round the corner.

The majority view might have been that the war was here for a while, although few could have predicted just how long it was going to take. Kitchener himself, often quoted as the archetypal 'long war' prophet, thought in terms of three years. The tragedy of the situation was that Germany did not just roll over and die some time in 1915 or 1916, or even 1917. If Germany could not win she was difficult to beat. Time and time again she demonstrated her resilience to keep fighting. More and more the local communities of the Halifax district were exhorted to provide more blood, more money and more production. Right up till the crisis point in the winter of 1917/18 the belief persisted that the end of the war was imminent.

The question of Belgium
Reading the pages of the *Halifax Courier* for 1914-18 it is difficult not to be impressed by the amazing display of communal solidarity that was buoyed up by an unshakable belief in the justice of the cause and a resolute determination to see the war through to nothing but complete victory. What secret force drove communities to maintain this solidarity to the very end despite the butcher's bill? Patriotism is frequently offered to explain this, but by itself seems to fall short of fully explaining the phenomenon. 'For king and country' had its appeal, but it is necessary to see patriotism in the context of one's own community as the centre of one's world. It was this local patriotism that proved to be an additional driving force that maintained communal solidarity, the belief that the people of the local communities were fighting to protect their very own 'hearth and home'.

The invasion of Belgium was a potent propaganda gift that operated at many levels, the moral gloss for going to war in the first place, as an appeal to uncommitted neutral nations, and also significantly it struck at the heart of local patriotism. What would happen if German militarism threatened to enter your own backyard? The answer was plain to see in Belgium, and the German Army was about to hand over yet another propaganda gift that would reinforce its image as the barbarous Hun.

The German Army invaded neutral Belgium on 3 August 1914, precipitating Britain's entry into the war on 4 August. Over the next two weeks the Germany Army proceeded to occupy most of Belgium. Fearing that the Belgians might employ guerrilla tactics to slow down the German Army's advance, it announced a policy of hostage-taking and reprisals to discourage this. Inevitably the war involved the displacement of considerable numbers of Belgian civilians, many of whom fled to Britain and other neighbouring countries, carrying with them alarming atrocity stories. Although it was subsequently revealed that some of the stories were layered with exaggerations, often of a perversely sexual nature, there remains ample evidence that the German Army was indeed brutally ruthless in its haste to pass through Belgium and get around the back of the French armies.

Several towns and villages in the path of the German Army were subjected to burnings, lootings and more alarmingly, executions of sizeable numbers of civilians. The pretext had been supposed small-arms fire on German soldiers. This was almost certainly mistaken fire in the confusion of battle. Whatever it was, it did not matter. The German troops were nervous, jumpy and under orders to deal severely, by example, in the event of any hint of civilian resistance. The end result was the indiscriminate massacre of about 6,000 civilians, including some women and children. The burning of the ancient city of Louvain, including its priceless medieval library, reported in both the *Halifax Courier* and *Halifax Guardian* at the end of August, came to symbolise what everyone believed they were fighting against.

Reports such as these found their way into British newspapers and clearly had a profound effect on the public. William Henry Stott writing in his diary on 2 September 1914 was moved to say:

Poor Belgium has suffered terribly, the barbaric Germans have burnt and murdered women and children, the passion of the civilised world is roused at this devilish work.

Germany was, yet again, playing into the hands of the propagandists.

By October 1914, the secretary to the Local Government Board had sent out information to local communities informing them that a large number of Belgian refugees were now arriving in England, and that offers of hospitality for them was needed. He asked that any persons able and willing to receive refugees should communicate with the War Refugee Committee based in London. Like many other communities, Halifax responded positively.

It seems likely that government involvement in the housing of 250,000 Belgian refugees throughout Britain was free of any propaganda intent. However, trainloads of forlorn Belgian refugees were despatched into countless local communities to be eagerly interviewed by local journalists all too willing to believe whatever stories they cared to tell. The *Halifax Courier* reported on 17 October 1914 that:

> Mr H. Van Dyke [...] welcoming them at the station [...] was afraid the reports of German atrocities as reported in the English press were only too true [...] The old man [a refugee] told him he personally saw four youths fetched out of a church and shot.

Every arrival was a walking propaganda poster to the evils of Hun barbarism. It had a local immediacy that the national newspapers could never hope to simulate. In the context of the ongoing recruitment campaign and the need to keep civilian morale firmly on course, it is difficult to find a more effective and wide-ranging propaganda tool. The mayor spoke to the people of Halifax:

> [...] we promise to stand by the Belgian people and to fight the cause until we have put down this military tyrant who has infested Belgium and would do the same with England (applause from the refugees).

The government could not have put it better.

Aliens: an unenviable situation
Britain in 1914 was not a good place to be if you were a German, were of German descent or even if you sounded vaguely German. Before August 1914, Britain had been a relatively open and liberal place to

Belgian refugees arrive at Halifax Station, October 1914. Calderdale Museum Services.

live. Almost overnight, following the declaration of war, it became increasingly xenophobic.

The Aliens Registration Act of 1914 was rushed through parliament at the beginning of the war and required all 'enemy aliens' over 16 to register with police. The Aliens Restriction Act gave the home secretary the power to order the deportation of enemy aliens if it was deemed 'conducive to the public good'. In practice, all 'enemy aliens' of military age were allowed to return to their country of origin. The problems lay with residents who were 'enemy aliens' but no longer regarded themselves as belonging to their country of birth. Some were British citizens, but others were not. Some were simply descendants of enemy aliens. Their presence clearly caused some discomfort amongst the native British population.

Alarmist stories of the 'enemy within' resulted in a wave of spy mania across the country. The *Halifax Courier* reported several spy stories from areas outside Halifax, but in 1914, stories such as these in Halifax's own back yard were virtually non-existent.

These stories were, nevertheless, probably sufficient to heighten people's anxieties. When a gas explosion occurred on the Ryburn Valley railway line on 27 August 1914, many people were prepared to believe the worst:

The bright lurid illumination [...] could be seen [...] for considerable distances. With imagination readily aroused [...] people living some distance away [...] evolved all kinds of alarmist theories.

The *Halifax Courier* continued to be unimpressed by spy mania. On 10 October 1914, it observed that elsewhere around the country 'the crusade against aliens and spies is increasing, and stories about them are so extravagant as to be beyond belief'. Of course in 1914 Halifax had no obvious reason to feel that it might be awash with spies. With the exception of the Halifax Barracks it had no naval or military significance. Neither did it have any significant German communities. The Yorkshire coast was far more jumpy and there were stories of 'mysterious lights [...] especially in Robin Hood's Bay [...] said to have been seen at sea [...] and apparently in correspondence with those on land'.

It may be that spy mania throughout the country has been overstated. Spy stories, both real and imaginary, found their way into newspapers and perhaps gave the impression that they were more common than was the case. Tellingly, the *Halifax Courier* reported at some length the exasperation of Mr McKinnon Wood, the Secretary of State for Scotland, in dealing with 'somewhat alarming statements' concerning aliens in Scotland made by the Earl of Crawford and Balcarres in the House of Lords in November 1914. The earl made claims variously to a 'German detected tampering with official messages', 'night signalling from our shores to ships in the Firth of Forth', 'illegal importation of dynamite', ships that must have been dropping mines because their coal bunkers were three-quarters full of sawdust, and an alien enemy allowed to 'reside at a spot commanding a view of the sea'. And so it went on. McKinnon Wood was unable to find any evidence to support the claims or, in some cases, to even find any evidence of existence of the stories.

It was to be 14 November 1914 before Halifax was to get its first genuine spy story. The *Halifax Courier* reported an 'unwelcome visitor' who seemed to take an over enthusiastic interest in military matters when talking with a wounded soldier on leave. When it was suggested that he should join the colours he exclaimed, 'You won't find me fighting the Germans [...] even if I was compelled to join under conscription I'd do all the damage I could by bringing about desertions.' Evidently this was enough to suggest he was a spy and he was promptly handed over to a constable. Despite the eagerness of others to fuel the story with anecdotal evidence that he had been seen 'studying war maps and making notes of his observations', his identity papers suggested he was nothing of the sort and he was soon released.

Anti-German sentiment, however, was rife and often in petty ways. Boycotting of German goods was perhaps understandable but castigation of existing ownership of anything German or a refusal to have German composed music played pushed intolerance to the limits. The *Halifax Courier* of 22 August 1914 reported:

> We regret to see that in some places German music is being boycotted at the concerts. Wagner, Strauss, and present day composers of German nationality have disappeared. Why not Bach and Handel too? Surely this is absurd. Are we to black out all the magnificent German hymns?

The case of a dismissed clock-winder at the Halifax Union Workhouse, as reported in the *Halifax Courier* of 3 October 1914, exemplified the pettiness. At a meeting of The Halifax Board of Guardians, Canon D. Foley of St Mary's Catholic Church, Gibbet Street, had asked:

> [...] whether Mr Faller [the clock-winder] had been dismissed from the service because he had not given satisfaction in his engagement or because he was a German? [...] Very exaggerated and wild reports had been put in circulation against this poor man [...] only the other day a rather respectable man told him [...] that Mr Faller had poison hidden under the floor of his house [...] poisoning reservoirs from which Halifax received its water supply.

After an attempt by Canon Foley to have the case re-opened and some stonewalling by the chairman, the motion was defeated by a majority of thirteen votes to twelve. Mr Faller did not get his job back.

Dismissal was not uncommon. On 5 September the *Halifax Courier* reported that ' [...] in Yorkshire some cultured and refined women and girls [...] dismissed through the outbreak of war, are now penniless and unable to go to their own country; they have had to take refuge in the workhouse'.

Anti-German or even anti-foreigner sentiment had certainly become a problem for many residents. William Dehner had emigrated from Germany in 1863 and come to Hebden Bridge where he set up as a pork butcher, and eventually became a naturalised British subject. He was one of many German immigrants from the Wurttemberg area. In 1914 he joined Hebden Bridge Council. Shortly after the outbreak of war he felt compelled to speak at a council meeting to affirm his loyalty to Britain. The *Halifax Courier* of 15 August 1914 reported:

> Councillor William Dehner said that as a naturalised Englishman he wished to publicly state his position. When 16 years of age he left Germany to escape the tyranny of military law, and for 34 years now he had enjoyed peace and contentment under English rule [...] to prove his loyalty to the British Crown he had sent his son to fight in the British Army and if necessary he was prepared to fight for King and Country under the same banner.

Two of his sons were to serve in the army.

Although there were no reported acts of overt hostility towards the Dehners, it is probable that people showed their disapproval in other ways, such as boycotting their shops. It is telling that William Dehner retired immediately after the war and that his two sons did not continue the pork butcher business.

Sometimes it was enough to have a name that merely sounded German. This was the case of John Chesswas of Greetland, who also happened to be a pork butcher. Sensing the circumstantial evidence building up against him, he wrote to the *Halifax Courier* on 18 August:

> You will readily understand my surprise when asked by a prominent local gentleman some days ago if I and my seven sons would be called back to my own country [...] and I now find the statement freely circulated [...] particularly annoying [...] I should be greatly obliged if you would give publication to the fact that, so far from being German there is no trace whatever of anything but true English blood in my family.

Herman van Dyk, professor of music and an immigrant from Holland, was a well-respected pillar of Halifax society yet was constantly troubled by what he sensed was a prejudice against him as a foreigner. His chairmanship of the local Foreign Circle (German Section) probably did not help. His diary displays constant worries and practical difficulties due to his national status:

> 3 September 1914 […] I am writing to the Home Office for conditions of naturalisation. In case Holland should be dragged into this war, if she should join Germany, or else, if Germany should conquer Holland, I should wish to become a British subject. I have lived in England nearly 27 years now.

> 22 June 1915 […] A Dutchman has been fined lately at Dublin £25 for not registering his name as an alien. I called therefore at the Police Station to ask if it was necessary for me to report myself.

He was advised that it would not be necessary because of his high standing locally. However, it seems that this did not last. At the beginning of 1916 he notes in his diary that 'We have had to register today as aliens!'

He experienced professional difficulties.

> 17 June 1915 [...] Mr Julian Clifford regrets very much that Harrogate Corporation will not sanction any foreign conductor or composer to appear this year unless they belong to the Allied countries. They are against foreign names. The letter is very kind and courteous. This is nevertheless very disappointing, and going a little too far, I think.

> 26 July 1916 […] Mr Julian Clifford writes that he regrets very much that he cannot perform any of my compositions this season! […] That's very disappointing, but not quite unexpected.

Occasionally it bubbled over into paranoia, real or otherwise:

> 3 August 1917 […] Mr Clifford's is the fourth refusal to play my works viz. Leeds Symphony Concerts, Halifax Choral Soc.,

Bradford Permanent Orchestra and Harrogate Kursaal, and although people are kind enough not to be personal, I am sure it is due to the fact that I am not British born.

He also experienced difficulties in his travels:

5 November 1918 [...] We gave the "Allies" lecture at Colne [...] But we had a lot of fuss with the Police who required all the details of our careers and our persons, because we had not slept in the locality before but had previously gone on to Nelson for the night. Neutrals are treated like enemies in this respect.

Even after the war his family was experiencing difficulties:

30 December 1918 [...] Mr Campbell [Campbell Gas Engine Company] has told Louis [Van Dyk's nephew] that he must look out for another place within six weeks, as he is only going to employ Britishers in future. I have mentioned this to Councillor Maud, a director of the firm, who does not agree at all with Mr C.

As late as 1935 Van Dyk still considered his nationality was a problem. The BBC returned his double concerto saying that they could not perform it in London. Van Dyk wrote 'no doubt the fact that I am not British-born has much to do with it, for I have had to suffer through this throughout my career, especially since the War!'

Being British also carried certain commercial advantages that Bovril was quick to turn to its advantage. Its advert of 31 October 1914 in the *Halifax Courier* proudly proclaimed its board were made of British nationals. Bovril was displaying its impeccable British credentials by emphasising that its creator was the British born John Lawson Johnston. This

When you buy

Bovril

you can be sure you are getting the product of a genuine all-British, and always British Company.

BOVRIL

always has been

BRITISH

and consequently there has been no need to make any change in the constitution or directorate of the Company SINCE THE OUTBREAK OF THE WAR.

The following complete list of the Directors of Bovril, Limited, since the formation of the Company affords the best guarantee of the entire absence of any alien influence or control:—

The Right Hon. Lord Playfair, G.C.B., LL.B.
John Lawson Johnston.
The Right Hon. The Earl of Bessborough, C.V.O., C.B.
Admiral of the Fleet Sir Edmund Commerell, V.C., G.C.B.
Frederick Gordon.
The Right Hon. Dr. Robert Farquharson, P.C.
George Lawson Johnston.
Andrew Walker.
William E. Lawson Johnston.
Douglas Walker.
The Right Hon. The Earl of Arran, K.P.
Sir James Crichton-Browne, M.D., F.R.S.
Prince Francis of Teck.
The Right Hon. The Earl of Erroll, K.T., C.B.

Insist on having Bovril
BRITISH TO THE BACKBONE.

Bovril announces its British credentials. Halifax Courier 31 October 1914.

was not so for its commercial rival, Oxo, whose founder was Justus Freiherr von Liebig, a German.

1915 was to provide further crass acts of German ruthlessness that made life for aliens even more difficult. The *Lusitania* sinking in particular incensed people almost to a frenzy. Aliens became an obvious target and were abused indiscriminately. Many towns and cities, including Liverpool, Newcastle, Manchester, Birmingham and Sheffield, experienced rioting, looting and vandalism. In Birmingham a restaurant was attacked even though its owner was of Norwegian and Swiss extraction. His 'crime' was that he had been born in Germany. The language was sometimes interesting. Corporal J. W. Grayson, writing to the *Halifax Courier* of 29 May 1915 in the aftermath of the sinking, 'We are wondering if you are having any troubles with the aliens in Halifax; we have just read of the riots in London, Southend, Liverpool etc.' His tag line was not 'trouble with rioters' but 'trouble with aliens' as if somehow it was their fault. In point of fact there were no reports of rioting, vandalism or looting in Halifax, but that is not to say that there were not some minor incidents or low level abuse. The latter may have been the case with Leonhardt Wennrick, as reported in the *Halifax Courier* of 22 May 1915. He was arrested for travelling without a permit more than 5 miles away from his place of residence. He had come to Halifax to work for Pohlmann and Son (themselves of German descent), had registered as an alien immediately on 8 August 1914, and had been interned for a period of about five months before release. He was described as having a 'quiet disposition' and had been 'no trouble'. 'When the *Lusitania* affair occurred people talked so, and he was considerably upset.' This had led to depression and caused him to wander outside his restricted area. He received three months in prison.

Government commandeering

One consequence of the outbreak of war was the need of the government to source supplies to support the expanding army. Because of the stage and screen adaptation of Michael Morpurgo's *War Horse,* there is some familiarity amongst the public with the story of the army's need go out and commandeer horses for war work. On 8 August the *Halifax Courier* briefly mentioned that the army was active in the Halifax district. The following week it reported:

[G]overnment officials are still busy securing horses and motor wagons for service in connection with the war. From Halifax and district about 300 horses have been commandeered. Those required so far have been chiefly draft horses and van horses [...] Several farmers have been called upon to contribute their share [...] Enquiring as to the prices paid, our representative was informed that there was not much to complain of in respect [...] Several firms are suffering much inconvenience as the result of the depletion of stables.

A less familiar story is that of the pigeon. The *Halifax Courier* of 8 August 1914 reported that:

[P]igeon fanciers in certain districts are expecting that they may soon be called-upon to furnish birds for a voluntary pigeon post service during the war.

In 1914, pigeons were still one of the most reliable methods of transmitting messages across the battlefield, and in consequence, the

Humorous cartoon by Alfred Leete of the London Opinion *depicting the government's thoroughness in commandeering.*

Drawn by Alfred Leete.   'Reproduced by courtesy of "London Opinion.'

" COMMANDEERED ! "

(A typical topical street scene.)

army formed a special Pigeon Corps. By the end of the war it consisted of 400 men and 22,000 pigeons in 150 mobile lofts. Killing, wounding or molesting homing pigeons could result in a six-month Imprisonment or £100 fine.

There was also anxiety that pigeons might be used by spies. Regulation 21 of the Defence of the Realm Act prohibited 'keeping, being in possession of, carrying or liberating any carrier or homing pigeon without a permit'. It is not clear if local authorities viewed this threat with any degree of seriousness or if the general public had any significant awareness of the regulations. The following case in the *Halifax Courier* of 10 July 1915 suggests neither:

> [A] case, the first of its kind in Halifax [...] was heard when Greenwood Dawson was summoned, under the Defence of the Realm Act, for carrying homing pigeons, without previously having obtained a permit from the police [...] He was seen by Inspector Beanland and Sgt Lee, in the Old Market with a basket containing 14 pigeons. There was another pigeon in defendant's pocket [...] He bought the pigeons, very cheap, for pie making [...] quite unaware he had to get a permit and had no idea he had done wrong.

He was fined a nominal £2.

Whether they liked it or not the residents of Halifax and its districts were now part of a major European war. For most of its non-militarist residents, more accustomed to industry and commerce, this was to be a completely new challenge. Many thought it would be 'business as usual', with the professional armed forces doing the fighting. They would be wrong.

CHAPTER 2

1914
A Call to Arms

Kitchener's new armies

On 5 August 1914, Lord Kitchener was appointed secretary of state for war, and on the same day attended the first cabinet War Council. By all accounts he was not the easiest man to work with and had his own very clear ideas on how things should be done. His first act was to announce that in order to defeat Germany the country would need to raise a mass army. By this simple and singular requirement Lord Kitchener defined Britain's war. In the long run, it was not going to be conducted in the time-honoured British way through the Royal Navy supporting small expeditionary forces. Britain was going to play hard ball, involving a major military commitment on the continent against the world's largest, best prepared and best trained army. For a society that was not organised on military lines and relied on a small professional army to do its soldiering, this was not going to be easy.

Kitchener's prediction at the War Council was a long war lasting at least three years. His vision was that the British should maintain a presence on the continent to support France, but think in terms of holding back the New Armies' until they were fully trained and equipped. They would then be ready to take the field some time in 1917.

He, himself, favoured conscription, but had to bow to the political experience of his Liberal cabinet colleagues who thought this would be too much too soon for the British public to accept. He therefore had to resort to raising a mass army through voluntarism. On 6 August, parliament sanctioned an increase of 500,000 men of all ranks. On 11 August, a proclamation was published entitled 'Your King and Country need you: a call to arms'. It explained the new terms of service and called for the first 100,000 men to enlist.

The 1914 recruitment campaigns
Halifax recruitment in the first few weeks of the war seems to have been a matter of the military authorities urging men to turn up at recruitment stations such as the Halifax Barracks or the Drill Hall in Prescott Street. The responsibility for Kitchener's New Army battalions fell on the shoulders of Lieutenant-Colonel Hayford Douglas Thorold, the depot commander of the Halifax Barracks and former commander of the 1st Battalion West Riding Regiment. Under the clarion call of 'Roll up Yorkshire Lads!', Colonel Thorold made his theatrical appeal in the *Halifax Courier* of 15 August:

> A new battalion of the Duke of Wellington's Regiment is being raised at the depot, Halifax. First class drill instructors are idle, waiting to drill recruits, to teach them how to defend their hearths and homes [...] Rally to your regiment, which has for more than 200 years fought for you in every quarter of the world, and in which officers and men are bound together in the closest ties of friendship and comradeship. Yorkshire mothers and fathers, do not hold your children back – your country needs them to learn to defend their homes.

Other parts of the country, particularly London, experienced a large surge of recruits immediately on the outbreak of war, but this did not seem to be the case in Halifax. On 17 August, the *Halifax Courier* was reporting a much more muted local response:

> Recruiting for the New Army is, we are sorry to announce, not making such progress as it ought to in Yorkshire.

Colonel Thorold proceeded to make an appeal to the paper's readership:

[…] at present only 10 have come forward in the large 33rd recruiting area in response to my urgent appeal […] Clergymen and ministers! I appeal to you to preach the right of every man to defend his own home […] Gentlemen of Yorkshire! Please lend your motor cars […] there is not a village which will give their quota of men if visited […] It will be a lasting disgrace if I have to appeal to other counties for men to defend Yorkshire homes.

There was then a suggestion from the newspaper that the civil authorities and the Mayor of Halifax in particular should perhaps be doing more to support the military authorities:

[…] we are assured Colonel Thorold will gladly address a public meeting to appeal for recruits. Surely a meeting could be arranged for Halifax […] in other towns, throughout the country, mayors have arranged meetings and the response to Earl Kitchener's appeal has been such as to gladden the heart of every lover of this country. Shall the country of Broad Acres be the only one in Britain to fail to send its quota?

Hint or not, a large meeting was organised by William Henry Ingham, the Mayor of Halifax, for 3 September in Halifax's Victoria Hall. This took the form of a rally with a heavy line-up of local dignitaries, patriotic music and strong motivational speeches aimed directly at eligible men of volunteering age. The speakers included J. H. Whitley MP, James Parker MP, Sir George Fisher-Smith and Colonel Thorold. It occurred at a seminal moment because, on 30 August, *The Times* had printed the 'Amiens Dispatch'. This had been unusually frank in its description of the British Army's first engagement with the German Army at Mons and how it had been forced to retreat. By the time the Halifax meeting was held, Lord Kitchener had announced an appeal for a further 500,000 men and Lord Derby had just delivered his famous speech in Liverpool on the concept of recruiting Pals battalions. There was, therefore, a renewed urgency for recruitment and the meeting was 'crowded to overflowing'.

On 5 September 1914, the *Halifax Guardian* reported the meeting in some detail. The mayor began by explaining that Colonel Thorold

T H E   **W** A R .

A YORKSHIRE CALL TO ARMS !
LORD KITCHENER'S APPEAL FOR
MEN.

Now that the services of every trained Soldier are
required either to defend this country or to under-
take the training of others for that purpose,

AN ADDITION OF 500,000 MEN TO
HIS MAJESTY'S REGULAR ARMY

Has been decreed to be immediately necessary, and
as Mayor of this town I have been requested to and
do hereby convene a

MASS   MEETING,
TO BE HELD IN THE
VICTORIA HALL, HALIFAX,
On THURSDAY, the 3rd day of September, 1914.
At 7.30 p.m.,

For the purpose of Appealing for Recruits from
Halifax and District.

The Meeting will be ADDRESSED by prominent
ARMY OFFICERS as well as by Representative
Local Gentlemen.

During the Meeting Mr. SHACKLETON
POLLARD will give Selections on the ORGAN.

Seats in the Dress Circle will be reserved for
Ladies.

WILLIAM HENRY INGHAM, Mayor,
Town Hall, Halifax,
28 August, 1914.

The mayor's appeal for a mass recruitment meeting in the Victoria Hall. Halifax Courier 29 August 1914.

had requested the meeting because he believed that 'the men of Halifax and district were not responding to the call as they should do'. Colonel Thorold spoke from the platform to say that he was:

> [...] enthusiastic in his praise of the 'Pals' companies and assured his hearers that if they should join in bodies of fifty or one hundred he would make it his duty to see that they were not separated. Now Yorkshire madams, hold not your children back when your country needs them.

Local Liberal MP J. H. Whitley then delivered the case for why the country was at war and why it was important for everyone to pull together. There had been an impression in some quarters that too many people did not understand the nature of the crisis and why it was necessary for as many men as possible to enlist:

We were in it for liberty […] the action of Germany gave us no option […] with France perhaps beaten to her knees […] where would England be? We should be but waiting for our turn for the same thing […] the issue in this case was whether the Prussian war lords were to dominate the whole of Western Europe […] we represented a free self-governing democracy […] the Germans had never had that. Would be God that they had. If the people of Germany had made their governments as we made ours there would have been no war […] we have no desire to wipe Germany off the map. No. We hope that a new and sober Germany will arise, where the people will take control […] and no longer will the Kaiser […] order them without a will of their own […] each and everyone [in Britain] must be at the service of the country in a crisis like the present.

James Parker MP (ILP) spoke of his conversion from 'man of peace' to his present position as a supporter of the war. The *Halifax Guardian* reported his beliefs:

His work for the last twenty five years had been well known to the people of Halifax […] and the stand he had taken against militarism and armaments […] As circumstances have come along he was heartily glad that their efforts for reduction in armaments had been unsuccessful […] glad that there was a bigger navy protecting our shores […] It was not an easy thing for him to talk like that for war to him was a horrible and devilish thing. But there was a price at which peace could not be purchased – the sacrifice of truth, honesty and personal honour […] there would be no peace, there would be no real reduction of armaments in Europe, until the cancerous growth of Kaiserism had been cut away.

Alderman C. F. Spencer appealed for recruits and pointed to the crisis developing on the continent. The newspaper outlined his arguments:

The Germans were nearing Paris, and it is no use saying the Russians are up behind. It was men who were wanted now for the British Army. Were Halifax people going to respond? It was no class war. All must make a sacrifice, rich and poor alike.

With a clear reference to what was happening in Belgium and France, former mayor, Sir George Fisher-Smith continued the theme. The newspaper reported that he believed:

> Civilised nations were at war […] standing aghast at the horrors and atrocities which were being committed under Kaiserism […] hell had been let loose and the devil himself had lost control. It was for the young men of Halifax […] to come forward solidly and give their aid in a war for the defence of liberty and justice.

The message was very clear and was to be vigorously reinforced throughout the war by both the *Halifax Courier* and *Halifax Guardian*. Significantly the civil authorities were now involved, something the War Office and many other areas of the country acknowledged was the way forward. Indoor rallies became more common in and around Halifax and shortly afterwards the Civilian Recruiting Committee was set up to further drive things onwards.

The speakers were drawn largely from the local elite and it is always more difficult to judge how far the message reached the wider Halifax population, composed mainly of the working-classes. It is unlikely that the newspapers would attach themselves to a viewpoint that was at odds with its readership, but to what extent did the local population embrace the war as something that should involve them? Supporting the war was one thing. Going out and doing something about it was another.

Slowness of recruitment

Cyril Pearce in *Comrades of Conscience* has collated much evidence in nearby Huddersfield of resistance to the recruitment effort there. He quotes a pro-war speaker, John Hunter Watts, who believed that Halifax was very similar:

> [E]ffort was most needed where there was a certain amount of hostility to recruiting. Huddersfield and Halifax ran one another very close in this respect.

Recruitment was far from being a disaster in Halifax and we should not run away with the idea that the area was a hotbed of war resistance.

Pockets of active resistance existed but it was far from a majority view. What Halifax may have had is a largely silent majority who, for a variety of reasons, were not in a hurry to hop onto the nearest recruitment bandwagon. The local newspapers made several references to this less-than-eager response to actually picking up a gun. 'An Old Volunteer' wrote in the *Halifax Courier*, 29 August, 1914 that:

> […] pleas of business or personal inconvenience must be treated as idle excuses […] Among village youths there is a curious shyness about joining […] they only want a lead.

Halifax's recruitment supremo, Colonel Thorold, let slip a story in the *Halifax Guardian* of 5 September 1914 that 'was enough to make a man's blood boil':

> [H]e had seen [men] clinging to the petticoats of a lass, and jeering at the men who were going out [to war] saying that 'There were so many fools going'.

Even after the alarms of the retreat from Mons, Colonel Thorold was having difficulty getting his message across in Brighouse. The *Halifax Guardian* of 26 September 1914 reported:

> [H]e did not seem to be able to bring home to them the fact that war was going on and that unless they came forward to defend their homes they would have no homes left to defend […] they all seemed so utterly apathetic.

By the beginning of October it seems that Halifax was continuing to have some difficulty in raising its (Service) battalions for Kitchener's New Armies (9th, 10th, 11th Battalions West Riding Regiment). The *Halifax Guardian* of 3 October 1914 reported:

> Owing to sufficient numbers not having come forward in time, the War Office has ordered the raising of the 11th Service Battalion West Riding Regiment to be cancelled […]

By 17 October, the *Halifax Courier* even ran a column headline 'A

Stigma on Halifax' and recorded Colonel Thorold's ever growing frustration:

> For the present, recruiting in the district is slack [...] supplying members for Lord Kitchener's Army, this district, Col. Thorold feels, has been somewhat lagging [...] authorities express great disappointment with the response of Halifax and district [...] we have a superabundance of hesitants.

In the same week's edition, the newspaper reported on George Stansfield's address to a Sowerby Bridge recruitment meeting:

> He had been told recently that the West Riding of Yorkshire was shirking its duty, but he did not believe that. If there did seem to be backwardness [...] he thought it was because [...] they had not realised the serious position the Empire stood in.

As the war moved into its third and fourth month some degree of soul-searching was going on. Some believed that many Halifax men were enlisting in other regiments. The Halifax Civilian Recruiting Committee believed the government was not making it easy and the *Halifax Guardian* of 7 November reported that it:

> [...] urges the Government to make better provisions for families of soldiers who have been killed or wounded [...] [there is a] belief that recruiting is retarded.

It must also be remembered that the local Territorial battalion (4th) was recruiting for its reserve battalion at the time and may have been drawing some of the potential recruits away from the service battalions. They were all valid arguments, but it did not entirely explain why other areas were being more successful. Perhaps J. F. Hirst, speaking in the *Halifax Guardian* of 24 October, was getting close when he was reported as saying:

> [...] he had tried to find out why certain young men in Halifax had not come forward [...] in England they had a bad habit of leaving other people to do what they did not care to do themselves.

There may simply have been a belief that 'soldiering' was someone else's job. For most British communities, 'national service' was not a part of the fabric of society as it was in France and Germany. Even the concept of 'voluntary national service' must have felt alien. Halifax was a manufacturing district and, arguably, may have felt its national contribution lay there. It is also possible that the various socialist groups of the area had generated a general feeling of anti-militarism, something that has a familiar resonance with 'hostility to recruitment', found in *Comrades in Conscience*. The reasons were clearly complex and it is something we will return to when we deal with the decline of recruitment in 1915 and later the local tribunal appeals against conscription.

Town Volunteer Guard
In the first few weeks of the war the country experienced the formation of various irregular 'local defence' groups. Indeed, there is an argument that they may even have deflected much local effort away from mainstream recruitment. In other towns and cities they were to serve as the inspiration for the idea of Pals battalions and the involvement of civilian authorities in recruitment. The *Halifax Courier* of 22 August reported that Colonel Thorold was anxious to form a local 'Shooting Committee' to train civilians in the use of the rifle. This was duly formed as a citizen's rifle club under the title of the Halifax and District Volunteer Town Guard and was initially based at the Halifax Barracks. In November, they moved to their own premises, loaned by Lumby, Son and Wood on Lister Lane, where they had several ranges for rifle practice setup. By then they had clear guidelines as to what they represented:

> No man will be admitted a member of the Halifax Volunteer Guard who is eligible for enlistment in His Majesty's Army […] The idea is train and form a corps of those too old, or for some reason, unable to enlist, and to train those from 17-19 in the use of a rifle and drill to fit them for service, for which they may be required later […] to form a national Defence Corps for home service throughout the country in case of invasion, with government recognition.

It was therefore fairly close in concept to the 'Home Guard' of the Second World War. Later, in February 1916 it received government recognition and was renamed the Volunteer Training Corps. One of its duties was to provide some introductory military training for men who had been granted a deferment from conscription by the local tribunals. Their existence was formalised even more when they were later rebadged as Volunteer Battalions and given designated battalion numbers. The Halifax Volunteer Training Corps became 8th Battalion West Riding Volunteers.

Why no Halifax Pals battalion?
The concept of the Pals battalions centred on the idea of friends coming forward in groups to enlist together and then being placed in the same units. It is often thought of as being based on the idea of recruiting men from the same locality but the real driving force was the grouping of men from a similar working background. Often they were one and the same thing, but it is important to recognise that the similarity of background was the bonding force.

The concept is often attributed to Sir Henry Rawlinson and Lord Derby. On 28 August, in the aftermath of the retreat from Mons, Kitchener had launched a further appeal for more men. That evening there was an 'emotional recruitment meeting' in Liverpool, where Lord Derby was reputed to have coined the term 'Pals Battalion' for the first time:

> We have got to see this through to the bitter end [...] if it takes every man and every penny in the country. This should be a Battalion of Pals, a battalion in which friends from the same office will fight shoulder to shoulder for the honour of Britain and the credit of Liverpool.

However, the idea seems to have been already taking hold in various forms and in many other localities. On 15 August, the *Halifax Courier* reported that Colonel Thorold himself had already expressed the wish that he wanted:

> [...] to organise the new battalion so as to keep all men from the same district together, under the command of officers who knew

them, and hope that Halifax and Huddersfield will furnish enough men to form a whole company.

Whether he had taken his cue from other localities or whether it was a case of 'great minds thinking alike', it is difficult to tell.

During the war the terms Pals or Chums seems to have been applied fairly freely wherever groups of men from similar backgrounds enlisted together, even if they represented only a portion of the unit. Today the term 'Pals Battalion' is generally reserved for whole units who were recruited as 'New Army' battalions and were composed almost entirely of men from the same background. In that respect it is not possible to identify a Halifax battalion that could be truly described as a Pals battalion.

Exactly why this never happened in Halifax becomes a matter of speculation. Several New Army battalions were initially formed in Halifax such as the 8th, 9th, 10th and 11th Service Battalions of the West Riding Regiment, and the 21st Battalion (Wool Textile Pioneers) of the West Yorkshire Regiment. The 8th, 9th and 10th Service Battalions moved out of the district in the early months of the war, presumably without having reached their full complement. Although they maintained a Halifax contingent, casualty returns suggest a fairly widespread geographical spread of recruitment. As noted above, the 11th Battalion was cancelled by the War Office because it had failed to reach its recruitment target and instead became part of the Training Reserve Battalions of 3rd Reserve Brigade, which did not serve abroad. George Holdsworth (of John Holdsworth and Co Ltd and chairman of the Halifax Recruitment Committee) played an important role in the formation of the 21st Battalion (Wool Textiles Pioneers) West Yorkshire Regiment. Initially, at least, it had a strong Halifax pedigree. Fairly soon afterwards, in February 1916, it moved to Skipton where its Halifax connection may well have waned. The *Halifax Courier*, however, continued to regard it as one of Halifax's own and regularly sent comfort parcels to it throughout the war.

In Martin Middlebrook's *First Day on the Somme*, the 12th King's Own Yorkshire Light Infantry (KOYLI) is curiously tagged as the Halifax Pals. This is an error because the battalion was raised in Leeds by the Mayor of Leeds and few if any of its casualties were Halifax men. Exactly how this myth arose, (and it is repeated in other sources) is uncertain. One possibility is that it was confused with the 21st West Yorkshire Battalion, which also had a connection with the Mayor of Leeds.

It is tempting to suggest that the absence of a Halifax Pals Battalion was because local recruitment was never vigorous enough to fill the ranks of any one battalion. Perhaps it was always necessary to complete the complement with outsiders. This seems to have been the case with the 21st West Yorkshire (Wool Textile Pioneers) Battalion. Another possibility is that recruitment for the Reserve 4th Battalion West Riding Regiment diverted many potential recruits. This required 1,000 men to be raised from virtually a standing start and was completed within a few weeks under the auspices of Lieutenant-Colonel William Land.

There were two proposals, which initially at least, seem to have matched the ideal of a Pals unit. Under a column headline 'Pals Corps idea', the *Halifax Courier* of 6 September reported that a:

> [...] meeting of those interested in another local corps was held on Wednesday at the Old Cock Hotel. The idea appeared to be to form an organisation in some way more advanced than the Volunteer Guard.

The idea came from local businessmen who wished to create their own unit, which would be prepared to join the national forces, 'if such circumstances should arise as a complete stoppage of business or conscription'. The military authorities did not like it because it smacked of a private army and the existing Volunteer Guard did not like it because it was too similar to what they were doing. It does not appear to have taken off and any further mention disappeared from the local newspapers.

The following week under 'Halifax Pals Battalion' in the *Halifax Courier* of 12 September, Colonel Thorold also proposed a Pals battalion based on the grammar and secondary schools of Halifax, which he said could be accommodated at the newly formed Lloyds Barracks (Highroad Well Tramshed):

> Harrison Road Lecture Theatre [...] Mr J. Walsh, who presided, said there had been great disappointment on hearing the Territorial Battalion (4th) for imperial service was up to full

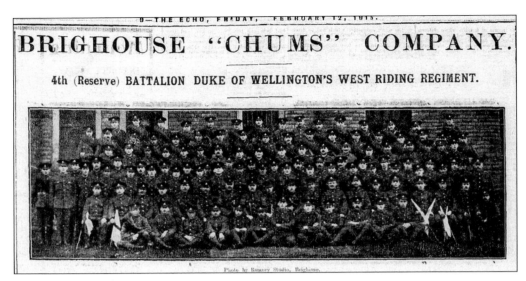

BRIGHOUSE "CHUMS" COMPANY.

4th (Reserve) BATTALION DUKE OF WELLINGTON'S WEST RIDING REGIMENT.

Photo by Ramsey Studio, Brighouse.

Brighouse Chums. Brighouse Echo *12th February 1915.*

strength [...] it was now proposed to form a Halifax Pals battalion for Lord Kitchener's army [...] Col. Thorold gave his assurance that they would be kept together.

The exact fate of this proposal is not known but a few weeks later Colonel William Land announced that 1,000 men were needed for the Reserve unit of the 4th Battalion West Riding Regiment. It is possible this became the channel for the new recruits instead.

This unit seems to have most closely fitted the ideal of a Pals battalion. Recruitment for the companies was very local, as can be seen by the photograph of the Brighouse Chums. Halifax, Sowerby Bridge, Elland and Cleckheaton also contributed their locally recruited chums companies to the battalion.

It was, however, the reserve battalion of a Territorial unit and, it seems, was raised mainly by the military authorities, so does not fit the classical mould of being a New Army unit. To further muddy the waters, the newspapers often referred to its recruitment as being part of Kitchener's 'New Army'. It did not arrive on the battlefield until early 1917 and so missed another frequently cited qualification for Pals membership – participation in the Battle of the Somme.

Campaigning methods

Civilian involvement from early September 1914 onwards brought something of a sea change in recruitment methods. Rallies using a greater variety of facilities and accompanied by civilian as well as military speakers became more numerous.

A 'novel recruiting campaign' involving three 'illuminated trams' was organised by the Civilian Recruiting Committee to conduct a recruiting tour of the Calder Valley from George Square in Halifax to Hebden Bridge. The idea was probably borrowed from other areas and took the form of a road show. The *Halifax Courier* of 26 September 1914 reported:

> All were studied [sic] with fairy lamps, gay with bunting and flashed appeals for service such as 'Serve your King', 'Your Country Needs You' and 'Now or Never'.

The first tram was a single-decker and carried Lee Mount Band. This was followed by a double-decker tram with the recruiting committee and friends. Bringing up the rear was a third single-decker tram with the 1st Halifax Troop of Scouts. The tour began with a bugle call from the scouts and the band played *Red, White and Blue*. First stop was at Station Road, Luddenden Foot, where a 'crowd of over 1,000 gathered' followed by stops at Mytholmroyd and Hebden Bridge, with crowds of 2,000 and 3/4,000 respectively. The following day the format was repeated on the other side of Halifax at Hipperholme, Bailiff Bridge and Brighouse.

Later in the year speakers became more pro-active and started to appear in schools, workplaces and even places of entertainment, such as cinemas.

Illuminated tram used for West Riding Regiment recruitment. Stephen Gee Collection.

The traditional image of mill owners and other employers is of hard-bitten, ruthless money-grabbers out to screw workforces for whatever they could get. The evidence of the newspapers runs contrary to this. There appears to be a considerable degree of paternalism exercised. When meeting to discuss the financial effects of the war on local communities, many employers saw relief of dependent families as their responsibility. Many also saw it as their patriotic duty to encourage men to enlist. Offering to keep jobs open for the men when they returned was one obvious gesture, but the patriotism extended to offering financial inducements. Ramsden's Brewery offered to pay anyone who enlisted with half wages as well as keeping their job open. Richard Thomas and Sons of Hebden Bridge pledged a bounty of £10. The Halifax Corporation passed a proposal to pay an army supplement of 5 shillings per week to the wife and 2 shillings per child. It is evident that employers used the workplace to encourage enlistment and there were even some reports of men complaining that they were being bullied into volunteering. John Mackintosh Ltd had to deny rumours that the firm was sacking men to force them to enlist. Those in charge were at pains to point out that they were paying half wages to a recruit's family and guaranteeing to keep the jobs open.

Of course, this degree of paternalism was unlikely to be universal. Ripponden Council found it necessary to send a circular round to employers asking them to support the war by topping up the army wages of an employee and also holding jobs open. Not everyone was being altruistic.

Departures

On 16 January, both Halifax newspapers reported that Colonel Thorold had been promoted to the rank of brigadier general and was leaving to join staff at the War Office. According to the report in the *Halifax Courier* of 16 January 1915, he had been:

> [... s]trenuously engaged at the Halifax Barracks raising service battalions for Lord Kitchener's Army. It is largely due to his strenuous efforts that local recruiting has been more successful than was anticipated.

This muted departure comes as a surprise and it is difficult to ignore the many reports that recruitment had been disappointingly slow. It becomes all the more mysterious to discover in the *Manchester Evening News* of 16 June 1915 that he had moved on to become the military officer for Didsbury District, and still with the rank of lieutenant-colonel.

Did he jump or was he pushed? No explanation was given for his departure except that it was 'for pastures new'. It may, of course, have been simply a routine transfer. But the lack of the usual effusiveness for occasions such as this, and the muddled information associated with his departure, cannot fail to fuel some doubts.

Another significant departure, reported in the *Halifax Courier* of 23 January 1915, was that of the Reserve 4th West Riding Regiment, who had achieved their full complement:

> Prior to their departure [...] they were accorded civic recognition [...] Great public interest was manifested and the streets from the Drill Hall to the Town Hall were lined with crowds of well-wishers.

Alderman C. F. Spencer was one of the speakers and provided yet another indication, if one was needed, that recruitment in the district had not been what everyone wanted or had expected:

> [...] one of the highest officials from the War Office [...] said though the numbers [of recruits] might not be as great as in other areas, the Halifax 33rd area was the best organised in the whole of the United Kingdom.

Alderman Spencer offered what might be regarded as a conciliatory view that: 'war could not be carried on unless war materials were made. Some had to stay at home for that purpose.'

These two departures signal a kind of watershed in the recruitment campaign. The early, sometimes frantic, months of calling the nation to arms would now give way to a more polarised struggle. Was the ideal of voluntarism going to be enough to furnish Kitchener's New Armies and could conscription be avoided? These were to be key issues in 1915.

CHAPTER 3

1914

Keep the Home Fires Burning

Employment problems and food prices

At the start of the war, the businesses around Halifax were already in the grip of a trade slump and the expectation was that this would become worse because of the loss of markets due to the disruption. Within a few days of the outbreak of war manufacturers were responding to 'the crisis'. The *Halifax Courier* of 8 August 1914 reported:

> Owing to the existing crisis in Europe and the temporary interruption of international trade merchants have signified their inability to accept deliveries of goods [...] In the circumstances manufacturers are unable at present to keep the mills open as usual... Ordinary contracts of service should be dispensed with, and [...] employers shall be at liberty to close the mills without the necessity of giving formal notices.

Unemployment was a problem in which the government had virtually no hand. Resorting to short time was considered preferable to dismissing men. At least that measure allowed the men to make some provision for their families, and the local authorities would not have large numbers of families to help who might become destitute. The newspaper continued:

> The Board of Trade issued last night a notice calling the attention of employers generally to the desirability of avoiding or limiting, in the public interest [...] the discharge of workmen. By working short time, it is suggested, it may be possible to retain man who would otherwise be dismissed.

In the first week of the war, the Halifax Chamber of Commerce convened a meeting 'to discuss the question of providing for families of reservists called-up [...] and the subject of employment for workers at home'. The varied views expressed were indicative of what was essentially a national problem being projected onto local communities, who were expected to pick up the tab. The chairman opened with the wish that:

> [t]hey could do something to mitigate the horrors they were called to pass through [...] whilst these men were away [...] their places should be kept open for them [...] they should make ample provision for their wives and families and dependants during their absence.

Some of the attendees thought the problems were the collective responsibility of all local companies, others thought it should be shouldered by the Halifax Corporation, and some ventured to suggest that it should fall on the government. Sir Algernon Firth, Chairman of Firth's Carpets, Bailiff Bridge, believed the important question was to keep the mills running as much as possible to maintain high levels of employment.

The outbreak of war also created an expectation that there would be an immediate hike in food prices. Inevitably there was panic buying, which in turn led to the very food shortages they feared and, of course, price rises. The *Halifax Courier* of 8 August 1914 reported:

> A special meeting of the Halifax and Districts Grocers and Provision Dealers Association was held on Monday at the Imperial Café [...] to consider the price question of food supplies

consequent upon the war [...] It was agreed by all that the public themselves are chiefly to blame for the rapid advances which have taken place in flour and sugar [...] many who have been in a position to do so have bought excessively [...] The result is that [it] has caused merchants and manufacturers to put their prices up [...] the public are consequently now suffering of their own folly [...] The poorest people, who cannot afford to pay the advance, suffer most.

The government clearly wished to dampen any fears of food shortages and moved to reassure the public.

The Board of Agriculture and Fisheries announced last night, that on the basis of more complete returns now available, it may be said with confidence that there is actually in the United Kingdom at the present time [...] five months' supply of bread stuffs.

Sugar, which many regarded as an essential foodstuff, was particularly vulnerable to shortages because most of it was imported from the sugar beet factories of Germany and Austria. The Economic Stores advertised in the *Halifax Courier* of 29 August that 'for the first time in history, sugar from Sweden'. This was interesting on a number of counts. Firstly, Sweden was not a major producer of sugar beet. Secondly, it has been established that some companies were exporting unusually large amounts of their commodities to Sweden where it would not be expected that the local market was strong enough. The export of chocolate by Cadburys is a case in point. The only satisfactory explanation is that Sweden, as a neutral, was a back door for both British and German firms to continue their pre-war trade with countries who were now the enemy.

Within a couple of months it became apparent that the expected problems of unemployment and rising food prices had largely evaporated. The war had, in some cases, generated extra work through government contracts, which sought to provide materials for the war effort. The sea lanes remained open and, with certain exceptions, foodstuffs were in plentiful supply. The editorial in the *Halifax Courier* of 3 October was upbeat:

The Economic Stores, Ltd

TEL. 303.   HALIFAX, BRADFORD, HUDDERSFIELD.

Our Telegrams from Copenhagen to-day announce that many more Food Ships have been despatched with much larger quantities of

Butter, Eggs, Provisions,

and for the first time in history, SUGAR, from Sweden.

The Economic has ever been the first to provide Popular Prices, and to place Pure and High-class Goods into the homes of the people, and always give the benefit of existing stocks in advancing markets.

BEST SWEDISH & DANISH BUTTERS 1/4 PER LB.

Fine Large DANISH EGGS, 12 at 1/-.

FINEST CHESHIRE CHEESE, 7½d. per lb.

English Refined Castor Sugar, 3½d. PER lb. or 2/0½ 7 lb. CALICO BAGS.

Best X.L. ROLLER FLOUR, 2/- for 16 lbs.

Best British YEAST, 4ozs. for 2d.   No advance.

Large English Baking Apples, 6½d. for 4 lbs.   Fine Victoria Plums, 7½d. for 4 lbs.

Best Yorkshire Potatoes, 7½d. for 16 lbs.   All the Best Sorts.

☞ ALL BREAD AND CONFECTIONERY REDUCED TO OLD PRICES.

These are about HALF THE PRICES usually charged by others who pose as friends of the people, etc.

ALL OUR GOODS ARE BOUGHT DIRECT FROM GROWER OR MANUFACTURER, WITHOUT ANY WHOLESALE AGENT TAXING US.

JOIN THE ECONOMIC and all its benefits, including a share in the profits. Over £6,000 will be divided next Bonus Day, and will be paid in coin.

Advertisement for the Economic Stores. Halifax Courier, *29 August 1914.*

It is very satisfactory that in regard to employment and prices, the homes of the people in this neighbourhood have not suffered a great deal yet through the war. The Government's demands have kept many employers busy [...] night and day work is increasing; and in some of the textile branches, chiefly woollens, work people are needed [...] The cotton mills appear to be worst hit of all. Dyers are finding plenty of work because of the war, though they report that certain dyewares, being scarce in this country, have more than doubled in price. Most of the engineering firms are also fully employed [...] The staple trades in this district are thus fairly well employed, and money is becoming more plentiful [...] the trade routes by sea being so well kept open, prices of foods have kept nearly normal.

Prince of Wales National Fund and the Mayor's Fund

Within the first few days of war, appeals were issued in places such as the *Halifax Courier* of 8 August 'by the Prince of Wales, the Queen and Queen Alexandra urging contributions to a National Fund for the relief of distress among the people of this country least able to bear it'. The money was intended to be used for both dependants of soldiers and distress caused by unemployment. The fund was very successful and raised £1,000,000 from the country very quickly. As the most prominent Halifax civic leader, the Mayor of Halifax immediately made an announcement (dated 10 August) 'to the inhabitants of the County Borough of Halifax' in the *Halifax Guardian*:

> In response to the request of His Royal Highness the Prince of Wales that I should assist his National Relief Fund by opening a subscription list in Halifax.

First on the list were local firms and men of substantial means including John Crossley and Sons Ltd (£1,000), J. H. Whitley MP (£500), Councillor John Mackintosh (£500). Many other benefactors, some of them anonymous, contributed shillings.

A local debate immediately sprang up over whether this was the most practical or desirable way of fundraising to alleviate local distress. The feeling was that local people were best placed to recognise the local needs and in some quarters others asked, 'why should we send our money to London?' There was a feeling that a central fund might delay the distribution of relief. Local committees were having to grapple with a complex set of issues. Indicative of this was a meeting held by Mytholmroyd War Distress Committee and reported in the *Halifax Courier* of 5 September. It faced a bewildering situation:

> They had before them the public invitation from the Prince of Wales to send money to the National Fund; there was an invitation from the Earl of Harewood to send money to the West Riding Fund; that day an invitation had been received to send money to the West Riding County Council fund, and the Mayor of Halifax was inviting people to support the fund which he had opened.

Mytholmroyd opted to look after its own local needs.

The Mayor of Halifax was also having second thoughts and issued another statement to the local newspapers including the *Halifax Courier* of 2 September:

> I feel […] that a large number have not yet subscribed […] many persons have intimated to me that they have withheld from

responding to my former appeal on the grounds that […] their gifts would be administered locally and not merged into the National Fund.

He continued that 'after careful consideration' he had decided to open a second fund called the 'Mayor's Local Relief Fund'. He was at pains to point out that he had no desire to 'divert subscriptions from the National Fund'. Despite these assurances, that particular boat had already set sail. Items continued to be published in the local newspapers detailing collections to the Prince of Wales National Fund but local effort had clearly shifted its focus from national to local appeals. The Mayor's National War Fund and the West Riding War Fund also became less noticeable on the front pages of the *Halifax Guardian* from mid-October onwards.

The Lady Mayoress's Lady Worker's Committee
The urge to support troops and the expected distress of their dependants was overwhelming and was being swept away in a feeding frenzy of committees. The *Halifax Courier* of 22 August 1914 reported on the battle plan of an organisation, which clearly was waiting for no-one:

> Notice is hereby given that at a Meeting of the Mayoress's Lady Workers' Committee […] it was decided to organise all Ladies within Halifax and District willing to give their services by making up good serviceable clothing for the use of Soldiers and Sailors serving their country […] making up of any articles […] which may be wanted by the Red Cross Society, Ambulance Brigade, Local Relief Committee, or similar institutions […] Dated this 11th day of August 1914.

Thirty-six districts were carved out and headed by women, whose addresses were littered with suffixes such as 'Hall', 'Vicarage', 'House',' Villa' or 'Royd'. Middle England was in charge. Instructions were clear and explicit. 'Any Lady willing to assist should at once communicate with the Head of the section in which she lives, and she will then be provided with material.' As carve-ups go it was clinically impressive. The military-like precision was not entirely accidental.

Punch Cartoon: September 1914. Artist, Arthur Wallis Mills. "Just the person I wanted to see. I've started ten committees in connection with the war and I want your help". "My dear! I've just started twelve and I simply counted on you!"

Subliminally, this was the Home Front equivalent of the men away fighting.

Initially, they had taken on the responsibility for making clothing for hospitals to deal with the wounded, but later expanded to include knitting and making garments for soldiers in training camps and at the Front. Their headquarters for storing materials and finished items was Holly House, Wards End (now a public house), which at the time had recently served as the Eye, Ear and Throat Hospital.

Some appreciation of the sheer scale and variety of goods that The Lady Mayoress's Committee produced and sent out can be gauged from this list published in the *Halifax Courier* on 26 September 1914. It also tells us how closely they worked with the Red Cross Society and the St John Ambulance Association.

To the headquarters of St John Ambulance Association [...] 25 bed jackets, 12 nightingales, 48 day shirts, 12 nightshirts, socks and scarves.

To the military hospital, The Barracks, 12 helpless shirts, 12

shirts, 24 pairs socks, 12 scarves, 12 body belts, two dozen handkerchiefs, 4 dressing gowns.
To Devonshire House [London] in response to her Majesty's appeal, 500 pairs socks, 60 body belts [see Kitchener's appeal later].
To Territorials, 180 pairs of socks.
To headquarters of Red Cross Society [...] Three finger splints, 60 'many tail' bandages, 4 rectangular splints, 30 flannelette bandages, 12 pneumonia jackets, 12 T bandages, abdominal pads, 15 calico bandages, eye pads, 42 bags of swaps.

Shirts, socks, scarves and woolly helmets were sent to 5th Battery 2nd West Riding Brigade, 4th Battalion West Riding Regiment, 3rd Battalion West Riding Regiment and 8th Service Battalion West Riding Regiment.

The knitting of socks for soldiers became a prodigious home industry, which came to symbolise how women in particular could support the war effort. Articles appeared in the newspapers, such as the *Halifax Courier* of 15 August, with all kinds of practical hints on how to go about this:

Many local ladies have now got well into work in the making of garments for soldiers, and in other cases provision is being made for "sewing meetings" twice or thrice a week with the same object in view. The correct patterns should be ascertained before any work is begun [...] Those who are equally good with the needle will do well to devote the chief part of their time to the making of garments for the hospitals, and keep their knitting for odd moments.

Nothing exemplified this more than a request from Lord Kitchener in response to the many shortages that the expanding army was experiencing. The *Halifax Courier* of 26 September reported the appeal:

Lord Kitchener has asked the Queen to supply 300,000 belts (knitted or woven) and 300,000 pairs of socks – to be ready, if possible, early in November. Lord Kitchener has promised that these articles shall be immediately distributed at the front. The Queen has willingly acceded to the request, and asks the women of the Empire to assist her in making this offering to the troops.

 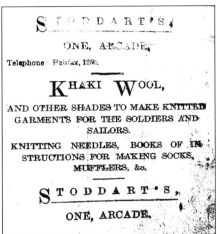

(Left) J and J Baldwin knitting booklet. (Right) Advert for knitting materials,
Halifax Courier, *1914.*

The Lady Mayoress's Lady Workers Committee rose to the challenge
and received the grateful thanks of the Empire. The *Halifax Courier*
of 3 October was able to report:

> The following letter has been received by the Mayoress this
> week: "Devonshire house, Piccadilly, – the lady-in-waiting
> presents her compliments to Mrs Ingham [Lady Mayoress], and
> is commanded by Her Majesty to thank the Lady Workers
> Committee for their magnificent gift of 500 pairs of socks and
> 60 belts for the soldiers at the front.

It seems that the whole of the United Kingdom answered the call, as
can be judged by the Queen's announcement, which was reported in
the *Halifax Courier* of 31 October 1914.

> So swift and generous response has been made by the women
> of the Empire to the Queen's appeal […] that it has been found
> possible to close the fund well in advance of the dates by which
> it was hoped sufficient gifts would have been received.

Punch Cartoon: November 1914. Artist, Fred Pegram. Humorous comment on the home industry of knitting socks for the troops.

Sock production became, for some, a badge of honour including this octogenarian, who had been born even before Queen Victoria ascended to the throne. The *Halifax Courier* of 8 July 1916 told her story:

> Few women, even in these days when they are tempting unheard-of things, are capable at 83 of rendering such service as Mrs Milnes [...] This week she completed her 106th pair [of socks], and it is well on with her next [...] With sight almost undimmed, and her faculties acute, this kindly lady, day by day, gives her quota to the general service [...] 'I can't remember the time when I couldn't knit' she said [...] 'I was knitting before I was seven.'

The *Courier* Comforts Fund

On 3 September 1914, the *Halifax Courier* had also entered the fray. Under the column headline 'Mayor's Local Distress Fund Courier Branch' the *Halifax Courier* announced 'We have pleasure in notifying our decision to try and assist our Mayor in building up a fund for the relief of distress caused in this neighbourhood by the war.'

On 5 September the *Halifax Courier* explained what it was setting up and why:

> In our midst vast numbers are suffering [...] through this dreadful war [...] some are soldiers' homes, others not. All must have our attention [...] immense means will be required to cope

adequately with the misery already inflicted [...] let it be clearly understood, that, as in the South African War, our branch is in aid of the struggling households of this neighbourhood [...] we have many more lads away than during the Boer War and therefore upheaval hits ever so much harder.

At this stage this fund's focus was very much on neighbourhood distress, but it was the beginning of what evolved into the *Courier* Comforts Fund, which went on to distribute large quantities of comforts to wounded soldiers in local hospitals and troops at the front and in prisoner-of-war camps.

On 12 September it began publishing its list of subscribers. It was a truly communal effort from the beginning, and was pro-active in its collecting activities. It was able to persuade many diverse individuals and institutions to arrange collections on its behalf including, according to its launch article, King Cross Orchestral Society,

Cartoon by J. J. Mulroy announcing the Courier's local war fund. Halifax Courier 5 September 1914. The use of the fund for helping soldier dependants at home is more in evidence at this stage of the war.

Queens Road United Methodist Church, Hanover Brotherhood Church and 'humourist Harold Foster'. Some of the helpers were people who went out with official *Courier* collecting boxes and actively canvassed for money around the streets of Halifax. The article listed eighty-five individuals and local businesses that held one of these boxes.

One notable aspect of the fund was the use of what amounted to an army of young children collectors. The most famous of these was George Bentley of the Commercial (Temperance) Hotel, Wards End. He first appeared in the *Halifax Courier* on 22 August 1914:

Halifax people will have noticed in the streets of the town during the past two days a little mite, dressed in khaki, carrying before him a collecting box inscribed 'for the Mayor's relief fund'. He is George Bentley, aged three, the son of Mr Bentley, of the Commercial Hotel, and the public are supporting his box freely. His first contribution will be found in today's list of subscriptions to the full.

By the 12 September he was appearing in the *Halifax Courier* subscription lists and was becoming something of a minor celebrity:

> 'Little Khaki George' is the name his father has given George Bentley, aged 3½ [...] The time and sacrifices of this parent are worthy of all praise; he must have spent scores of hours walking the little chap round [...] in three trips he landed 696 pennies. And last evening, not tired – no not by any means, he sat on our office counter while we counted his collection and prepared him a new box.

How did the idea of children dressing in such outfits for fund collections evolve? Certainly the idea of dressing up children in military or naval uniforms was not new. This had been part of the repertoire of photography portrait studios for years. George Bentley recalled many years later:

> I never knew how the affair started. I believe that my parents knew Mr. Denison [editor of the *Halifax Courier*] and can only assume that in conversation with him an idea germinated that they could somehow help with the collection of money. Just how this crystallised I can only imagine but the outcome was that I being small, therefore likely to arouse the maternal instincts of the citizens, was detailed to do the collecting [...] a war theme should be employed [...] Sam Stocks, considered to be Halifax's leading tailor [...] was brought in to make a uniform small enough.

There had been a similar use of a juvenile called Percy Wilson setup by the *Halifax Courier* during the Boer War, so we may assume that the idea came from Denison.

The use of juvenile collectors in this way was not unique to Halifax. Jennie Jackson ('Young Kitchener') in Burnley is sometimes quoted as the most famous of all, but in the 5 December 1914 issue of the *Burnley News* she is reported as submitting only her 'third instalment', suggesting a much later starting date than Little Khaki George who was reported in the *Halifax Courier* as early as 22 August 1914. Is it possible he was the model for Burnley and maybe others?

Whether original or not, the *Halifax Courier* seems to have industrialised the idea. The subscription list that launched its local war fund contained the names of at least four juveniles. By 24 October there were twenty-three juvenile collectors. They included Leonard Haigh, who went under the name of 'Little Scottie'. The *Halifax Courier* of 12 September reported:

Master Haigh aged 3 [...] He is dressed as a Scotch-boy. His mother writes [to] us [...] 'of course I do not let him go out without myself or his big brother. Wishing you all success.'

Postcard of 'Little Khaki George' produced by Lillywhite: Calderdale Museums Service.

George Bentley continued with his collections until mid-1916. According to his recollections he started school that year and also had outgrown his outfit. He did pass one important milestone in April 1915 – Percy Wilson's record of £84. By the time he hung up his collecting box, Khaki George had collected £150 (£12,500).

The *Courier* War Fund had taken its inspiration from the newspaper's experience in the Boer War when it had supported soldier's dependants. The new fund, supporting a much larger war, involved virtually everyone, and started to take a different direction quite early on.

The 12 September issue of the *Courier* carried a request from the Great Coates Camp, where the Territorials of the 4th Battalion West Riding Regiment were stationed:

Leonard Haigh ('Little Scottie') Halifax Courier.

"EACH OF 'EM DOING 'IS COUNTRY'S WORK."
— ABSENT-MINDED BEGGAR.

J. J. Mulroy cartoon depicting everyone pulling together, including the children. The small boy with the collecting box is presumably George Bentley ('Little Khaki George'). Halifax Courier *19 September 1914.*

[T]there is a rumour that a fund is being started in Halifax to get tobacco to the Terriers. We hope so! If the rumour is unfounded, perhaps it has arisen because the wish is father to the thought, and if it is not true, it certainly ought to be.

The *Halifax Courier* reacted immediately by placing a special box for tobacco contributions in two streets close to the newspaper's office. This was the beginning of a regular flow of tobacco and cigarettes donated by local residents and sent out by the *Halifax Courier* to the district's soldiers.

The Halifax men of the 10th (Service) West Riding Regiment put in a request for tobacco through the *Halifax Courier* of 3 October:

It has come to our knowledge that the Courier has opened a fund to supply troops with tobacco and cigarettes. In this regiment there are about 80 Halifax men, the majority of whom have received no pay. We would be very grateful if the Courier would be so kind as to remember them when apportioning cigarettes.

The public were being made aware of these requests through the letters that the *Halifax Courier* was publishing, so it is perhaps not surprising to find readers spontaneously sending in comfort goods to the *Courier* Office. The *Halifax Courier of* 19 September reported:

> We have been overwhelmed with kindness in other directions this week, gifts of all sorts from Testaments to blankets and cigarettes [...] and they come without having been asked for.

J. J. Mulroy Cartoon depicting the new Halifax Courier *initiative, the 'Tobacco Fund'. 26 September 1914.*

The *Courier* reported on 3 October that the variety of goods being despatched had also become more varied:

> We intend, as soon as we can accumulate a parcel big enough to go round, sending to the West Riding Regiment now fighting at the front, woollen socks, toffee, cigarettes and tobacco [...]

Local firms such as John Mackintosh also pitched in:

> We notice you have added Toffee to your list of presents for the Soldiers. We are quite sure, Halifax Soldiers at any rate, will appreciate a present of Toffee and we have pleasure [...] sending you one hundred 6d tins of Toffee.

It was also evident that the impetus for sending comforts was coming from the battalions themselves. The custom grew for commanding officers to find out the needs of their own battalion and send in what was effectively a wish list. The *Halifax Courier* then did its best to source these requirements. In 1915, the newspaper was working with local businesses who were ordering goods from wholesalers, who then sent the goods directly to the battalions. The list below, taken from the *Halifax Courier* of 5 May 1915, provides us with a vivid idea of the kind of things soldiers were asking for:

By November 1914 the net was widening. Comforts were being sent out to 'Camp, Front, Hospital and Prison'. The latter was a reference to prisoners-of-war from the Halifax area and was about two years ahead of the Central Prisoners Committee, who later instigated a similar service nationally. As the prisoner-of-war stories were to later testify in 1918, these food parcels were for many a morale booster and for some a literal life saver.

It was in everyone's interest to keep up a dialogue between donor and recipient. Even allowing for an element of official encouragement in the writing of 'thank you' letters, there is little doubt that the goods were very much valued by the troops. The following appeared in the *Halifax Courier* of 26 September:

The consignment comprised the following goods bought out of the Fund:—

24,000 Cigarettes.
10,000 Sheets Foreign Notepaper.
5,000 Envelopes.
5,000 Pencils.
5,000 Boxes of Safety Matches.
2,000 Handkerchiefs.
2,000 lbs. of Carbolic Soap.
1,576 Clay Pipes.
1,000 Bags of Biscuits.
1,008 Packets of Tobacco.
500 Wood Pipes.
720 Socks.
300 lbs. of Candles.
96 pairs of Braces.
£5's worth of Sweets.
£5's worth of Dates.
£5's worth of Nuts.
£5's worth of Keating's Powder.
48 Electric Torches.
36 Spare Batteries for Same.
50 Razors.
96 Tins of Salmon.
48 Tins of Crayfish.
48 Tins of Whole Pineapples.
48 Tins of Pineapple Chunks.
48 Tins of Pears.
24 Tins of Lobster.
24 Tins of Sardines.
24 Tins of Herrings.
24 Tins of Apricots.
24 Tins of Peaches.
12 Medicine Chests.

Sir, – I should be pleased if you will insert the following in a conspicuous place in your newspaper

I am a private in the West Riding Regiment, and we are indebted to the townspeople of Halifax for their kindness in providing us with shirts and socks. A pair of socks has been handed to me by company Quartermaster Sgt. Dolby, and attached is a piece of paper bearing the following words:

"Cissie Whiteley, aged 11 years, Halifax Yorks. Wishing you the best of luck: down with the Germans."

As the address of this kind stranger is not given, I shall be pleased if you will insert the episode, as otherwise I have no means of acknowledging her kindness. The socks are warm and comfortable, and will come in handy for the coming cold winter. We shall all do our best to carry out Miss Whiteley's wishes, and trust she will remain in the best of health to see England victorious.

Yours faithfully, H. Newton, Belton Park, Grantham, September 23, 1914.

We believe this was Harry Newton who served with the 8th Battalion West Riding Regiment and went to Gallipoli in July 1915. Afterwards, the battalion took part in the Battle of the Somme and unfortunately this is where Harry met his death on 30 September 1916. 'Cissie' was Elizabeth Ann Whiteley and was born at Southowram Bank, Halifax. She married and lived at Nottingham for a while before emigrating to Australia. Her nephew, Peter Whiteley, described her as 'small, slim and fiesty' and said that her comment 'down with the Germans' was totally in character.

The *Halifax Guardian* Prisoners of War Fund

In June 1916 the Halifax Guardian announced its own initiative to help prisoners-of-war. It explained that the fund was being opened 'For starving prisoners of war [...] against the brutality of the Hun'. It was roused to action by:

VISITING OFFICER. "You'll get the D.C.M. for recapturing all that ammunition in the face of the enemy."

WOUNDED TOMMY. "Ammunition, Sir! Not much, Sir. Why, it was a crate of comforts from the Halifax Courier!!"

Appreciation of comforts being sent to soldiers.
Halifax Courier *17 April 1915.*

[…] the disclosures which have recently been made concerning the treatment of British prisoners of war in Germany have created a feeling of deep concern the country through […] it is neither more nor less than contemptible cruelty.

German prisoner-of-war camps were administered by the military and treatment of British servicemen varied enormously. Newspapers may have over-egged the situation but the fact remained that conditions and treatment were well below what was expected by The Hague Convention. Brutality and starvation were rife. More than anything, a lack of food was the problem and deaths due to starvation were not infrequent.

The *Guardian* continued:

We have been specially requested to render all assistance possible in this matter of giving relief to starving prisoners and particularly for the men of the local regiments, the 8th, 9th, and 10th Duke of Wellington's Regiment […] 'GIVE US FOOD!' is their request [their emphasis].

A parcel depot was setup in the York Café on King Edward Street and an army of mainly women volunteers was employed to do the packing. As with the practice of the *Halifax Courier* the newspaper called for voluntary donations to its fund and printed a subscription every week. It regularly claimed that around a thousand parcels were dispatched every fortnight.

With a clear nod to what the *Halifax Courier* was already doing, it was at pains to point out that 'THERE WILL BE NO OVERLAPPING' [their emphasis]. Despite this assurance the boundaries could be very blurred. Both claimed they were officially authorised funds to the exclusion of all others and both could be found apparently servicing the same battalions. Was this something of a turf war?

It is an area that needs more research, but if we attempted some generalisations we could say that:

The *Courier* was servicing troops at the front and wounded servicemen at home; the *Guardian* concentrated on prisoners-of-war.

The *Courier* was delivering different kinds of comforts; the *Guardian* concentrated on food.

The *Courier* concentrated on local men only including those in other regiments; the *Guardian* serviced all members of the West Riding Regiment.

Rivalry?

In May 1917, the *Halifax Courier* announced its own important new initiative for prisoners-of-war that extended what it was already doing. This was the 'Soldiers' Parcels Depot':

> [...] to take the parcels of the relatives or friends of any soldier or sailor [...] strongly packed [...] fully addressed; it will be our business to check the addresses, detect faults in them, add to each parcel's covering and finally affix our official label [...]

It proclaimed that its fund was:

> Amongst the first in Britain initiated [...] but the warriors and prisoners' needs have grown so prodigiously by reason of the increased numbers [...] that we find it impossible to do anything really tangible for them [...] All this neighbourhood's men in these units and over a thousand isolated men besides, will [now] equally share in comforts.

'These units' were:

2nd Battalion West Riding Regiment
4th Battalion West Riding Regiment
Reserve 4th Battalion West Riding Regiment
8th Battalion West Riding Regiment
9th Battalion West Riding Regiment
10th Battalion West Riding Regiment
5th Battery of 2 Brigade (West Riding) Royal Field Artillery
21st West Yorkshire Battalion (Wool Textiles Pioneers)

They represented the units which had been 'raised' initially in and around Halifax, even though by this time (1917) the numbers of Halifax men in them had been considerably diluted.

In effect what they had done was to organise the parcels from individuals into a single depot and deliver then by a single parcels convoy. Photographs exist showing the Comforts Fund committee and its lady packers seated in front of the Blue Coat School, which once stood on Harrison Road. It seems likely that this is where the packing took place. It cannot be said with absolute confidence that this was also what the *Courier* called the 'Parcels Depot', although it must remain a strong candidate.

According to the *Halifax Courier* itself and the 'Certificate of Thanks' issued at the end of the war by the Red Cross Society, the authority to do this came from the Central Prisoners of War Committee. This was a national body administered from London by the Red Cross and the Order of St. John, and set up in mid-1916 to put prisoners' parcel distribution on a more serious footing. Quite what authority the *Halifax Guardian* had is unclear, but curiously J.J. Fisher, in his *History of the Duke of Wellington's West Riding Regiment*, also credits them with the authority from the Central Prisoners of War Committee.

One assumes that the *Guardian*'s continued activity led the *Courier* to regularly issue announcements like:

> Halifax men interned [...] are entirely dependent upon the 'Courier's' subscribers, because nobody, neither organisation, friend, nor relative can send direct to them. If they or anybody else would help them, they must, by the regulations of the Central Prisoners' Committee, send their contributions to us and as this help reaches us we send sustenance to them. If this help fails, then 'our' prisoners could have no parcels from Halifax [...] because nobody is authorised like we are, to do just this work.

Belgian Refugee Fund and Belgian Famine Relief Fund

Belgian refugees who were accommodated in the Halifax area were assisted by the establishment of the Belgian Refugee Fund. Later in the year, a Belgian Famine Relief Fund was organised to tackle the shortage of food in occupied Belgium. As might be imagined, the supply of food relief to an enemy-occupied area posed particular diplomatic problems. The German Army of occupation refused to take any responsibility for supplying the 7,000,000 population of Belgium with the necessary food. They argued Belgium should import her own food as she had done before the war. The British naval blockade prevented this, insisting that any food allowed through would simply be requisitioned by the Germans. The problem was finally solved by a compromise agreement brokered by the American Herbert Hoover. Britain agreed to allow food to enter Belgium and the Germans agreed not to seize it.

Wherever there was a need, it seems a committee was setup to organise a fund. As with so many needs, local communities looked after their own. It was the way they did things then. Government involvement was minimal.

St John Ambulance Brigades

Before the outbreak of war, the local St John Ambulance movement consisted of a few enthusiastic individuals who trained men and women to render first aid in case of accident, usually civilian injuries in workshops and on the street. There were firms in Halifax where accidents were almost a daily occurrence. The outbreak of war led to an expansion in their services and numbers. A large number of the members volunteered for active service, mostly with the RAMC and something like 200 men were drafted away from the town. Some served on hospital ships such as HMS *Oxfordshire*.

The women's section also expanded, leading to the formation of the famous Voluntary Aid Detachments (VAD). They supplied nurses to the various military hospitals at home, and to the clearing and base hospitals abroad. In Halifax, several VADs were attached to St Luke's Military Hospital (former Halifax Union) when it opened in December 1915. They were also in great demand for the many auxiliary hospitals that were set up in the Halifax area between 1915 and 1917.

Men of the St John Ambulance Brigade turned out on convoy nights at St Luke's Military Hospital when they assisted with the transfer of wounded soldiers (totalling 17,384 overall) from the local railway station to the hospital.

St John Ambulance man, James Brockless, with family group circa 1916. He served on the hospital ship HMS Oxfordshire: *Courtesy of David Nortcliffe.*

The outcome

As events were to prove, Halifax was to enter a period of unprecedented prosperity on a scale nobody could have anticipated on account of the increase in government orders. Unemployment was never a problem and the government also began to shoulder greater social responsibility through increases in separation allowances. The plethora of fund and support committees was a testament to the self-help ethic that swept through Halifax, as it did over most other parts of the country. In May 1919, the Halifax Union Guardians were able to report:

> At the start of the war prophesies had been made that there would be a significant increase in cases of local distress who needed Poor Law assistance but the local communities had responded to such an extent that there were fewer cases of distress post-war than pre-war.

It is tempting to be drawn into clichés such as 'finest hour', but the support activities of the local Halifax communities demonstrates how war can sometimes bring out the best in people. It was not only the soldiers at the Front who helped win the war.

CHAPTER 4

1914–15
Realisations

The first convoy of wounded soldiers

During the first few months of the war the readers of the local Halifax newspapers had received a sanitised view of the military situation and had been able to largely stand aloof from the realities of war. It is true the first significant clashes around Mons and Le Cateau in late August had aroused alarm at the German advance, but details in the form of casualty lists and soldiers' letters had not yet become common. For most of the time the two established hospitals (St Luke's, Salterhebble and The Halifax Royal Infirmary) had been receiving nothing more than a trickle of wounded soldiers since quite early in the war.

During late October and into November, the British Army had been involved in some desperate fighting around the Belgian city of Ypres where the German Army was making its last attempt to break through to the Channel ports. The battle, later designated First Ypres, had resulted in casualty figures that were five times greater than Mons and the subsequent retreat from the city. They included 30,000 wounded, a relatively large proportion of the army at the time. Many of these found their way back to hospitals in the UK. On 21 November, Halifax was to have its first real taste of what modern war could be like, when it received a convoy of nearly 100 wounded soldiers that arrived at the Halifax Railway Station. The *Halifax Courier* reported:

Comfortably seated in an easy chair, reading the War story, one gets but a faint idea of its sad realities. Happily our insular position has for very many years prevented such experiences being brought to our own doors [...] there was quite a different scene at Horton-Street Station on Tuesday night when a hundred wounded soldiers came showing unmistakable signs of having been amongst the shrapnel [...] sixty of the patients were taken to the Infirmary, and forty to Salterhebble Hospital.

Ten ambulance carriages from around the districts and five tramcars were assembled to transfer the wounded to the two hospitals.

[...] some with several weeks growth of beard looked foreigners [...] all came from Ypres where the fighting, said one of the men to our representative, was 'something awful'. Most of the wounds he said had been inflicted by parts of shells which flew in all directions [...] some seemed too ill to care [...] the hands of a few were almost completely covered in bandages [...] The procession of wounded [...] was a sight not seen in Halifax before and those who witnessed it must have been impressed with the horrible danger to life in the trenches [...] these men are fortunate to return [...] One said a group of comrades, only 50 yards from him were laughing and joking in a trench when a shell burst right over them, and not one of them was left.

Soldiers' letters were now appearing more regularly in the *Halifax Courier* and could be surprisingly graphic. Their publication followed announcements in the *Halifax Courier* requesting both casualty details and soldiers' letters. Many of the letters were coming from hospitals elsewhere in the UK and as such were not subject to military censorship. Sergeant Ernest Jackson of Boothtown wrote to his sister from hospital in Lincoln:

I have seven shrapnel wounds [...] I was hit in the right shoulder, thigh and knee, left upper arm, wrist, knee and foot. The left upper arm is not so smart as it might be, and the left foot is bad. I have to undergo an operation this week. Otherwise in excellent health.

He went on to describe the action he had been in where his unit had been told to hold their position:

> It was about this time the enemy's artillery opened on us [...] one [shell] came straight into our pit. Six were in, and four were wounded. I am the luckiest of the lot. One poor chap had his side face blown off and the other two had arms and legs broken [...] I got the hospital train for Boulogne [...] I was glad when I got aboard the St. David hospital ship. I got a change of underclothes there – the first since I left England, and a bed. I thought I was in Paradise.

Also from hospital (Bristol), Private J. Coates wrote to his mother:

> It is not war, it is a first class slaughterhouse. It is sickening to see the killed and wounded lying around us. It is simply awful.

Carnage on the battlefield may have been coming home to Halifax but at least civilians could console themselves they were not suffering like the French and Belgians on the continent.

Bombardment of Scarborough, Whitby and Hartlepool
This security was shattered on 16 December 1914 when German battlecruisers stole up in the early morning mist to pour hundreds of heavy calibre shells into the three east coast towns of Whitby, Scarborough and Hartlepool. Not since the Jacobite uprising of 1745-46 had mainland Britain tasted war on its own soil. It was, however, all part of a cat and mouse game to lure the British Grand Fleet piecemeal into the North Sea to be ambushed. The niceties of naval strategy were of no immediate relevance to the inhabitants of these towns. Shattered buildings and 592 casualties were. If you were in the wrong place at the wrong time you were struck down. The deaths amounted to 137 and no distinction was made between men, women or children.

Scarborough was a popular seaside destination for many Halifax people and was only a few hours away by rail. It received a bombardment of 200 shells resulting in eighteen deaths, including 14-month-old John Shields Ryalls. With an eye for a telling phrase,

THE HALIFAX COURIER, SATURDAY, JANUARY 2, 1915.

DISHONOURED.

Captain of the Emden : "Dirty Work."

[Reproduced by permission of "Punch."]

Punch cartoon reproduced in the Halifax Courier *of 2 January 1915. Artist, Leonard Raven Hill. It depicts the German captain of the Emden, who was widely admired by the British public for his daring yet honourable campaign sinking British merchant ships. The propagandist message is that his ideals of honourable warfare were sadly lacking in the actions of the German High Seas Fleet.*

Churchill dubbed the Germans 'the baby killers of Scarborough'. This early morning bombardment had brought the war uncomfortably close to Halifax. It also furnished a number of 'near miss' stories for the local Halifax newspapers.

William Foster of Queensbury, who was visiting Scarborough, was in the bedroom of 48 The Esplanade when:

> [...] one of the first shells fired by the Germans struck the wall to the left of a big window in the drawing room below [...] The wall was shattered [...] Had the shell struck the house a little higher it would have entered the bedroom.

He was later to give a graphic description of his experiences in Scarborough at a special service in Halifax's Victoria Hall.

There were a number of boarding schools at Scarborough where several Halifax children attended. Interestingly, some girls had already been sent home because the authorities thought a bombardment was a possibility. Orleton School on the south front contained the sons of Prebendary Andrew Burn (vicar of Halifax), Dr John Woodyatt (Halifax surgeon), Revd Frank Elam Wheatcroft (vicar of All Souls Church), Charles Shoesmith, and John Brooke Dewhirst (department manager at Crossley Carpets). Their 'adventure' was reported in the *Halifax Courier* of 20 December. They were having breakfast at eight o'clock when there was 'a terrific clatter. The pottery rattled and the ground shook.' They were promptly told to get dressed in whichever of their clothes that came to hand for immediate evacuation. 'Master Woodyatt came home in his football jersey and pants.' As they crossed some fields heading for Seamer Station, they witnessed some of the shells and some exploded 'within two or three hundred yards of them'. They arrived home with a few extra days of Christmas holiday.

Thirteen-year-old Joyce Dewhirst was attending Highcliffe School on the South Cliff. She was in bed when the shelling began and claimed that the school was in the direct line of fire. One shell landed in the school gardens but did not explode. Opposite their school a postman was delivering letters to a maid. Both were struck and killed. At first the schoolgirls, still in their nightclothes, took refuge in the basement, but later were dispatched to Seamer Station by cab.

A daughter of Dr Woodyatt was at St Margaret's School, which was actually struck by shells after the children had been evacuated. The school was later relocated to Scotland.

There was a certain amount of morbid fascination with this act of war so close to everyone's 'hearth and home'. The Christmas editions of the *Halifax Courier* reported trainloads of people tripping up to Scarborough from all over the country to see the damage, with a particular interest in the Grand Hotel. The *Halifax Courier* proudly displayed 'shell relics from Scarborough' in its window on Regent Street. Two men from Elland journeyed to Scarborough to inspect the damage. When they were about to set off home again they found the police inspecting their car. Much to their disgust they found the

Scarborough police had received some sort of tip-off from the York police that they might be spies.

Of course, the main message to emerge was that the war was on everybody's doorstep. Women, children and even babies were being killed. It was a propaganda gift. Churchill wrote to the Mayor of Scarborough:

> [...] practically the whole fast-cruiser force of the German Navy [...] utterly irreplaceable has been risked for the passing pleasure of killing as many English people as possible irrespective of sex, age or condition [...]

It reinforced the propaganda message that had been established by the German invasion of Belgium. The Hun was barbarously ruthless in pursuit of his ambitions to dominate the lives of all Europeans.

Not surprisingly army recruiters were the main benefactors. The *Halifax Courier* reported on 20 December:

> A bit of effective recruiting was done in Halifax on Saturday by Major Hallett who exhibited pieces of German shells fired on the Castle Hill at Scarborough [...] as Mr Whitley said, in his recruiting speech [...] Scarborough and Whitby call loudly for Yorkshiremen to take their place in defence of their homes. And the most urgent need at the moment, to assist in that end, is to volunteer for service at the front.

A typical recruiting poster that played on the barbarity of the war on women and children.

Poetry contributions were a common feature in the *Halifax Courier* during the Great War. Miss E. Todd of the Rook Hotel, Queen's Road, typified the mood:

But Scarborough – he loved the place
That happy haunt of summer revels
Bombarded! – Blood rushed to his face –
   'The Devils'
To the recruiting shop down town
He strode – he almost seemed to run it
'I want to dot them one,' said Brown
'That's done it!'

Zeppelins

Charles Tetley was born in Halifax but living in Hartlepool at the time of the naval bombardment. Perhaps with an eye for the theatrical, he penned a 'war report' direct from 'the front' for publication in the *Halifax Courier* of 24 December.

> I did not get hit, but people were dropping down all about and shells were whistling and bursting all around me […] guns were going a hundred a minute all told.

He then went on to give his thoughts about the Zeppelins threat:

> Well they will have to be right over our heads to do any harm. I should enjoy seeing a fight with Zeppelins; you can dodge them.

Despite Charles Tetley's reassurances, Zeppelin bombs were not easily dodged, and were to become a serious psychological menace.

Even at the beginning of the war, Halifax civilians were jumpy about Zeppelins. In the early hours of 27 August a gas explosion in a Ryburn Valley railway siding led to wild rumours. The *Halifax Courier* reported the incident on 29 August 1914:

> Early on Thursday morning […] residents had a rude awakening by successive explosions. In the minds of many people there were at once imaginings of terror – visions of [a] Zeppelin dropping bombs, and there was a sudden rush to bedroom windows […] a huge flame was seen amid the trees […] meanwhile a buzzer was sounding from a local mill […] the valley was pitch black, relieved only by the glare of the fire and weird continuous sheet lightning.

Despite this early over-reaction, the use of Zeppelin bombers against Antwerp in early October 1914 confirmed that they had more than fantasy status.

The British government imposed blackouts on all centres that they considered to be potential targets. The *Halifax Courier* of 31 October 1914 reported that:

> The more powerful lights in the main streets of Halifax have been subdued since Monday and even the Town Hall clock is in darkness. The police also request that tradesmen who have outside illuminations to their shops will shade them as much as possible [...] the chance of a hostile aeroplane, much less a Zeppelin, paying us a visit is remote. It is a compliment to the importance of Halifax that the Home Office authorities deem that a reduction in lighting is expedient.

Initially, Zeppelins were intended to attack military targets, but the blackouts, navigation difficulties and the woefully clumsy aiming technology meant they hit just about anything. Inevitably this meant civilians. The first 'successful' raid on the British mainland occurred on the night of 19-20 January 1915. While attempting to raid Hull, they killed four civilians in the Norfolk towns of Yarmouth, Sheringham and Kings Lynn.

There were two or three occasions when alarms were sounded and Halifax was plunged into complete darkness, but the nearest any Zeppelins ever came was a few miles away in the neighbourhood of Leeds and an unconfirmed report of one passing near Pecket Well (near Hebden Bridge). Most raids were on the eastern side of Britain, although some raids made it to places such as Liverpool and Manchester.

The *Halifax Courier* noted that many people 'grumbled as they groped'. Indeed, the Lighting Orders concerning private houses were regarded with some resentment, particularly when the private individual could see brightly lit trams and munition factories nearby. Nevertheless, they were imposed and were strictly enforced. The *Halifax Courier* of 4 March 1916 was full of convictions that its citizens were forced to accept. Excuses, hard luck stories and plain hostility were evident.

Samuel Crossley of the Royal Oak Inn, Haugh Shaw, blamed one of his lodgers. William Wood of South View Terrace was caught pulling up his blind before switching off his lights. Harold Marshall of Park Road was ordered to cover all of his forty-four windows. He employed a professional blind-maker who forgot two of them. Fred Dolphin of Swaine's Terrace protested that light was needed to illuminate some dangerous steps. Best of all was James Fox of Marvel Square. When apprehended by the police for not covering a fanlight he remarked, 'Rather funny that I had to turn the gas up so that you [the police sergeant] could see to write my name in your book.' All were fined 7s. 6d. James Ashworth, a shopkeeper of King Cross, perhaps said it for everyone. Previously cautioned and told he might be reported, he simply said, 'Report it. I'm fed up.' He was fined £1.

Inevitably there were complaints that the blackouts were causing accidents. Alderman Morley in the *Halifax Courier* of 8 May 1915 thought 'the death of a little child at King Cross was largely owing to bad light', and asked when Halifax was 'to resume its old position as a decently lighted town'.

The Zeppelins never did come to Halifax.

The horror of gas

Gas is so synonymously associated with the Great War that it is easy to think that it must have been a legitimate and acceptable weapon of war. However, even then it was in theory banned (in this case, under The Hague Convention). The Germans began using it as a mass weapon of attack around Ypres early in 1915. The 2nd Battalion West Riding Regiment consisting of many Halifax men was caught on the notorious Hill 60 by one of the gas attacks on 5 May 1915. When reported in Halifax, it came as a profound shock and rocked everyone's sensibilities about the nature of the men they were fighting against. The death toll alone was enough to make it newsworthy, but it was the horror of the gas that seemed to usher in a new era of barbarity. The war had shifted up a gear.

The shock and revulsion is evident in C. D. Bruce's history of the 1st and 2nd Battalions of the West Riding Regiment.

[…] a cynical and barbarous disregard of the well-known usages of civilised war, and a flagrant defiance of The Hague Convention […] On came this terrible stream of death, and

THE TOLL OF THE WAR.

Many Sorrow-Stricken Homes.

WELL-KNOWN LOCAL FAMILIES BEREAVED.

Headline from Halifax Courier *29 May 1915.*

before anything could be done, all those occupying the front line over which it swept were completely overcome, the majority dying at their posts [...] The battalion suffered over 300 casualties that morning, large numbers dying as a result of this barbarous gas.

A letter from Lance Corporal Greenwood to the *Halifax Courier* of 22 May 1915 brought home the experience at first hand:

Then the most terrible scene I have ever remembered began [...] the poor beggars were staggering along the trench choking and gasping. Some dropped but were walked over by chaps endeavouring to get out [...] when the gas gets into the system it terribly weakens the limbs. My knees were very near collapsing.

Some of the gassed were also present in the second consignment of about 100 wounded that arrived at Halifax Station in May 1915. As before, they were convoyed to the local hospitals through the Halifax streets and under the gaze of its residents. There was a mixture of motor and horse-drawn ambulances and they were assisted by 150 men of the St John Ambulance Brigade, including for the first time members of the ambulance section of the Halifax Volunteer Corps.

The *Halifax Courier* of 22 May described its impact:

On Tuesday night Halifax was provided with another glimpse of the real meaning of war. Individual wounded soldiers are common enough in our streets but the arrival of a trainload, 50 per cent on stretchers, is a saddening sight bringing home the horrors of the conflict more thoroughly than could otherwise be the case. Previous wars have been so far away [...] the wounded have not come before our gaze [...] it has not been felt to the extent it has now [...] most of the men have come from Ypres [...] many of the men were smoking cigarettes but some looked too weary for anything but sleep [...] There were several cases of gas poisoning and these sufferers appeared to be especially languid [...] some have bronchitis, an after effect of the poisoning [...]

As the war progressed, the British and French learned to counter the effects of gas and, of course, developed their own weapons. Despite this, the horror and revulsion is still evident, even at the end of 1915. Bales in his *History of the 1/4 Battalion Duke of Wellington's (West Riding) Regiment* wrote of the gas attack on 19 December:

> [...] the Battalion was bearing the full force both of the gas and the bombardment [...] many men had been gassed before they could do anything, and among them the sights were ghastly. They lay in agony on the ground, sickly greenish white in colour; they foamed at the mouth and gasped for breath; some even tore open their own throats [...] none will ever forgive the enemy who first made use of such fiendish means of destruction.
>
> [...] the battalion's first stay in the Ypres Salient came to an end. It had arrived at the beginning of July, inexperienced and practically unknown [...] it left towards the end of December [...] But it had paid the price. There in the vicinity of Ypres, the original Battalion which had mobilised, trained and gone out to fight, was disbanded. Its men were scattered in a dozen cemeteries and scores of hospitals.

The sinking of the *Lusitania*

The sinking of RMS *Lusitania* in 1915 was, likewise, a severe jolt to people's perception of civilised behaviour. In fact the whole concept of sinking civilian ships without warning or any attempt to evacuate their human cargo was highly controversial. The *Lusitania*, however, was big and carried a large number of women and children. It was this more than anything that caused enormous emotional outrage. The liner had been torpedoed by the German U-20 off the southern coast of Ireland and had gone down within eighteen minutes. The speed of the sinking had made it difficult to get many of the lifeboats away and out of a total of 1,959 souls on board, 1,201 perished. Many of the bodies, including large numbers of women and children, were washed up on the Irish coast, showing the horrific effects of time in the water and eyes pecked out by seagulls. For identification purposes they were photographed. To the British public, the sinking was an obscenity that fuelled the 'Beastly Hun' stereotype.

Walter Dawson of Fixby Avenue, Halifax, was one of the lucky ones. He had been working in America and was on his way home to visit family when he was caught up in the tragedy. He told his story in the *Halifax Courier of* 15 May 1915.

He was interviewed 'in bed' and the *Courier* noted that 'the young man showed direct signs of the terrible hardships he faced'. His claim that he 'actually saw the periscope of the submarine' is perhaps questionable, but nevertheless he had a dramatic story to tell. He went on to say (very precisely) that the ship was travelling at 16 knots and the torpedo struck a little forward of where he was standing. The explosion 'threw up a huge volume of water', which drenched him. He returned to the starboard side but the ship had taken a heavy list. In order to get to the port side he had to crawl up the deck. The ship started going down by the nose so he ran to the port bow deck and dived into the water. From here he witnessed the ship go down and thought he stood no chance of survival because he had no lifebelt. He managed to reach a waterlogged boat and was pulled onto it. There he remained for five hours before being by picked up by a torpedo boat which took him and others to Queenstown, County Cork, Ireland. He paid tribute to the way in which all had behaved, adding (almost reminiscent of the *Titanic*) that there was no panic.

As a footnote to what was already a remarkable story, Walter Dawson later became a soldier and served on the Western Front. He was eventually captured and spent much of his war in a German prisoner-of-war camp.

The second reported story was not so happy. George Arthur Smith was a native of Sowerby Bridge where his fiancée lived. He had been working in America for two years in Rochester, New York. He had written home at the end of April to say that he had booked his passage on the *Lusitania* and expected to be home by the weekend of 8 May. By the time that the weekend had arrived, the news of the sinking was on the streets of Halifax. The *Halifax Courier* reported that for the Smith family 'there was great anxiety in both homes respecting the fate of the traveller'.

The Cunard Steamship Company issued passenger lists that featured two George Smiths – a third-class passenger reported as rescued and another, a second-class passenger, listed as missing. For a while, which must have felt like an eternity, George Smith's family would have suffered the agonising uncertainty of not knowing their son's fate. They were soon to hear what they had dreaded and had probably secretly expected. Their George Smith was not the survivor.

The brother of George went to Liverpool and established that his brother's photograph was not among those posted. He was informed that George Smith's body had not been recovered and he was probably one of several hundred who would never be found. The *Halifax Courier* of 22 May reported that Sam Smith and his wife had 'resigned themselves to the certainty' that their son had perished in the sinking.

Condemnation was vigorous and widespread. Halifax born preacher Dr J. H. Jowett, whose main childhood influences had been at Square Congregational Sunday School, preached from his New York Church saying the disaster was 'a colossal sin against God; it is premeditated murder; it is a relapse to dark, savage barbarity.'

Like the atrocities in Belgium, the bombardment of Scarborough and Whitby, the Zeppelin bombing raids and the German use of gas, the sinking hardened people's perceptions of the Germans. Not only did it assist the recruitment campaigns, it made people more determined to pursue the war with the utmost vigour. Corporal J. W. Grayson, writing to Chief Inspector Gledhill of the Halifax Borough Police clearly took it very personally. His letter in the *Halifax Courier* of 29 May 1915 showed how the *Lusitania* sinking hit home with everyone:

[…] we have exacted the first toll for the Lusitania. The boys used it as a battle cry, whilst charging the German trenches, and gave them a taste of cold steel in fair exchange for their cold water and gas.

Lance Corporal Frank Mitchell, writing to the *Halifax Guardian* of 22 May from a military hospital in London, was even more direct:

We attacked […] giving the Westphalians a taste of our bayonets. They shouted 'Mercy, comrades.' We yelled 'Lusitania, you beggars,' and killed them.

As 1915 drew on, people were getting a clearer picture of the type of war they were in. Few still saw it as either adventurous or glorious.

CHAPTER 5

1915
The End of Voluntarism

The struggling campaign

The recruitment arguments remained the same for 1915. Was the message getting through to the young men of Halifax? Did the young men of Halifax think their job was soldiering? To what extent was it necessary for men to remain behind to manufacture the munitions? Above all, was voluntarism enough to satisfy the demand for 'men, more men and more men'? The authorities kept beating the drum, but the recruitment story in 1915 increasingly became a matter of diminishing returns.

Things began brightly enough. In the early months, weekly recruitment numbers in Halifax were around the 400 mark. By May the tide was turning and newspaper reports were featuring increasingly negative reports. The *Halifax Guardian* of 1 May reported a motor car tour of Greetland and Stainland, accompanied by a band and a veteran of Mons and Ypres. The speakers compared the local villages to what was happening in Belgium, but the Belgian card was not always working. Some did not see why they should be fighting for Belgium when they considered what that nation had done in the Congo (a reference to Belgian atrocities against ethnic natives in the Belgian Congo). One recruitment speaker 'deplored the apathy to be met with in some quarters'.

The Civilian Recruiting Committee had numerous propaganda gifts

THE TENNIS SEASON HAS COMMENCED.
SPORTIVE SLACKER : " Service."
PASSING TOMMY : " Yes, but who's—yours or the country's ?"

J. J. Mulroy Cartoon, highlighting what was seen as the selfish attitude of 'the slacker'. Halifax Courier *8 May 1915.*

to call on, including the recent sinking of the *Lusitania*, but recruitment continued to disappoint. The *Halifax Guardian* of 22 May reported what recruiters were finding in Brighouse:

> [...] the Germans' latest outrages should have convinced everyone that it was not only the Army and Navy which was at war but the whole people [...] It was only a question of getting them to see that it was their duty to go.

One speaker referred pessimistically to a 'barrier of complacency which had been much in evidence lately'.

One stumbling block to recruitment was a concern amongst workers that enlistment would lead to a loss of their jobs when the war was over. The Halifax Chamber of Commerce had received a circular from the War Office urging them to get all employers to guarantee jobs. The local newspapers had published the names of many who had offered to do this, but the *Halifax Courier* of 29 May reported that Alderman F. Whitley-Thompson was sorry to say that some firms were 'unwise, un-English and unpatriotic' and had not agreed to do this. One committee member drew their attention to 'a very ridiculous article [...] by some Piccadilly newspaperman [...] that they (in Yorkshire) were not enlisting'. Sir George Fisher-Smith believed:

> It was becoming increasingly difficult to get recruits in Halifax because, comparatively, there are few to enlist. In Halifax they were engaged to a considerable extent upon the manufacture of war munitions.

By mid-summer the numbers were drying up. The *Halifax Guardian* of 24 July reported that 'recruiting has been very slack in the Calder Valley (Hebden Bridge and Sowerby Bridge) and only two recruits have been enrolled'. It was a problem that was not unique to Halifax and the conscription lobbyists started to become more vocal at all levels. There was a need to know how many eligible men were still out there, and to rationalise where they were best placed. On 15 July 1915, the government sought to create a national register of all males between the ages of 15 and 65 and their occupations by the passing of the National Registration Act. The coalition government dressed it up as a means to help industry and, rather unconvincingly, as a means to stave off conscription. It fooled nobody. Whatever the short term benefits, the information collected was going to be a very useful tool for implementing conscription. The register took some months to compile but eventually showed there was a pool of about 5,000,000 males of military age who were not in the forces. Of these, 1,600,000 were in so called 'starred' occupations, which were deemed to be of 'national importance'. This left a potential of 3,400,000 other men who could be enlisted into the army if conscription was introduced. Recruiting officers continued to bang the drum for volunteers but sensed that conscription was coming, and were not above using this as a lever to persuade eligible men.

August 1915 brought the first anniversary of the outbreak of war and an opportunity for the Civilian Recruiting Committee. A week-long jamboree of events was organised 'to secure further enlistments'. The *Halifax Guardian* of 7 August reported on the huge procession that began the proceedings from George Square:

> This demonstration [...] was in a manner, symbolic of the authorities going on their bended knees and begging the enlistable young men to come to a sense of duty [...] there were innumerable potential soldiers lining the pavements on the route of the procession, and if their consciences were not touched by all that they saw they were tackled by the many recruiting officers [...]

The procession itself was nothing if not impressive:

> In the van [...] was the [Second Reserve 4th Battalion West Riding Regiment], with the depot and Territorial Bands [...] then came the first of several vehicles which had been transformed by an artistic treatment of posters [...] Following on were three vans of soldiers' children [...] several of the little ones carried aloft legends stating 'My Dad is at the front; where's yours', 'Remember Scarborough', 'I wish I were old enough', 'Our King wants you', 'Have I to go?' The Volunteer Training Corps with their honourable band [...] succeeded, and then came another touching sight, a van load of wounded heroes. Six more vans of soldiers' children and a recruiting pantechnicon were succeeded by a splendid array of the Boys' Brigade [...] after the King Cross Band [...] came yet another five vans of laughing and chatting children and a recruiting vehicle and then eight further loads of youngsters, interspersed by the Church Lads' Brigade [...] Boy Scouts [...] Catholic Boys Brigade [...] Southowram band [...] four vans of heroes' offspring, two recruiting vehicles, and a collecting donkey made up the rear of a long and imposing procession.

In all there had been 'twenty-six of these van loads of bubbling life, representing nearly eight hundred children', and the 'collecting donkey' was presumably occupied by Little Khaki George. The procession toured the town before heading west to the open spaces of

Savile Park, 'where there was a march past of the military and the VTC (Voluntary Training Corps).'

A spectacular military tattoo was organised at Thrum Hall, home of the local rugby football club. The *Halifax Guardian* reported it in terms that we might associate with an Olympic Opening Ceremony:

> The spectacle of 400 torches forming fantastic figures was one of bewildering brilliancy. To swinging martial music [...] the air of the ancient Roman amphitheatre [...] National Anthems of our French, Belgian, Russian and Italian Allies [...] massed bands [...] the mournful note of the 'Last Post' [...] grand display of aerial fireworks [...] gymnastic display [...] bands of the two regiments.

Despite the splendour of it all, recruitment officers voiced familiar frustrations:

> 'We have been down on our knees as it were, to beg for recruits for the Army,' said Capt. Moorhouse of the Halifax Recruiting Depot [...] he said he was afraid there were people who were thinking more of cricket and of going on holidays than of the safety of our country. 'Do you realise the seriousness of the position? Conscription is not far off and then you will be driven in!'

Their pessimism was not misplaced. The *Halifax Guardian* reported that 'The great effort locally to secure further recruits concluded on Thursday evening, and the results are by no means satisfactory.' The total for Halifax was twenty-nine.

The following week the *Halifax Guardian* commented that these were:

> [...] not striking results particularly when we remember with what energy the campaign was conducted [...] to stir up enthusiasm in the district. True this is a munitions area [...] but we cannot close our eyes to the fact that to many young men the appeal has gone out in vain. The general excuse is that they have good jobs [...]

One recruiting officer put it more bluntly:

> [...] there are hundreds of young fellows in the town slinking behind a badge of some description.

In another attempt at a mass recruitment drive, the Reserve 4th Battalion West Riding Regiment paid a visit to the Halifax districts and was employed as a 'Flying column' to tour local communities. The *Halifax Guardian* of 2 October reported that it attracted 'large numbers of people [...] many fluttering flags that hung from bedroom windows'.

At Hebden Bridge, the battalion's commanding officer, Colonel Land, was in critical mood and willing to use the veiled threat of conscription. The *Guardian*'s report continued:

> It is a disgrace [...] that such a large proportion of the men who had joined were married [...] that was not right.

Many men were wanted for munitions, but were all the men who could join [...] on munitions. Recently a register had been taken [...] he doubted very much if one in twenty of those who were eligible for the Army were engaged on munitions [...] the names of the eligible men were on the pink forms [...] If volunteers did

RECRUITING WEEK.

Poor Response in Halifax.

Only Twenty-Five Men Join.

Twenty-five recruits have been induced to join the Third Line of our Territorial Battalion as an outcome of last week's oratory and inducement held out to men to join the colours. These, on the face of it, are not striking results, particularly when we remember with what energy the campaign was conducted and the thoroughness of the effort to stir up enthusiasm throughout the district.

True, this is a munition-making area. A great many men are held back through employment in that capacity; true, too, that many prospective recruits have found and are finding their way to Huddersfield, Bradford, and such places, to the detriment of the local battalion, but we cannot close our eyes to the fact that to many young men the appeal has gone out in vain.

"The general excuse is that they have good jobs and do not see their way clear to throw up that work for 1s. a day," is the impression of an officer who has taken a leading part in the recruiting of men in the borough throughout the past twelve months, and who forms the opinion that there are hundreds of young fellows in the town slinking behind a badge of some description.

The rise and drop of the recruiting thermometer at the Drill Hall reads:—

Saturday, July 31st	3
Sunday, August 1st	1
Monday, August 2nd	9
Tuesday, August 3rd	3
Wednesday, August 4th	3
Thursday, August 5th	4
Friday, August 6th	2
Saturday, August 7th	0
Sunday, August 8th	0

Recruitment returns. Halifax Guardian *7 August 1915.*

COLONEL LAND'S FLYING COLUMN

Visit to Halifax.

STIRRING SCENES.

The Camp on Skircoat Moor

Halifax Guardian
2 October 1915.

not come forward the time would come when compulsion would have to be used.

Another recruiting officer remarked that 'the young eligible men were conspicuous by their absence from that meeting'.

The column proceeded down the valley to Halifax where, on the borough boundary, at Pye Nest, it was met in the middle of the road by a ceremonial greeting party. The mayor gave the battalion 'a most hearty welcome back to the ancient town of Halifax'. He proudly emphasised the unit's Halifax roots, '1,200 men raised out of this district,' before boarding a car to lead them in towards Halifax and on to Savile Park where they paraded and pitched camp.

The *Guardian* reported one strange aspect of the battalion's arrival. Despite the fact that 'the police had to cope with a crowd several thousand strong' and the crowds on the ropes were:

> [...] so dense they were met with a deplorable reticence [...] the crowd held back its cheers [...] scarcely a cheer was raised as they marched into the enclosure.

No explanation for this was offered by the newspaper.

A platform was improvised and the now familiar addresses were given. The mayor wanted 'to put every ounce into our exertions [...] we want every man', drew attention to the 'sorry plight of Belgium' and asked 'what would be our position if the Germans secured a footing in England?' Colonel Land asked them to:

> [...] fill up our ranks and expedite our going. They had to realise what they had never realised before that this is a life and death struggle [...] for their homes, their hearths and their very existences [...] the fate of women and children would be too horrible to contemplate ...

With a nod to some of the disappointments of 1915 and the 'shell scandal' (see next chapter), Colonel Land reassured them: 'They all knew that mistakes had been made but they were now assured that munitions and guns would be forthcoming.' Hinting at what was now becoming more inevitable by the hour he added, 'if the government demanded conscription there was not a man worthy of the name of an Englishman who would oppose it.'

The criticism continued in Elland:

> [...] there had not been that response from Elland that there ought to have been. There were many sheltering as munition workers.

He claimed to have received 'anonymous communications' telling him that:

> [...] at least a hundred eligible young men, tradesmen and the sons of tradesmen who had not come forward [...] names of various places where these men could be found, and the graphic description given of them was not very complimentary to Elland men.

The mood of the army recruiters now seemed to have a bitter edge to it. One speaker was moved to say:

> If ever there was a blot on Yorkshire it was today to think of the disgrace of sending round soldiers to beg, plead and fawn to men to help their country [...] a lot of slackers were sitting at home smoking their pipes or sitting in pubs drinking their beer.

The 'slackers', who were sitting at home smoking their pipes or in the pubs drinking beer, were not by any means a small minority, as the National Register was about to establish. They represented millions who, for a variety of reasons, did not want to go to war.

The Derby Scheme (Group Scheme)
A final attempt to tap into some of these 'missing millions', and maintain a semblance of voluntarism, was attempted by Lord Derby who was appointed Director-General of Recruiting in October 1915. Eligible men (those aged 18 to 40) were to be visited by canvassers who were to invite them directly ('without bullying') to voluntarily attest to serve in the army. Those who agreed would be allowed to return to their current occupations, but would be obliged to come

forward if called-up later on. Attesting under the Derby Scheme had a number of benefits. The men were allowed to wear a special armband, indicating they had shown their willingness to serve, so avoiding accusations of being slackers. They were also assured that they would be allowed to appeal when called-up. They were to be placed into groups according to marital status and age. The single men would be called-up first, starting with the youngest age groups. It was made known that voluntary enlistment would end on 15 December 1915.

The *Halifax Courier* of 27 November reported:

> The Halifax Civilian Recruiting Committee has arranged […] a recruiting office under Lord Derby's scheme at York Café (Alexandra Buildings), Commercial Street […]

Local MP James Parker thought that this scheme would make it possible to avoid conscription. The vicar of King Cross believed: 'It goes very near compulsion but it still has the merit of allowing men the chance of saying "I come" rather than saying to them "you must".' On 4 December, the *Halifax Courier* noted that there was 'A busy time at the new office'.

Despite some encouraging early signs, the Derby Scheme failed to enlist the numbers hoped for. Having tried many approaches to raise the necessary numbers for Kitchener's New Armies through voluntarism, the government had to turn to its only remaining option: conscription.

Postscript: The strange case of Lieutenant Richard Flanagan
A regular figure at the recruitment meetings was an officer called Lieutenant Richard Wycliffe Flanagan. The local newspapers reported his recruitment activities and frequently described him as a popular speaker. There seems little doubt he was an asset to the service, but it appears he was a complete fraud. He was not a commissioned officer and had been given no authority to be recruiting on behalf of the Halifax military authorities. He was born in Halifax in 1895 and attended the Crossley and Porter Orphanage and School. A school's roll of honour, published in the *Halifax Courier* early in the war, lists him as having joined the Leicester Regiment in 1914 as a private. It appears that he went absent without leave from his regiment in January

1915, and turned up at the Halifax Drill Hall dressed in an officer's uniform. Incredibly he managed to successfully persuade the military authorities that he had been appointed to assist in recruitment. At one point he even had himself promoted to the rank of captain. By September 1916, his deception caught up with him, and he was arrested for impersonating an officer. His subsequent trial was extensively reported in the *Halifax Courier* and he was sentenced to six months imprisonment, after which he appears to have been returned to the Leicester Regiment. His records indicate that he also served with the North Staffordshire Regiment and was eventually discharged from the army for medical reasons.

CHAPTER 6

1915–16
Preparing for Total War

In 1914, Britain had gone to war reluctantly and, in many quarters, with an unclear idea of how it was going to be conducted. Prime Minister Asquith famously said 'Business as usual', as if adding the conduct of the war to his existing portfolio. By 1915 the nature of the war was becoming more apparent and it was evident there would need to be changes.

Shell Scandal and the coming of the Ministry of Munitions
Lord Kitchener had already broken with tradition by declaring that Britain would require a large army to help defeat Germany, and had called for a massive recruitment programme. Its natural consequence, a radical rethink to the supply and equipping of this vast army, was slower in coming.

By 1915, the British serving soldier was forced to face up to an unpalatable truth: the German Army was better equipped. He seemed to have a plentiful supply of hardware, such as bombs, mortars, machine-guns and heavy artillery. More importantly, he had a seemingly inexhaustible supply of shells to feed his war machine. Tommy firmly believed he was a superior fighting man to Fritz, but his constant need to rely on homemade grenades and mortars undermined his efforts.

1915: British soldiers improvise by making 'grenades' out of tobacco tins.
The Illustrated War News.

The issue began to gain momentum in mid-March when the British Army launched its first offensive on the Western Front at Neuve Chapelle in support of a major French offensive. It was a relatively modest affair compared to the activities of its allies. Nevertheless, there was an air of optimistic expectation that the attack would break through the German trench positions. Things began quite well with British troops breaking into the German positions on the first day. Then it all went pear-shaped in a fashion that was to become wearily familiar. The British were unable to exploit their success quickly enough before the Germans were able to reinforce, and the offensive ground to a halt. Recriminations and excuses abounded. The real culprit was poor communication and a muddle over deployment of reserves, but the commander-in-chief, Sir John French, had another scapegoat in mind and began to voice it – a shortage of shells.

Things came to a head in May 1915 with more failed attempts to break through, this time at Festubert and Aubers Ridge. An air of frustration prevailed. Sir John French leaked a story to the press blaming the War Office for failing to supply his army with the necessary goods to do the job properly. The 'Shell Scandal' row that ensued caused political mayhem, which fatally damaged Asquith's Liberal government, and in the long run, Kitchener and Sir John French himself. Someone else's star, however, was in the ascendancy.

Lloyd George's vision
On 1 March 1915, Lloyd George spoke to his constituents in a speech at Bangor:

> The reason why we should triumph is that the resources of the allies were overwhelmingly greater than those of the enemy [...] The allied powers had at their disposal more than twice the number of men which our enemies could command [...] We had since raised the largest voluntary Army that had ever been enrolled [...] we want more [...] This is an engineer's war [...] we need men but we need armaments even more.

It was a blueprint for total war. His audience may not have fully grasped where Lloyd George was taking them, but he himself was very clear. The whole of Britain was to be reorganised into a full time war machine on a scale it could never have imagined. Nearly every corner of British Society was to be organised, manipulated and squeezed to one aim: the defeat of Germany. The process began with the setting up of the Ministry of Munitions on 6 June 1915, with Lloyd George as its first minister. The Munitions of War Act gave the ministry extensive powers and became law in July 1915. This laid down the fundamental shape of the way things were going to be. The single-mindedness of the vision was staggering.

The munitions problem
The initial catalyst for the creation of the Ministry of Munitions had come from the Shell Scandal. The Great War was, if nothing else, an artillery war that consumed prodigious amounts of ordnance. Shell production needed to be increased by anything between 500- and

1,000-fold and this was not something that would be achieved easily. There was a number of challenges that needed to be faced. The pre-war British Army had been geared to the use of mainly shrapnel-type shells designed as anti-personnel weapons delivered by emitting a shower of lethal spherical bullets. The artillery pieces used to fire this type of shell were relatively light because of the requirement for mobility. In the first few months of the war this had served its purpose well, but once the armies became 'dug in', the war took on an entirely different texture. Siege warfare replaced mobile warfare. What was predominantly required were heavier guns to fire shells that would be earth movers, high explosive rather than spherical bullets. British ordnance factories capable of producing the high explosive itself, let alone the heavier shell, were extremely thin on the ground. Starting virtually from the ground up was to be the first challenge. The second challenge was that modern ordnance technology was a complex business involving many different production processes. Different components had to be separately produced, distributed and delivered to the appropriate plant.

Perhaps the greatest achievement of the Ministry of Munitions was that it achieved all of this and on such a prodigious scale. It was not just a matter of making all available industries more co-ordinated and efficient. It had to also set about converting existing peacetime industries into producing different goods. This was particularly true of munitions. Although the building of entirely new factories was commissioned, a portion of munition production came from workshops normally used for something else. Often there existed a core pool of related skills and an infrastructure that could be adapted. Part of the equation was to expand these existing premises. As we shall see later, this was particularly true of Halifax firms, and affected such companies as W. H. Asquith Ltd, J. Butler and Co, Campbell Gas Engine Co, John Crossley and Sons Ltd, Drake's Engineering and many others.

Controlled establishments and employment control
The Ministry of Munitions was given far reaching powers to control whole swathes of British Industry that went way beyond the existing armament production companies, which were insufficient to satisfy war on the scale expected. Its controlling hand stretched to research and development, the procurement of raw materials and machinery,

and the power to make any company a 'controlled establishment'. This effectively gave control of the company to the Ministry. With the negotiated support of the unions, it was also able to take control of working practices in a way that would have been impossible before the war. Strikes were made illegal, arbitration became compulsory, munition tribunals had powers to fine unsatisfactory workers and they could not move from one firm to another without a leaving certificate. Above all else the unions were persuaded to accept dilution. This was the practice of allowing unskilled workers to do what was regarded as skilled work. Pre-war this had been one of the sacred cows of the engineering industry, so the negotiating skills needed to achieve this were considerable. Most industrial disputes had traditionally been related to this principle and to demarcation (who was allowed to do what). The union's co-operation, built into the Munitions of War Act, was bought on the back of 'the national good'. In exchange, the government agreed to confine dilution to war work only, to end this at the successful conclusion of the war and, most importantly, to limit company profits.

The virtual nationalisation of the country's means of production was Britain's first step towards a truly national war. The second step, nationalisation of its people for both industry and the military, was more difficult to take, but it was coming.

Drink licensing regulations
Even before the outbreak of war, drunkenness was a major problem throughout Britain with convictions regularly exceeding 200,000 every year. As David Lloyd George began unfolding his plans to re-organise British industry, he personally believed that productivity, particularly in munition works, was affected by excessive drinking:

> I hear of workmen in armament works who refuse to work a full week for the nation's need […] What is the reason? Sometimes it is one thing, sometimes it is another, but let us be perfectly candid. It is mostly the lure of drink […] Drink is doing more damage in the war than all the German submarines put together.

There was also a belief that drunkenness amongst soldiers on home soil needed curbing. New regulations came into force in January 1915.

BIBULOUS BENJAMIN, at 9.3 p.m. : " Nah, then, wot's it goin' ter be, George 'Erbert—Coffee or Ice Cream."

Bibulous Benjamin, at 9.30 p.m.: 'Nah then, wot's it goin' to be, George Herbert – Coffee or Ice Cream.' J. J. Mulroy cartoon reflecting humorously on the new drink regulations. Halifax Courier *23 January 1915.*

The *Halifax Courier* of 23 January 1915 reported their arrival:

> The official orders affecting licensed premises issued by Col Thorold, as the military authority for the district, under the Defence of the Realm Consolidation Act, 1914 directs that the premises shall be closed.
> 1. For the sale or consumption of intoxicating liquors at 9 p.m. daily.
> 2. As respects H.M. Forces, except during the hours between 12 noon and 1 p.m., and between 6 p.m. and 9 p.m. daily.

The regulations went on to reduce alcohol strength and prohibit the habit of buying rounds of drinks – the so-called 'no treating order'.

The conscription debate
The concept of compulsory military service in Britain did not suddenly appear on the agenda during the Great War. Militarism had been a fact

of European politics for decades and the trend towards greater expenditure on armaments made sure British organisations such as The National Service League always had a voice even if it could command little support. At a Huddersfield meeting in February 1914, local MP Charles Trevelyan (Elland), proposed a motion 'That this mass meeting of Huddersfield citizens declares its emphatic condemnation of all forms of compulsory military service'. He had little difficulty in gaining the approval of both audience and local newspapers. That was the nature of peacetime Britain. The increasing demands of the war and the struggles of the recruitment campaign changed all that.

The debate over whether voluntarism was enough or whether the country needed compulsory military service continued to tax the minds of many. The returns supplied by the National Registration Act had established that there was a considerable number of men who the state had not been able to persuade into the armed forces. The Derby Group Scheme using voluntary attestation had barely touched this untapped source of manpower.

By January 1916, when compulsory military service was being debated in parliament, the pendulum of opinion had moved dramatically away from the anti-conscription argument. Opinions on the streets became severely polarised and increasingly embittered. The *Halifax Courier* of 8 January 1916 reported that 'great indignation' was caused in Todmorden when masses of 'down with conscription' posters appeared on billboards around the town. It continued that 'Many people became so incensed that they set about defacing the bills'. How much this was newspaper bias and how much was a genuine public reaction is unclear but on 12 January, the second reading of the Military Services Bill was carried by 431 votes to thirty-nine. Charles Trevelyan (Elland) and James Parker (ILP, Halifax), a tireless campaigner for voluntary recruitment, were two of the thirty-nine. The tide of events was now moving in one direction, certainly at the level where decisions were made. The kind of anti-conscription support that Trevelyan had been able to call on at the beginning of 1914 had evaporated.

Meetings were convened in an attempt to counter the conscription threat and are particularly instructive because they give us an important and rare glimpse into people's attitudes to the war.

One such meeting was held on 18 January 1916 at the Friends Meeting Place (Quakers) on Clare Road and was reported in the

Halifax Courier of 22 January. The No-Conscription Fellowship had been unable to persuade any bill posting companies to circulate details of their meeting and the local newspapers refused to accept advertisements, telling us immediately of the practical difficulties the No-Conscription Fellowship was having just to get itself heard. The fact that uniformed police were present suggests that the meeting was well-known in advance, and that it was likely to be disrupted, possibly with violence. The account also hinted that the police presence was not an entirely unbiased body of bystanders.

There is an interesting sub-plot to this episode. Letters exist in the National Archives showing that the editor of the *Halifax Courier*, William Denison, was corresponding directly with the Press Bureau over how the meeting should be reported. Denison explained that he had refused to carry any advertisement for the meeting because he thought it was 'prejudicial to the country's interests' and thought it best to not report the meeting at all. What does this tell us about censorship of local newspapers? One interpretation is that many newspapers were probably not in need of any censorship in the first place. Denison, a Liberal let it be remembered, appears to be acting entirely off his own convictions. If the *Halifax Courier* was typical of the country as a whole, then we are looking at a remarkably compliant local press, requiring only the occasional piece of advice or at worst some gentle suggestions as to what might be expedient. In the event, the *Courier*, did report the meeting and at some length but it is probably safe to assume that it highlighted as many negative aspects of the meeting's cause as it could.

The meeting was packed and significantly included a contingent of khaki-clad soldiers. The views exchanged, as reported by the *Courier* were not always related directly to the subject of conscription.

Presiding over the meeting was a mix of socialists, pacifists and suffragette sympathisers who argued that conscription was a mark of militarism and a violation of civil liberties. Many of the speakers were heckled and disrupted by what the *Courier* described as 'the opposition'. Much of this came from the soldiers but it was clear that 'the opposition' consisted of many elements who appeared united in one thing: the war had to be prosecuted with all vigour.

The chairman was Edward Whiteley Collinson, a Quaker. He had already put his name to the Neutrality League advertisement carried by the *Halifax Guardian* and *Evening Courier* in the opening week of the war. He was greeted with what seemed to be a well-prepared question meant to cause him as much discomfort as possible. The *Courier* reported the line of questioning:

> [...] in 1914 he published a letter in the newspapers calling on all to stop the war. Had he [...] since changed his views, seeing that he had accepted catering contracts for the Army? If not, he should like to know how he could conscientiously make money out of these contracts at the same time that he was trying to induce men not to serve their country. Was it consistent that people should allow their sons to go and fight in order that he might live comfortably out of contracts for the Army. The matter, he could assure him was causing considerable talk in the town.

His position was clearly going to be a difficult one to defend. Collinson explained that he was a director on a board whose other members did not share his views.

> I have no objection to feeding men but I have to killing them.

This was greeted with laughter and cries of 'what is the difference between killing men and in feeding men to kill others?'

Alderman Morley also had a rough time being heckled by soldiers who asked why his company had declined to make any shells. After some more taunting it seems he was drawn into a bad-tempered slanging match where he eventually gave vent to his frustrations.

> You have got conscription in your ribs [...] Talk about Germany, why you are degrading British liberty [...] where were your military service men when Labour men in the House of Commons were fighting for your dependents being kept out of the workhouse [...] who were fighting for the dependants of soldiers having a decent living whilst their soldiers were away at the front? Not Lord Derby, not Lord Milner, none of those fellows. It was working men who got you the separation allowance.

It all fell on deaf ears and he was forced to sit down.

Lavena Saltonstall, suffragette and socialist sympathiser, had even less success. She was greeted with cries of 'no suffragette' and protests that the motion before the meeting had nothing to do with women. She abandoned her speech without even managing a word.

Given that the nation's remaining eligible men did not particularly want to join the colours, it is sometimes difficult to accept that no-conscription meetings were given such a hard time. We cannot rule out that these soldiers and other staunchly pro-war elements had been organised to come and disrupt the meeting.

On 27 January, the Military Service Act was passed and single men between the ages of 18 and 41 (except widowed men with children or ministers of a religion) were deemed to have enlisted in His Majesty's forces as from 1 March 1916. Mindful of the sensitivities of Britain's treasured principles of individual freedom, there were certain provisions built into the Act to make it more palatable. Its most significant was the inclusion of the Military Service Tribunals. These were to operate at local level and adjudicate on civilian claims for exemption on the grounds of domestic hardship, health, occupation of national importance and, most controversially, conscientious grounds. It says volumes for the liberal principles of Britain at the time that no other country had any such mechanism in place. Ironically the tribunals' legacy has been to draw attention to the extent of the problems involved in forcing civilians to fight against their will. One thing the tribunal evidence does tell us is that there was a considerable number of people who indeed were being made to fight against their will. Only a small proportion of these objected on grounds of conscience. The vast majority of appellants in Halifax were motivated by a simple and understandable reluctance to be a soldier but also in many cases for very real practical reasons.

There are various estimates for how many conscientious objectors were dealt with by the tribunals. Adrian Gregory, in *Britain's Last Great War*, puts a national figure of 2 per cent percent on it. Others put it slightly higher. Whatever the figure it was small minority. Halifax, for a variety of reasons, probably exceeded this figure.

The Military Service Act went through several additions before the war ended. Initially it encompassed eligible unmarried men, but from June 1916 it also included married men. Other groups were drawn in as the manpower situation became more pressing. The die was now cast. Britain had been forced to become, albeit temporarily, a militarist state. The fears of some were that this would infuse British society so much that it would become permanent. The arguments rumbled on, supressed to a considerable extent by government control, but nevertheless still there. On some occasions they exploded into public view.

In April 1916 two diametrically opposed camps squared up against each other in Halifax. The Anti-Conscription Council for Halifax was set up in February 1916 with the avowed purposes of forcing the repeal of the Military Service Act and resisting any extension to it. The socialist William Richard Stoker was its first secretary. John Selwyn Rawson came from an eminent local family with an established military pedigree and served as the military representative for the Soyland Military Service Tribunal. They each represented a totally different world and there was really no common ground between them. Each of them, in their own way, represented an extreme position. A violent clash of views was inevitable, and in April 1916 it spilt into the local newspapers. Stoker and the Anti-Conscription Council for Halifax passed a motion objecting to the arrest of a group of conscientious objectors who had defied their call-up. Rawson made no attempt to disguise his feelings and wrote with clear anger to Stoker:

> [...] the childish and senseless resolution passed by a few irresponsible renegades does not interest me. I am content to leave the cases of any self-styled 'Conscientious Objectors' in the hands of the Local Tribunals believing that they are quite able to deal in a proper manner, with cowards and traitors who skulk behind the hypocritical garb of religion and my only regret is that steps have not already been taken to bring to justice members of a body who are a disgrace to the country which allows them that protection and liberty to which they have no moral right [...] PS If you wish to send copies of this correspondence to the press by all means do.

And that is what Stoker did. His reply appeared in the *Halifax Guardian* on 14 April 1916:

[…] the general tone proves that all the Huns are not in Germany and that had our own Military Representative had a free hand without any restraining influence of such organisations such as ours the people of this country would have no need to look to Germany and Russia for undisguised brutality. They would find it in their midst […] it proves to me that militarism and brutality are inseparable. Mr Rawson leaves our cases […] to the mercy of the Tribunals. Their operation and abuse of the act have been a scandal and even the President of the Local Government Board admitted in the House last month 'that in certain cases respecting conscientious objectors, the Tribunals had taken a wrong view both of the Act and of the regulations' […] we are fighting the extension of the very militarism at home which so many have died to destroy in Prussia. In our different ways our members are working for a system of society where wars would be impossible […] through an attempt to introduce by constitutional means an International Socialist Republic.

In principle Stoker and his group had a case. But in practice Rawson was always going to be the winner. This was wartime. British public opinion and the state were on his side. The logical outcome of Stoker's position, if universally adopted, was that the war would be lost. Germany would triumph and impose its militarism on Europe. That was something the country had long-since decided should not be allowed to happen.

The year of 1915 had been a period of realisations and a readjustment to make it possible for Britain to pursue Kitchener's policy of confronting Germany with a continental style army of millions. Voluntarism had not been enough to raise the necessary manpower, and free market trade and industry had been insufficient to support it. By the beginning of 1916, the necessary changes were largely in place, and Britain and Halifax prepared themselves for what they believed would be the big push that would bring the war to a close.

CHAPTER 7

1916
A Town Transformed

During 1915-16, the Halifax district changed beyond recognition. Regulations controlled more of everyday life, voluntarism had been abandoned in favour of compulsory military service and the manufacturers of Halifax were made to turn their skills to war work. The whole social and industrial landscape of Halifax was robustly dragged from 'business as usual' into a life of total war that would touch nearly everyone. It did not happen overnight, of course, and the process continued beyond 1916 and right up to the Armistice of November 1918.

Halifax was a substantial town but not one of the major cities of Britain. Apart from the Halifax Barracks, she did not have any high profile involvement with the military. There were no centres of armament production to catch the mood of the moment. She was best known for textiles and machine tool industries. On the face of it she was not a prime target for a war transformation. But in many ways she epitomised Lloyd George's mission statement. Everyone and everything was going to have its place in total war. Halifax firms variously expanded their existing trade or adapted their products to war work. Some quite simply changed completely. All became much busier, and by extension, much more prosperous. The worries over lost markets and disrupted trade, so anxiously felt on the outbreak of war, had become a distant memory.

W. H. Asquith Ltd (Highroad Well Works at the junction of Gibbet Street and Warley Road)

Machine tools

In the new order, it soon became apparent that machine tools were pivotal to the Ministry's plans. They were needed to make all kinds of war goods in the new factories that the Ministry of Munitions required. This was particularly true of lathes needed for the many factories that had to produce shells in prodigious quantities. Consequently, the Machine Tool Department was set up within the Ministry of Munitions, to rationalise and regulate the production and distribution of these. Halifax had a number of firms that specialised in their production.

The story of William Asquith Ltd is a good example of the diverse way in which Lloyd George's vision panned out at the grass roots level.

In more recent times W. H. Asquith Ltd has merged with J. Butler and Co Ltd and moved to different premises. The name Asquith, however, can still be seen clearly marked on a nearby building.

Prior to the war the firm produced high speed radial drilling and boring machines. As a measure of the scale of these machine tools, it should be noted that Asquiths was commissioned in 1924 to provide all the drilling gear for the construction of the Sydney Harbour Bridge.

On the outbreak of war the company faced a problem that was to become typical for many manufacturing firms. It began to lose its skilled workers. Mobilisation of the Reservists and Territorials caused

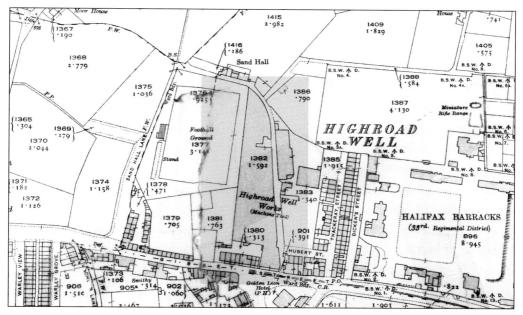

W. H. Asquith location. OS Map 1919.

W. H. Asquith Ltd, armour plate drilling machine advertisement. The Engineer *1914.*

an immediate loss of some 15 per cent of these. Others were later recruited into established private and government ordnance and naval shops. Not surprisingly, production at Asquith's slackened.

The advent of the Munitions of War Act in July 1915 changed everything. As was noted previously, machine tools, particularly lathes for shell manufacture, were in great demand. The shortage of skilled men was an initial problem, but that had been solved by the acceptance and implementation of dilution, the practice of allowing unskilled workers to replace skilled workers. From 5 August 1915 onwards, Asquith's allowed women to do what had been traditionally accepted as the work of skilled men. This was a pattern repeated elsewhere, both locally and nationally, strengthening women's demands for voting parity with men in a way perhaps even the suffragettes had not imagined. In the first election after the war, women were partly rewarded by the grant of voting rights for those aged over 30 (with certain property qualifications). Greater equality had to wait another ten years.

Machine tool prices were strictly controlled, and any uneconomical and unnecessary finishing work was stopped. Paint was reduced to a single serviceable coat of chocolate colour. Machines did not need to look good, they were for function only. By the end of the war, Asquith's had produced approximately 3,000 tons of machine tools for the British war effort.

The Machine Tool Department of the Ministry of Munitions insisted that the production of the vital machine tools should not be compromised by replacing any of its capacity with munition production. It is possible that Asquith's was already involved in the production of munitions before this directive. However, they were able to adapt some unused buildings (on the east side of Bob Lane) and new plant was specially installed. Significantly, female labour was used from the very start, albeit under the supervision of skilled male labour.

Although the type of shell produced in the Halifax factories was by no means uniform, the most common types were the smaller calibres (18 pdr, 4.5 inch and 6 inch). For reasons that have not been established, Asquith's also received contracts directly from the government to produce the very large 9.2 inch shells, which were used by the heavy artillery to smash defences.

9.2 inch Howitzer in the Imperial War Museum. Author's collection.

Work began on the erection of a new 4,800 sq ft workshop that was capable of producing 1,000 9.2 inch shells per week. This became operational in March 1917. Like all the shell-making workshops, they remained very busy throughout the war, requiring two sixty-hour shifts per week. Employment levels increased from a pre-war level of 373 to 1,310. Of these, 610 were women. They were even employed in the

'Asquith girls' photographed on an artillery piece in West View Park. Stephen Gee Collection.

9.2 inch shell workshop, despite having to handle shells of several hundredweight, where lifting devices were required.

The reputation of Asquith's 9.2 inch shell factory was such that for a long time after the war it was referred to as the 'nine two' factory. It would be nice to think that the souvenir photograph above depicted some of the 'nine two' girls, but unfortunately it is not possible to establish this.

At the end of 1917, there was further expansion with the acquisition of the Sandhall football field from the Halifax Town Association Club. By this time Asquith's workshops had expanded to 10 acres. By the end of the war the firm was also producing chemical shells.

Asquith's 9.2 inch factory was regarded as something of a model for the employment of women, being considered 'one of the best examples of female labour dilution in the North of England'. Following guidelines laid down by the Ministry of Munitions, they appointed a lady welfare supervisor to consider the special needs created by the employment of women in large numbers. Her role was to monitor working conditions and individual suitability, provide attention in case of sickness and accident, and institute savings and holiday clubs. She was also responsible for a library, and for gymnastics, swimming and ambulance classes. A large canteen was opened in January 1918. Young boys were also employed, and had a boy welfare supervisor.

Buildings formerly occupied by John Stirk and Sons Ltd. Author's Collection.

Location of Crown Works. Calderdale Maps Online OS 1908-12.

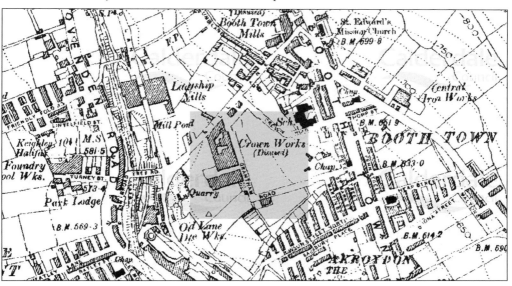

J. Butler and Co was also a major producer of machine tools, producing gun boring lathes. Their story probably had considerable similarities with W. H. Asquith Ltd, but so far research has not uncovered as detailed a picture as the latter.

John Stirk and Sons Ltd (Crown Works, Grantham Road, Boothtown)

Before the war, John Stirk provided the massive lathes needed to make brass screw propellers for some of Britain's largest warships. HMS *Lion*, Admiral David Beatty's flagship, launched in 1910 at Devonport, had been fitted with the propellers supplied by J. Stone and Co of Deptford, using lathes made by John Stirk.

With the advent of the Great War and the increased demand for machine tools, the firm expanded its business, erecting more machine shops, acquiring extra warehouse space (at Horton Street) and taking on additional branch works at Maude and Turner Ltd, Northern Engineering Co and William Copley and Son. As was the case with Asquith's, the Ministry of Munitions insisted that John Stirk concentrated on its core activity of machine tool production (ranging in size from 2 to 50 tons). Initially the firm's production concentrated on shell lathes, but later they moved to the production of larger gun lathes. One national artillery production centre in particular contained a battery of forty-two John Stirk planing machines.

Francis Berry and Sons (Calder Dale Iron Works, Walton Street, Sowerby Bridge)

This firm was also a big player in the production of machine tools, particularly lathes and shipbuilding tools. They were very much at the heavy duty end of the range, with some machine tools reaching 100 tons each. The most common type of lathe was for 9.2 inch shells, but others were used for anything from 8 to 18 inches in size. In the last two years of the war there was an urgent need for shipbuilding tools and Francis Berry reverted to the production of these.

Dilution was necessary, although the employment of women was not as extensive as other firms in the Halifax area (15 per cent of the workforce). In *the Halifax Courier* of 25 January 1919, it is interesting to note that:

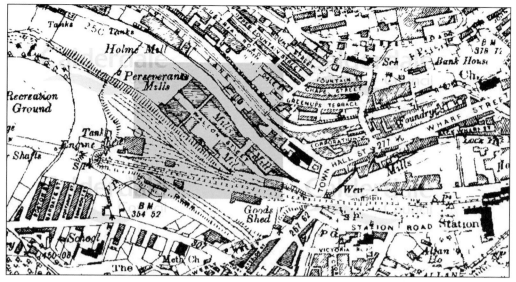

Former location of Francis Berry and Sons of Sowerby Bridge. Calderdale Maps Online OS 1908-12.

Owing to the variety of tools, the heavy nature of the work and the lack of repetition, the employment of women was not entirely successful. The work was rather too much for them.

Smith, Barker and Willson (Forest Mills, Ovenden)

This firm proudly bore the slogan "We make nowt but lathes!" In 1914 it was headed by George H. Willson, husband of the locally famous suffragette Laura Willson. The factory has since been demolished and its site is now occupied by a housing estate.

As with other machine tool companies, the firm was directed to continue making lathes rather than shells, particularly for munition and gun work. Productivity rose threefold, necessitating expansion of premises. They later supplied 50,000 cast iron shell noses, 10,000 mine sinkers and aeroplane engine parts. At the war's end there were 200 people employed, including seventy-four women. George Willson remarked that the firm had been as successful as many other machine tool firms in the employment of women. In December 1918, the firm was hoping to retain its women until they were replaced by the returning men.

The *Halifax Courier* of 21 December 1918 reported:

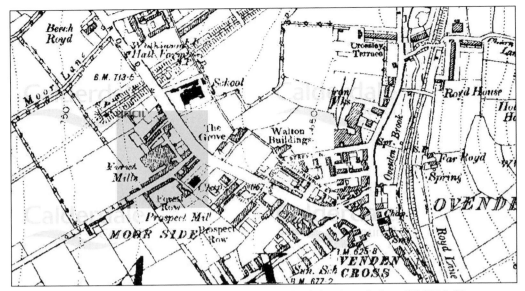

Location of Smith, Barker and Willson. Calderdale Maps Online OS 1908-12.

Much of the success of the employment of women has been due to the endeavours of Mrs Willson, upon whom, by the way, the King bestowed the Order of MBE for her services in connection with women munition workers.

The article described in some detail how Laura Willson had been active in organising the firm's welfare services for its women munition workers, something that had acted as a model for other companies. After the war she became the president of the Women's Engineering Society from 1926-28 and also pursued a very successful career as a local property developer. She was a very accomplished and versatile woman whose pioneering spirit epitomised the need to challenge the conventional view that women were, in various ways, merely accessories to men.

Other machine tool firms
There is much evidence in the local newspapers that war production became an almost universal activity amongst Halifax firms, although details for the individual firms are variable. Other machine tool firms that have all been identified from one record or another include J. Butler and Co, Carter and Wright, H. Holmes, C. Redman and Sons, J. Sagar and Co, Siddal and Hilton, and Frederick Town and Sons. No doubt there are many others yet to be identified. Some of the

firms already mentioned were involved in other capacities, and these will be dealt with later in the chapter.

Halifax munitions

The Ministry of Munitions did not attempt the day-to-day administration of munitions production from a single central office. It recognised that this could not cope with the administration pressures of such a radical and wide-ranging brief. Therefore, it divided the country into administrative districts. Halifax came under the Leeds office, which also administered Barnsley, Bradford, Huddersfield, Sheffield, Keighley, Rotherham and Wakefield. Each of these towns or cities had its own board of management, which dealt with the government contracts for munitions work.

In May 1915, Sir Algernon Firth had already fostered the idea of cooperative munitions work within the area. A committee was formed, which thrashed out a scheme and later a delegation was sent to meet government officials at the War Office for their approval. This was duly granted by Lloyd George who urged that it should begin as soon as possible. On 18 June the Halifax Munitions Committee met in the Mayor's Parlour and elected a 'Board of Management', which was tasked with dealing directly with the government contracts and ensuring fulfilment of orders. Its head office was 'Field House' Ovenden and consisted of J.W. Wallis (Drakes Ltd), H. Campbell (Campbell Gas Engine Company), J.W.S. Asquith, (W.H. Asquith Ltd.), H. Butler (J. Butler and Co), G. Stirk (John Stirk and Sons Ltd) and J. Sagar (J. Sagar and Co Ltd). They were in many ways the great and the good of Halifax engineering. J.W. Wallis was elected as its chairman probably because of his prominent position as chairman of the National Engineers Federation. J. Sagar was later replaced by his son H.G. Sagar.

The other members of the Halifax Munitions Committee consisted of W.H. Ingham (Mayor of Halifax), J.H. Broadhead (R Dempster and Sons), E.E. Pollitt (Pollit and Wigzell), J.E. Shaw JP (President of the Halifax Chamber of Commerce), F. Whitley Thompson JP (ex-president of the Halifax Chamber of Commerce), J.H. Howarth JP (ex-president of the Halifax Chamber of Commerce) and James Parker MP. From mid-1915 onwards they probably had little to do with the day to day running of the scheme although they nominally 'assisted'.

The firms who became part of the cooperative effort were:

W. H. Asquith Ltd.
J. Butler and Co.
Campbell Gas Engine Co.
Carter and Wright.
J. Crossley and Sons Ltd.
Robert Dempster and Sons Ltd.
Drake's Ltd.
Greenwood Standard Gear Cutting Co.
Charles Horner Ltd.
J. Sagar and Co. Ltd.
United Brassfounders and Engineers.
Wood Brothers.

The munitions work was not uniformly spread. Each firm had its own particular facilities and adapted as it could to the requirements of the cooperative scheme. An essential requirement of the scheme was provision for a central store for the inspection and collection of the shells. So far it has not been possible to establish where this was. As far as is known, fulfilment of shells (the adding of explosives to the shell casings) took place elsewhere outside of the Halifax district.

The Board of Management enjoyed a fair degree of autonomy from the Leeds area office, and this contributed in no small measure to their enthusiasm for the way the members approached their task. In many ways they regarded the extra layer of administration as an intrusion between them and the Ministry of Munitions.

Campbell Gas Engine Company (Gibraltar Road as it crosses Hopwood Lane)

The Campbell Gas Engine Company was a good example of a wartime company called on to satisfy a huge variety of different engineering needs, including shell production.

It was headed by Hugh Campbell and prior to the war occupied the Kingston Works (built in 1892). At the time the area was regarded as a garden suburb. A little further down Hopwood Lane was the firm's own iron foundry at Kingston Iron Foundry, and some of this structure remains today. The main Kingston works has, however, been demolished, and is now occupied by housing.

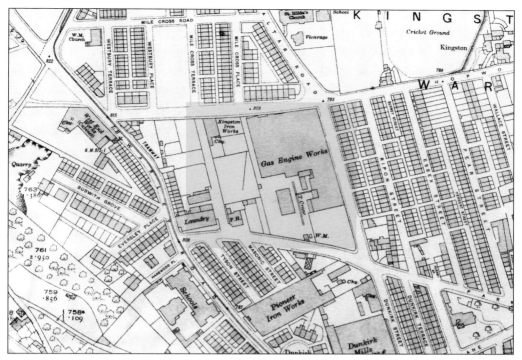

Location of Campbell Gas Engine Company Kingston Works. OS Map 1907.

Pre-war, the Campbell Gas Engine Company workforce was 600, but the extra work generated by the war expanded the firm to 3,000 (men and women). To accommodate this business, the firm purchased Albert Foundry (used for production of shell castings) and, additionally, also made use of Wade's Foundry at Dunkirk Mills.

Former location of Kingston Iron Works, at junction of Hopwood Lane and West End Road. Author's Collection.

The company's main line of business was the manufacture of engines driven by oil derivatives. Many of these engines were used to drive various types of smaller boats. Early in the war, Campbell's received orders from the Admiralty for submarine engines, but later more orders were received for oil engines to propel landing boats, transport vessels and patrol boats. The orders ran into millions of pounds. One of the most interesting projects was the manufacture of engines for some of the landing craft (called Lighters), which were used in the Gallipoli landings in 1915 at Suvla Bay. One of these continued its service in Malta during the Second World War (X-127), where it was sunk in Valetta Harbour. Today, the wreck is accessible to divers and the X-Lighter has been extensively filmed and studied.

When it came to Halifax munitions production, the Campbell Gas Engine Company had to be one of the area's great successes. The number of shells produced was greater than all the other Halifax firms put together. However, in terms of tonnage produced, Asquith's was the league leader. From 1915 onwards, the Campbell Gas Engine Company became one of the firms operating under the Halifax Munitions Committee, producing HE munition shells including 18 pdr (155,000), 4.5 inch (30,000) and 6 inch (85,000). Later in the war it diversified into cast iron shells for trench mortars, poison gas and smoke shells. It also made gaines (a tube for containing explosive) and 270 lathes for other shell makers.

Wartime contributions do not end there. The firm became involved with some of the gear that the early minesweepers used. Initially the British Government had turned its attention to the trawler fleet, which had a natural affinity with the technology involved in dragging submersed nets and cabling. The trawlers were adapted to drag paravanes, a kind of miniature underwater glider whose cabling could catch round marine mines and was able to cut their moorings. Campbell's supplied 200 of the winches needed for this improvised minesweeping fleet to operate the paravanes. Some of their winches were also used to raise kite balloons for submarine reconnaissance. Perhaps as a further development of this involvement, their engineering technology became more directly involved with anti-submarine work. They claimed to be the first company to make 'blue pigs' or 'blue otters', which were anti-submarine paravanes. These were full of explosives and were dragged by cables from small ships in such a way

Campbell Gas Engine Company Open Day, December 1918. Stephen Gee Collection.

that they tangled with submarines and exploded on contact. More prosaically, Campbell's also supplied engines for central electric stations needed by aerodromes.

The company was clearly proud of its achievements and in December 1918, shortly after the Armistice, it threw open its doors to the public to exhibit its workshops, which were specially decorated for the occasion.

The *Halifax Courier* of 21 December 1918 reported a huge celebration party at the Halifax Victoria Hall. 'It was the occasion of probably the largest Christmas party ever held in Halifax.' All 3,000 of the company's employees were invited to celebrate the completion of the company's war work. When you consider that the theatre today has a maximum capacity of 1,860 (part standing), it becomes apparent what a packed event this must have been. Entertainment was provided by various musical acts and dancing. During an interval there was a special ceremony in which Hugh Campbell awarded pocket wallets to fifteen of the firm's longstanding employees who had been with him since the company's foundation. The wallets contained pound notes to the value of the number of years' service of each man. In total this amounted to £450 (approximately £36,000 in today's terms). Hugh Campbell went on to say:

[T]he future years would be strenuous and there would be difficult problems [… his wish was] that the workpeople would […] keep their heads [… he believed] they would be able to do that at Kingston.

Former location of Drakes Ltd on Foundry Street North, Ovenden. Author's Collection.

Sadly this was a case of 'as good as it gets'. His words came back to haunt him only seven months later, when he became locked in a prolonged and bitter strike over the employment of ex-servicemen. The firm closed in 1926. It seems that the unity of purpose generated by the war evaporated with the return of normality.

Drake's Ltd (Foundry Street North, Ovenden)

Pre-war, they advertised as gas engineers and made condensers. Statistically, the firm was a large producer of the 18 pdr, 4.5 inch and 6 inch shells. Some of its buildings can still be seen today.

Charles Horner Ltd (Gibbet Street, opposite Newstead Avenue)

Charles Horner Ltd was a world famous jewellery-making firm located at the purpose-built Mile Cross Factory. Here is another illustration of how every nook and cranny was sought out and adapted to help the war effort. It is difficult to imagine exactly how a jewellery manufacturer might fit into the total war concept, yet parts of the factory was turned over to making cap chambers. These were small components used in the detonation mechanism of shells, so perhaps the employment of jewellers, with their expertise in delicate metalwork, is not so surprising after all. Incredibly, the firm produced 207,053 of them.

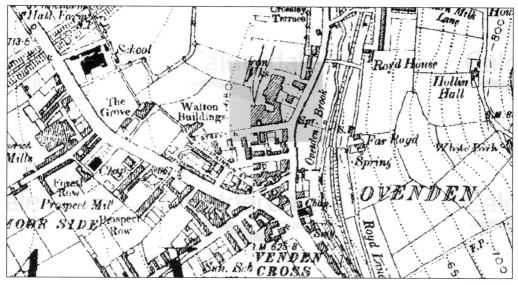

Location of Drake's Ltd. Calderdale Maps Online, *OS 1908-12.*

Group photograph of some of the munition workers at Drake's Ltd. Calderdale Museums Service Collection.

Mile Cross Factory today. Original location of Charles Horner Ltd. Author's Collection.

Location of Charles Horner Ltd, Mile Cross Works, Gibbet Street, Halifax. OS 1907.

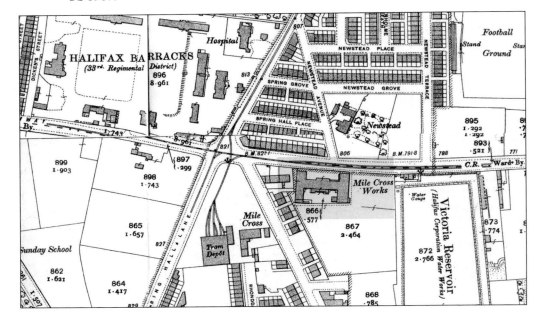

J. Sagar and Co Ltd (Canal Works, Water Lane, Halifax)

This was another firm that became involved in munition production but had other interesting war work contributions to make. The firm's main business was the manufacture of woodworking machines. One machine of interest was used to shape the wooden propellers of the Royal Flying Corps aircraft (later renamed the Royal Air Force).

These were the major Halifax players, but there were five other firms, including John Crossley and Sons Ltd, that added to Halifax's munition productivity. If we were to draw up a league table based on the number of shells produced, then it would look like this:

Summary of Halifax shell production

(source *Halifax Courier*, 15 March 1919)

Company	Shells produced	Tonnage produced
Campbell Gas Engine Company Ltd	787,157	12,106
J. Butler and Company	269,957	1,870
Drakes Ltd	182,380	5,635
W. H. Asquith Ltd	130,880	1172
J. Sagar and Company Ltd	63,323	656
J. Crossley and Sons Ltd	52,775	862
Greenwood Standard Gear Cutting Co	33,301	344
Carter and Wright	32,312	320
Wood Bros	21,809	220
Dempster and Sons	8,160	54

This does not include shells produced for contracts outside of the Halifax Munitions Committee scheme.

W. H. Asquith Ltd. was, for example, involved in the production of 26,510 tons of 9.2 inch shells (quantity, 123,642).

Campbell Gas Engine Company also produced 1,237,856 shell castings.

Explosives Factories

A somewhat separate part of the Halifax munitions story involved two other firms which also operated outside of the Halifax Munitions

Committee. These were the munitions factory at Greetland (Copley and West Vale) under the management of Sharp and Mallett, and Brookes Ltd of Lightcliffe. Both were involved in the production of picric acid, which was the bursting charge used in HE (high explosive) shells. The Greetland plant was an HMEF (His Majesty's Explosives Factory) meaning it was purpose-built for the government's munitions programme (between 1915 and 1917). Some sources suggest that it was used only as a store, but correspondence between Brookes and the government makes it clear that picric acid was produced there.

Greetland Explosives Factory (HMEF) (by Greetland Railway Station)

Efforts were made by the Ministry of Munitions, from December 1916 onwards, to increase the supply of picric acid for use as an explosive. They sought company management who had already proved to be a satisfactory contractor.

The *History of the Ministry of Munitions* wrote:

A Messrs Sharp and Mallett undertook to erect and manage a factory at Greetland (Yorkshire) and an agreement was drawn up on the same lines as that for the Lytham factory [near Blackpool] [...] They were to erect and equip a factory in the shortest time possible [...] in return for a fixed sum [...] to appoint and train the appropriate necessary staff.

Using the powers of the Defence of the Realm Act they took possession of a site owned by the Halifax Corporation and the Lancashire and Yorkshire Railway, situated next to the River Calder and Greetland Railway Station. Some operations took place at the Copley Chemical Works, because we know this is where an explosion took place in December 1917.

Work began building the factory in January 1917, and it went into production the following August. It proved to be very efficient, producing picric acid more cheaply than its model at HMEF Lytham. There were some difficulties in getting sufficient labour, and for a while in November 1917 production was limited. The problem was eased 'after the closing down of neighbouring works at Copley and Wyke', presumably releasing some labour.

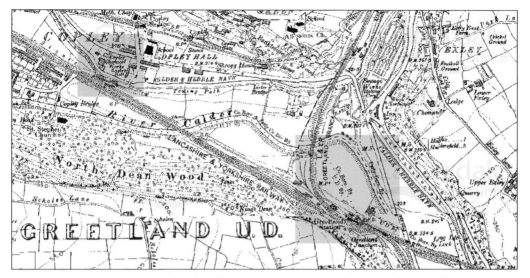

Location of the Greetland Explosives Factory next to Greetland Station (North Dean) and Copley Chemical Works. Calderdale Maps Online OS 1908-12.

Composite picture of the Greetland National Factory using images from the Stephen Gee Collection and Halifax Courier.

[…] dilution was carried out to a considerable extent, the women proving quite satisfactory on the lighter kinds of work.

This hints that the official attitude to the employment of women still remained ambivalent. In common with the firms operating under the Halifax Munitions Committee, the proportion of men munition workers was still greater than women, which runs contrary to the common belief that munition factories were filled almost exclusively with female staff. According to the official account in the *History of the Ministry of Munitions*, the proportion of women at Greetland was just over 24 percent. The photograph below, however, perpetuates the myth, because for some reason the group consists of slightly more than 50 percent women.

Munition workers thought to be at Greetland Explosives Factory. Stephen Gee Collection.

The demand for picric acid as an explosive became less towards the end of the war, because TNT (a preferred choice) was by then becoming available in larger quantities from other national suppliers. Production at Greetland then switched to 'undried service picric acid for poison gas manufacture'. Greetland thus has the dubious distinction of having once been home to a 'chemical warfare site'.

A few years after the war, HMEF Greetland was dismantled, and all but disappeared from the record.

Brookes Ltd of Lightcliffe (Brighouse Road, running from Hipperholme to Brighouse)

Brookes Ltd was a quarrying and stone business that made much of its

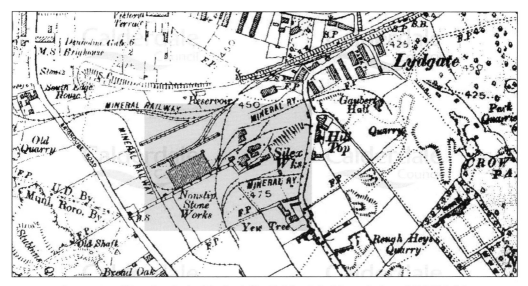

Location of Brookes Ltd of Lightcliffe. Calderdale Maps Online OS 1908-12.

money from artificial non-slip stone flags. The original buildings have been demolished, and the site is now occupied by Crosslee PLC.

The manufacture of completed shells was a multi-faceted process involving supplies from different sites around the country. It was not possible to marry quantities exactly, so temporary storage was required before distribution to the relevant plant. In 1915, Brookes Ltd wrote to the Ministry of Munitions, offering some of their premises for storage, demonstrating that the conversion of peacetime industrial Britain was not an entirely passive process. For many it must have been a business opportunity not to be missed. However, following an inspection in September 1915, Brookes Ltd was considered unsuitable for this. For a while the Ministry of Munitions constantly changed tack on what to do with these premises. Use as a filling factory (factory for filling up the empty shells with explosive) was even considered but also abandoned.

The sequence of events then becomes unclear, but it is known that at some point Brookes Ltd handed over some premises to a subsidiary company (probably Brookes Chemicals) for the manufacture of picric acid.

There is an interesting footnote to the story of picric acid production at Brookes. After the war, the Crow Nest Estate, which was located next to the Brookes Chemicals factory, took Brookes to court in an effort to obtain compensation for damage caused by the fumes from the picric acid production.

The *Halifax Guardian* of 5 July 1919 reported the plaintiff's case:

[I]t was alleged that in the course of the manufacture of picric acid […] clouds of noxious fumes were allowed to escape and that these caused damage to the plaintiff's vegetation, trees and waters […] The trout in the ornamental lake were killed […] White cows in the neighbourhood became yellow […] pigs were stained the same colour, and were known as 'canary pigs'. A swan was also affected […] and turned from white to yellow.

Later in the year, the *Halifax Guardian* of 15 November 1919 reported the evidence of the farm bailiff:

The fumes were so bad […] He had to keep the doors and windows closed. Brass and silver were turned black […] Grass was burned up, and dogs which ran through the grass became yellow.

The outcome of this case is not known.

Textiles

Any description of war production in Halifax cannot pass without reference to its textile industry. The huge expansion in the army placed considerable demands on the production of khaki uniforms and their ancillary textile-based webbing (belts and straps to hold weapons, ammunition, tools, water bottles, etc). The type of webbing used by the existing regular army servicemen in 1914 was called Web Pattern 1908. It proved both efficient and popular.

The immediate problem was that the two traditional suppliers, Mills Equipment Company and M. Wright & Sons, were too small to produce enough of this webbing. Consequently the War Office had to resort to companies able to offer leather copies. This was to be Web Pattern 1914. The leather version was not as popular as the substitute because it was clumsier to fit and handle. It also marked out its owner as a new recruit. As the war progressed, more companies were found that were

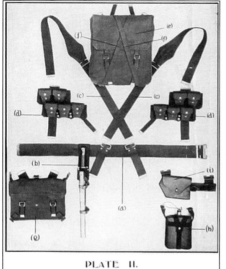

PLATE II.   PLATE III.   PLATE IV.—FIG. I.

Web Pattern 1908: From 'The Pattern 1908 Infantry Web Equipment '. War Office Publication HMSO.

able to make the more efficient textile webbing of the original Web Pattern 1908. Some of them were Halifax-based.

John Crossley and Sons Ltd

The Crossley family dominated Halifax. Their huge complex at Dean Clough was the largest carpet-making factory in the world, employing 4,000 people, and occupying thirty mills, warehouses, sheds, and dyehouses. The firm's normal peacetime production of carpets was inevitably hit by the outbreak of war. Raw materials became more difficult to obtain and carpets were generally regarded as a luxury item. The firm had no previous involvement with government contracts, but this was to change dramatically with the conversion of several departments to war production. Khaki yarn for uniforms was inevitably needed in huge quantities, but there were other less obvious needs, such as spun hemp and linen yarns for the fabric of tents and aeroplane coverings. Blankets were also required, and John Crossley and Sons was to turn out a million yards of cloth for these.

Crossley's was also required as one of the firms to produce textile based webbing, and this required the installation of new equipment. 'H' Shed was turned over for this.

In common with several other factories with workshops, Crossleys was able to take on some shell manufacture. Although not a big player in this field, they produced 60-70,000 shells (18 pdr, 6 inch and 4.5 inch).

John Holdsworth and Company Ltd

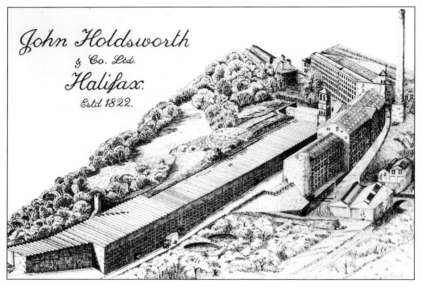

John Holdsworth and Company Ltd. Holdsworth Family Collection.

Like many textile companies, John Holdsworth and Company Ltd was in the grip of a trade slump in 1914. The sudden demand for wartime khaki and other textile goods radically changed the industrial landscape, and they entered a period of wartime boom. Overtime was worked throughout the mill from mid-December 1914 until November 1915. Later in the war, the government took control of the supply of wool and restricted its consumption, causing a reduction in working hours. Despite this, Holdsworth's had a very profitable war, reaching record levels by 1918.

Late in 1917, the Army Ordnance Department took temporary

possession of several floors of the warehouse at Shaw Lodge Mills for the duration of the war, and used these as a boot repair depot. There does not appear to be much known about this facility, but the reason for siting it in Halifax may have been because of the presence of a large number of 'shoe factors' in the area. There is a reference in the *Halifax Courier* of 4 April 1918:

> On Saturday the quarterly meeting of the Yorkshire Council of Boot Trades Association was held at Halifax Town Hall […] Halifax was the principal shoe factoring town in Yorkshire […] It had twice as many shoe factors as Leeds, twice as many as Bradford and four times as many as Huddersfield. Prior to the war, nearly 30 travellers left Halifax every Monday morning representing local boot and shoe firms.

S. Clayton and Company (between Beech Street and Fleet Street, off Pellon Lane)

This company was located at Beech Hill Mills. Nothing of the company or its buildings remains today.

This relatively small firm had already been involved with

Location of S. Clayton and Company off Pellon Lane. OS Map 1907.

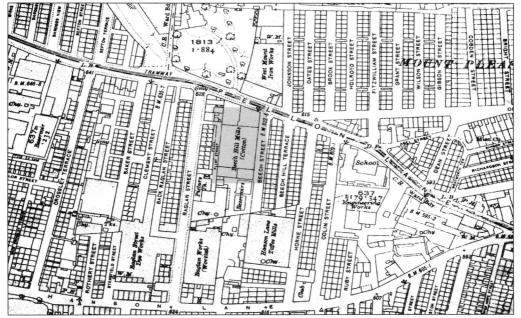

government contracts before the war and its peacetime work had been described as 'elastic webs and smallwares'. Their government contracts became greatly extended and included the production of webbing, to help with the shortfall experienced at the start of the war. They also handled orders for braces, belts, tapes for puttees, and even hospital bandages.

Fleming Birkby and Goodall (New Bond Street, Halifax)

They occupied West Grove Mills, and had branches in Brighouse and Liversedge. The firm still exists today and is now located in Bingley.

Fleming Birkby and Goodall: Advertisement for Teon in The Engineer.

Location of Fleming Birkby and Goodall in West Grove Mills. OS Map 1907.

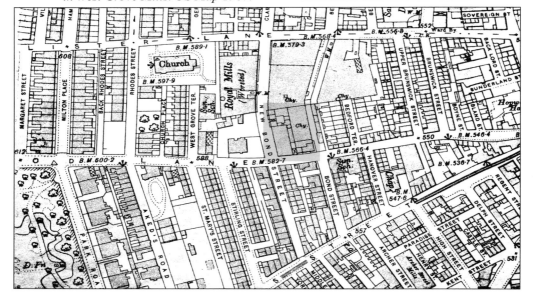

In peacetime they produced industrial belting for a variety of types of machinery. The business, however, was clearly transformed by wartime experience:

> [...] never in its history has such reconstruction of its business been necessary to meet the needs of the times as during the past four years.

During this time the firm was almost wholly employed by government contracts. Webbing material for uniforms was very scarce at the beginning of the war and, as mentioned above, the government had to resort to leather as an alternative, provided by companies such as Fleming Birkby and Goodall. The sheer variety of other goods that the firm produced for the government also serves to illustrate how the creation of a British industrial war machine was not just about armaments and munitions. There was a need for the ancillary equipment that made it possible for the soldiers and armaments to function. These included 40,000 blacksmiths' aprons, 100,000 scabbard leathers, 250,000 mess tin covers, over 1,000,000 square feet of upper leather for army boots, 100,000 leather gloves for protection from liquid gas, and several thousand cartridge cases for the Admiralty.

Animal transport requirements also rose astronomically and somebody had to provide the basic accessories. The business produced 25,000 sets of reins for driving mules and 250,000 nosebags for horses. Domestic industry also had its requirements. Every week the company produced 10-20,000 pairs of leather gloves for shell-filling factories, as well as industrial belting for the increased number of arsenals.

Every little helps
One further example will illustrate how the drive for total war was indeed total. Archer and Tempest's peacetime trade could not have been more unwarlike if it tried (Victoria Works, Adelaide Street, Gibbet Street). They made fancy furniture for theatres, such as palm stands, music stools and artistic tables. The immediate effect of the outbreak of war was that this market dried up completely, because the products were deemed luxury goods. What possible use could a business like that be to the war effort?

The works was turned over from these artistic products to making locker cabinets for hospitals, field service bedsteads, and recreational tables for huts and billets used by soldiers. Someone had to make them. Furthermore, boxes were used to store shells and these were needed in droves. Why not ask a cabinet maker? The firm was awarded a government contract to produce boxes for 18lb shells to the tune of 30,000.

Halifax technology and inventions
Apart from machine tools, engines and munitions there were also many examples of firms producing niche technological items for the war effort. The winches and paravanes of the Campbell Gas Engine Company have already been mentioned. Two other remarkable contributions were bomb release mechanisms and flame projectors (throwers).

G. H. Gledhill and Sons Ltd (Trinity Works, Harrison Road, Halifax)
On 8 November 1918, three of the RAF's largest and most up to date bomber aircraft, the Handley Page V/1500, were authorised to go and bomb Berlin. Each of them had a payload of 7,500lb of high explosive bombs. They were fitted with precision bomb-release systems developed and manufactured by G. H. Gledhill and Sons Ltd.

These aircraft were a far cry from the flimsy box-like machines used only for reconnaissance in the early days of the war. Some measure of the crudity of these early aircraft can be appreciated from the fact that the first crossing of the English Channel by a powered aircraft had taken place only five years previously in 1909.

As much as anything, the November 1918 raid was a political gesture. It was now time to pay back the Germans for the aerial raids that Britain had suffered since early 1915, when Zeppelins, and later Gotha bombers, had been employed. The Handley Pages suffered a number of serious delays before they were ready. As the mission was finally about to take place the orders were received to abort. The Armistice had just overtaken events. Berlin had to wait a further twenty-two years to experience its first aerial bombing raid.

Gledhill's played a pivotal role in the development of these bomb-release mechanisms, which at the time would have represented some of the first excursions into what would later be dubbed strategic bombing. Delivering aerial bombs had at first been a simple matter of throwing them by hand over the side of the aircraft in roughly the right direction. However, it was becoming apparent that the driving principle of the aerial bomber was to deliver as many bombs as possible at an enemy target with as much precision as possible. All of this required a mechanised control system capable of releasing the aircraft's bombs at exactly the point required by the crew. It was this mechanical precision in which Gledhills excelled. The firm was world-famous for designing and manufacturing intricately engineered time-recorders.

Gledhill's had begun developing their bomb-release mechanisms in 1917. Following a lack of encouragement from the Inventions Board, Arthur Gledhill had gone and personally demonstrated the bomb-release mechanisms to the Air Board. This had been received favourably, prototypes had been tested, and variants were ordered in numbers for the bomber aircraft coming on stream, such as the DH-4, DH-9, DH-10 and Handley Page bombers.

Hartley and Sugden Ltd (Gibbet Street)
In 2011, *Channel 4* broadcast an extraordinary story by the *Time Team* crew about a British weapon that has remained virtually unknown since it was first used on the Somme in 1916. This was the Livens Large Gallery Flame Projector, which was intended as a reply to the famous German flamethrower (the Flammenwerfer). Named after the Royal Engineer officer who designed them, Captain William Livens, these flame projectors were monstrous contraptions that were installed in underground tunnels and squirted a huge jet of liquid fire over a considerable distance. The Halifax firm of Hartley and Sugden Ltd may have been, at some stage, involved in their development, and/or supplied some expertise. The *Halifax Courier* of 24 January 1919 reporting on the wartime activities of Hartley and Sugden said:

> The Ministry of Munitions [...] suggested the manufacture of flame-projectors on the model of the German 'flammenwerfers'. Two types were eventually produced – the portable and the stationary [...] those manufactured by Hartley and Sugdens are spoken of as the finest type of portable 'flammenwerfer' yet manufactured.

The *Halifax Courier* article implied an involvement between Hartley and Sugden's and the flame projectors:

> [...] the stationary type were first used on the Somme and have been improved by Messrs Hartley and Sugden on their own designs [...] the portable type [...] in the Zeebrugge raid were employed by the landing party.

The evidence, however, is not entirely satisfactory because most accounts credit Ruston, Proctor and Co of Lincoln, a firm that belonged to Livens' father, as the manufacturer of these flame projectors.

The stationary projectors were cumbersome to assemble, difficult to move around, labour-intensive and had only a limited operational timespan. They hit a development dead-end. Consequently, the military abandoned them in favour of simpler and more cost effective cylindrical mortars designed to hurl barrels of flammable substances, which were ignited by bursting charges and dispersed over enemy trenches.

Here the evidence for Hartley and Sugdens' involvement is more clear-cut. The *Halifax Courier* was able to be very specific:

> [...] Other weapons of modern frightfulness [...] were contributed by the Atlas works in the form of gas drums, oil drums and ammonial drums. These drums were a species of shell fired from trench mortars and held more gas, inflammable liquid or explosive, than could be fired out of any gun [...] (over a) range of 1500 yards [...] at the start, the firm made the trench mortars for the shell, but later concentrated on the drums which they manufactured in their tens of thousands.

The Livens Large Gallery Flame Projector makes for a spectacular story, but the mortar-fired drums were a more successful and practical weapon that the army went on to use on a regular basis. Hartley and Sugden have an unambiguous claim to be part of this, but the intriguing question remains: How much were they involved with the monsters depicted in the *Time Team* programme? There's a tantalising reference in the *History of the Ministry of Munitions* to the early development of the stationary flame projectors:

Captain Vincent of the Trench Warfare Department evolved a four cylinder apparatus, or quad battery in collaboration with a firm which had already had experience in the manufacture of compressed air machinery.

Frustratingly the firm is not named, but Hartley and Sugden had the necessary expertise with compressed air boilers.

Alfred Bates (Willis and Bates, Pellon Works, Reservoir Road, Halifax)

Based on an obituary in the *Halifax Courier* of 22 October 1929, David Glover of the Halifax Antiquarian Society made a claim in 2008 that Alfred Bates should be credited as the designer of the famous British tin helmet. The story was in circulation amongst many newspapers throughout the UK in 1929. It is even possible to find references in Canadian newspapers (*Montreal Gazette* and *Ottowa Citizen*). Curiously, the story then seems to fade from the records. Current references now universally credit the design to John Leopold Brodie who held two patents for it. In fact the helmet is often referred to as the 'Brodie Helmet'. How could this be so and why the two claims?

LOCAL WAR INDUSTRIES.

More Instances of Inventive Genius.

HALIFAX FIRM'S SHARE IN PERFECTING THE STEEL HELMET.

(NO IV.)

Banner headline in the Halifax Courier. *11 January 1919.*

The *Halifax Courier* of 11 January 1919 carried a lengthy article on Bates and his contribution to the war effort. It refers to his experimental work, explaining that he was something of an inventor, and listing a number of technological items devised by him. The article went on to claim that the Trench Warfare Department, a sub-division within the Ministry of Munitions, had sent a copy of the existing French helmet to him for his opinion. Bates had concluded that he could invent a better one that could be made more easily, quickly and cheaply. Key to this was the use of a suitably strong sheet of steel that could be metal-stamped into the helmet shape.

All of this seems reasonably plausible on a number of counts. Bates' firm (Willis and Bates) was already shaping metal objects by metal-stamping, he had considerable expertise as a metallurgist, and was conveniently placed to investigate different types of steel at nearby Sheffield. Anyone looking at his firm's advertisement for the lanterns he was producing cannot fail to see that they were already producing components that bore a remarkable likeness to the future shape of the iconic tin helmet.

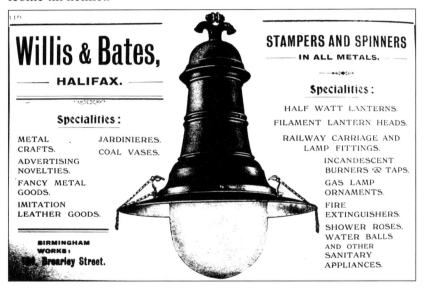

Advertisement for Willis and Bates Lantern. Halifax Chamber of Commerce booklet 1915.

At face value, John Leopold Brodie would appear to have a more cut-and-dried claim because his two successful patent applications are a matter of public record. Any modern day research, using, for example, *Google*, will always lead you to a Brodie attribution. Even the Imperial War Museum refers to the helmets as Brodie Pattern and cites the patent.

However, reading both patents you are left with little doubt that the chief subject of Brodie's patent is the design of the lining and its cushioning features. His British patent (filed 16 August 1915) makes no mention of the important manufacturing process – metal-stamping a helmet shape from a single sheet.

Perhaps, like many inventions in wartime, there were several contributors to its design. These would have been processed at the Ministry of Munitions, culminating in the British Steel Helmet Mk 1. It is quite possible that Alfred Bates contributed the iconic shape and the basic manufacturing idea and then John Brodie would have added important improvements, such as the cushioning device and the use of stronger manganese steel.

Nevertheless, Brodie's claim had the built-in advantage that he left an important paper trail in the form of the patents. It is probably this more than anything else that has convinced later generations (including the Imperial War Museum) that he was the inventor of the tin hat. In the meantime Alfred Bates, with only newspaper reports to support him, has slipped into obscurity.

Sir Leonard Bairstow
Another relatively unsung Halifax hero is the mathematician Sir Leonard Bairstow. He was born, raised and educated in Halifax before gaining a scholarship to the Royal College of Science and later becoming head of aeroplane research at the National Physical Laboratory. He was a member of the Advisory Committee for Aeronautics, set up in 1909 by Lord Haldane (Secretary of State for War) to act as a kind of think-tank co-ordinating the research of the Admiralty, War Office and National Physical Laboratory. Bearing in mind the relative infancy of the aeronautics industry, the influence of this body on the development of fighting aircraft used in the Great War must have been significant. Leonard Bairstow is credited, in particular, with important research into aircraft stability. Much of what he and his colleagues did was 'classified information', so this may have contributed to the general lack of public recognition for their work. In the final analysis, Sir Leonard Bairstow may actually have been Halifax's most significant individual contributor to the war effort.

Josiah Wade and the *Arab* printing press (Dunkirk Mills, Dunkirk Street, Halifax)
It is also possible, although this cannot be verified, that the 'Arab' printing press made by Josiah Wade of Halifax was the press used to

Dunkirk Mills today, where Josiah Wade's firm manufactured the 'Arab' printing press. The building is in the process of being restored to its former glory. Author's collection

produce the iconic trench newspaper, the *Wipers Times*. This story gained some currency with the broadcast of the TV film shot by *Trademark Films* for BBC2 in the autumn of 2013. Written into the script was a very clear accreditation to the 'Arab', although it now seems that the motive was to match script with the actual machine prop used. Unfortunately, there is no known written or visual evidence that an 'Arab' was indeed used. However, it can be said that if you were looking for a best guess candidate then you need look no further than the 'Arab'. It was a machine, so named for its portability, which was sold worldwide and in huge numbers.

The ones that got away
The Inventions Department of the Ministry of Munitions had to deal with a hoard of submissions from inventors hoping they had what the War Office or the Admiralty had been looking for. Most of them were, for all sorts of reasons, discounted. These are two Halifax contributions that seem to have fallen into that category.

Michael Holroyd Smith submitted a scheme for the destruction of Zeppelins. In principle, it had similarities to the naval paravane. Nothing is known of the outcome of this idea.

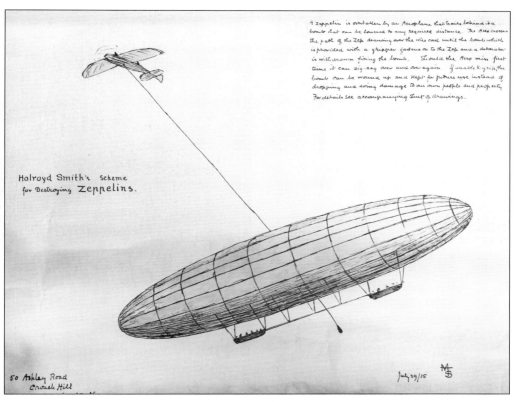

A zeppelin is overtaken by an Aeroplane that trails behind it a bomb that can be lowered to any required distance. The Aero crosses the path of the Zep drawing over the wire cord until the bomb which is provided with a gripper fastens on to the Zep and a detonator is withdrawn firing the bomb. Should the Aero miss first time it can zig-zag over and over again. If unable to grip the bomb can be wound up and kept for future use instead of dropping and doing damage to our own people and property. For details see accompanying Sheet of drawings.

Holroyd Smith's Scheme for Destroying Zeppelins.

50 Ashley Road Crouch Hill

July 29/15

Michael Holroyd Smith's Zeppelin destroyer. West Yorkshire Archives (Calderdale).

The GREENWOOD BULLET DEFLECTOR — (PATENTED) —

TO HELP THE TROOPS.

A Shield for the Soldiers.

Interesting Halifax Invention.

Above we give a sketch of an invention by Ex-Hon. Lieutenant and Quartermaster J. H. T. Greenwood, of Halifax. The idea is to protect the soldier with the rifle. The shield placed on the rifle would not weigh more than a couple of pounds, could be carried on the arm, and would be bullet-proof. It is claimed that it would assist in careful and deliberate shooting, and would greatly minimise the danger to troops in the firing line.

It is also claimed that the Shield would be of exceptional value in storming or attacking the enemy's position ; men trained with it would be able to take cover behind it in creeping across the open to attack.

Our soldiers in the trenches being in greater safety behind it would eventually dominate the enemy by the more careful, deliberate, accurate shooting obtained.

Our Snipers would have a far more dangerous weapon and screen for their work ; the shield could be coloured or made to represent the surroundings, and they would thereby be able to enlarge upon their particular usefulness.

Inner View, showing : Sighting Aperture :

J. H. T. GREENWOOD, 28, Union St., Halifax. Tel. 1069.

J. H. T. Greenwood's protective armour for riflemen. Calderdale Museums Service.

Halifax dentist, J. H. T. Greenwood sought to find ways of protecting soldiers with some form of body armour or shield. He made the claim that this protection 'would neither be cumbersome nor mean that he would carry very much more weight'. He also believed, somewhat dubiously, it could be used when charging the enemy. Nothing is known of the outcome of this specific protector, but body armour/protectors were a common theme for inventors and were used by the army in a limited capacity.

British Summer Time

The idea of advancing clocks during the summer months had already been suggested by William Willett some years before the outbreak of war. The idea was to add extra hours of daylight in the evening for the benefit of agricultural productivity. Successive British governments, however, did not take up the idea until 1916, when its adoption was seen as a means of saving fuel in addition to the agricultural benefits. The Summer Time Act came into force in 1916. The hour was advanced between the dates of 21 May and 1 October. William Henry Stott recorded in his diary:

> 21 May 1916 [...] Daylight Saving Bill came into operation today. All clocks were put forward one hour until October, this scheme is supposed to save 2½ Millions in coal & gas. I hope it will prove true.

All hands to the pumps

Many of the details of Halifax's wartime activities still remain buried within archives or have simply disappeared. Sadly, the majority of the businesses described here have also ceased to exist. It is apparent, however, even from this incomplete survey, that virtually all of the area's manufacturing processes were changed over to

William Henry Stott diary depicting the introduction of British Summer Time daylight saving. Stephen Gee collection.

war work. It also has to be said that, for many, it was a period of unprecedented prosperity, which came as a welcome relief after what had been dire trading conditions before the war. William Stott recorded in his diary on 5 January 1914:

> Trade very depressed all over the country, cotton just now is very bad indeed. I have my warehouse full, nobody wants anything.

By 1917, as he fought with the local military tribunals to keep his son from conscription, he remarked how much his son was needed to manage the factory because 'every spindle was on government work'. By 1917 it was total war in every way.

CHAPTER 8

1916
For Gawd's Sake
Don't Send Me

Local tribunals

Napoleon once famously described the British as a 'nation of shopkeepers'. His observation was that the British were more concerned with industry and commerce than acquiring land on the continent of Europe by military means. Most of Britain's army was, in essence, a 'global police force', which was stationed around the empire and used for suppressing indigenous tribes with disciplined firepower. The British regarded war as something for professional soldiers. By and large it did not involve you or the people in your street. It happened somewhere else, usually a long way off. It was an attitude of mind that was going to present a number of challenges to both Lord Kitchener's plans and the Military Service Act.

For many in Britain, the initial expectation had been that the present war would be waged in the time-honoured way: through the Royal Navy, with small expeditionary forces, and by bankrolling Britain's allies to do most of the fighting. The War Office had already created a small, highly trained mobile force of six divisions for deployment to the continent in support of potential allies such as France. Lord Kitchener recognised that this was going to be insufficient to wage war on a highly militarist state such as Germany. He planned for a prolonged war of about three years, and called for the raising of a mass citizen army whose scale would approach that of the other continental armies. As was noted earlier, the government approached this in a quintessentially liberal manner – volunteers only. To countries like France, desperately fighting for survival in their own back yard, this was madness, British madness. Inevitably she leaned on Britain to take the one step that all continental countries had long since recognised as essential to their security – compulsory military service.

With hindsight we can now see that voluntarism, under the circumstances of total war, was a pipedream. Sir Henry Wilson, the sub chief of staff of the British Expeditionary Force dispatched to the continent in 1914, scornfully said:

> It took the German army forty years of incessant work to get an army of twenty five corps [Kitchener's target] with the aid of conscription. It will take us to all eternity to do the same by voluntary effort.

Voluntarism, on its own terms, was in actual fact very successful. Over 2,000,000 men came forward who believed they either wanted to or had a duty to take the king's shilling. By mid-1915, it had already become apparent that the willing volunteers were drying up and those that were left had, for a variety of reasons, little or no intention of becoming soldiers. By the time Britain had passed through a couple of tentative measures intended to persuade this reluctant body to come forward of their own accord, she was left with the unpalatable task of using coercion by means of the Military Service Act. Even then Britain did not take an absolute path. To soften the blow she added procedures that allowed certain exemptions from conscription. These were to be dealt with by the Military Service Tribunals, which were panels of selected representatives who, in theory, were a cross-section of the local community. They could grant certificates of exemption to men on the grounds of conscience, family hardship, business difficulties, or if his work was 'in the national interest'. These certificates could be absolute, conditional, or temporary. They could also defer decisions to a later date. A military representative attended to look after the army's interests, and could lodge appeals against the tribunal's decisions.

Far from being the province of a handful of cases, applications to these tribunals were the norm. Tribunal members were kept very busy indeed. Gordon Corrigan in *Mud Blood and Poppycock* quotes some interesting statistics on this. During the first few months, when the first call-up papers had been sent out (March to July 1916), 43,000 men had been successfully conscripted, 93,000 had ignored their call-up papers, and a staggering 750,000 had applied to a local tribunal for exemption. This was partly because the government had failed to make it clear to the tribunals that they were intended to grant exemption in exceptional circumstances. The consequence was that the tribunals were flooded with many complex applications covering a wide spectrum of circumstances. James McDermott's study of the archival records from Northamptonshire points out that at no point was the Military Service Act able to recruit the kind of numbers that the government had envisaged.

The principles behind the system were, in many respects, surprisingly fair-minded, even if they were somewhat unevenly applied. This unevenness was perhaps not surprising, given that the tribunals were manned by amateur volunteers who frequently had to use their own initiative in making decisions based on vague legislature and frequently shifting guidelines. The occupants of the panels were often between a rock and a hard place. They had to grapple with complex regulations from the government and were often presiding over desperate people in no mood for compromise. Not surprisingly the members of the tribunals have been described as 'a much abused people'.

The reported findings of these tribunals make fascinating reading, and provide an illuminating snapshot of British society coming to terms with total war, or in many cases not coming to terms with it. Most of them were held in public and were reported in the local newspapers, often at length. In the Halifax area they generally took place in local council chambers. The Halifax local tribunals took place in the mayor's parlour in the town hall, as did many of the appeal tribunals. Several newspaper reports underlined the genuine difficulties that compulsory military service posed for many people. Some applications smacked of desperation and others were quite comic.

Reluctant soldiers
The story of the tribunals is, in many ways, a continuation of the

recruiting story. Men who wanted to join the army had, by and large, already done so. Those that remained did not want to be soldiers for a variety of different reasons. In many cases there were marked practical reasons or deeply felt ethical reasons for this, and the creation of the tribunal system was intended to deal with it. On the other hand, there were large numbers of men who, living in a non-militarist society and accustomed to an absence of compulsory national service, were reluctant to take on the mantle of a soldier. The following is an extract from a letter reported in the *Halifax Courier* of 18 March 1916. It had been read out to a tribunal from a Halifax applicant who had already been refused. Although ludicrous in its tone and far from typical, it illustrates ways in which this reluctance could surface:

> I have received your insulting verdict on my exemption case and shall only excuse it on the grounds that I did not make my points quite clear in the last letter to you. I appealed chiefly on the grounds that it was to the national interest that I should stay in my present position, pointing out at the same time my abhorrence of any form of compulsion, which means that if compelled to enter into the army it would be a question of doing pack drill or being shot [...] I know what you want. You want me to come whining about my widowed mother and perhaps bring her before you to cry a bit [...] I do not admit the right of King George or Lloyd George or any other 'George's' to make me a soldier against my will [...] I have no desire to throw myself into the maelstrom of muddledom. In conclusion I will give you the opportunity to reverse your decision, if not I shall get the exemption other ways and expose the Tribunal as a set of dumberheads (who cannot form an unbiased judgement) to the whole country.

Similarly, this applicant, reported in the *Halifax Courier* of 4 March 1916, wished to point out how unsuitable he was:

> 'I couldn't kill a rabbit, never mind killing a German.'
> 'Supposing a German was trying to kill you?'
> 'I'm soft hearted. I couldn't kill a hen.'

"And what work are you doing of National Importance?"
"Why, I'm rearin' eight children an' helping to make airyplanes!"

Humorous postcard depicting a civilian pleading with a Military Service Tribunal for exemption from conscription. Tony Allen Collection, www.worldwar1postcards.com

The tribunal's reply that 'there was an art about killing a hen, but not about killing a German' demonstrates that these exchanges were often not without their humour. The application was refused.

The testimony of Edgar Robinson's mother, in the *Halifax Courier* of 29 April 1916, demonstrates a good example of someone refusing to accept the logical outcome of a society waging total war. At first her application seemed to be based on financial reasons. But the military representative pointed out that she would actually be better off financially with her son in the army. Then came the crux of the argument:

'Yes, but that is not having my lad, when he is all I have.'
Councillor Burke explained to her that there were many mothers in the same position.
'Yes, but supposing he comes back crippled?'
'That is the risk everyone has to take.'

The key word was 'everyone', and this was something that all members of the local communities were being made to face. The application was refused.

Conscientious objectors

There seems to have been a fair degree of misunderstanding on both sides of the table of exactly how the exemption criteria should be applied. Nowhere did this apply more than with the applications on the grounds of conscience. Whilst both the tribunals and the government had a fairly clear understanding of the Quaker's position, they were less-prepared for similar conscience arguments from other religions such as the Christadelphians and members of New Connexion. To compound this even further, there were numerous applications from people with a conscience argument based on moral grounds rather than religious, as was the case with many socialists.

In the early months, tribunals were overwhelmed by the number and variety of conscience applications. This is clearly evident in the pages of the *Halifax Courier* where it was easy to get the impression that tribunal activity was dominated by these cases. Part of this was the tendency of the *Halifax Courier* to pay more detailed attention to these cases, maybe in an attempt to discredit them. Nevertheless, there were, indeed, large numbers applying on the grounds of conscience. The tribunals were somewhat surprised by this, and initially reacted with a mixture of hostility and cynicism.

In the *Halifax Courier* of 11 March, it was reported that John Selwyn Rawson, the military representative for Soyland, began proceedings with the declaration that 'I am going to object to every fellow who comes along with a conscientious objection.' His line of questioning was fairly typical of the robust approach to conscientious objectors particularly at this early stage:

'Did you ever express any conscientious objection to fighting before the war?'

'No.'
'Would you fight for your property or your women, if the Germans came over?'
'No.'
'Would you fight for yourself?'
'No.'
'You would let them run a bayonet into you?'
'I would protest with voice.'
'Do you think the existence of the independence of this state is essential to our liberty?'
'Yes.'
'And are you letting other people fight for you?'
'Yes.'

The applicant repeated that he had an objection to combat service. Rawson replied: 'I dare say lots of people have. I expect the Belgians had when the Germans were near.' The application was refused.

Sometimes the arguments were badly presented and received little sympathy from the tribunals. The case of two brothers, reported in the *Halifax Courier* of 11 March 1916 illustrates how easy it was to confuse a dislike of soldiering with a moral objection to killing. The first brother, Jonathan Riley, said he had:

> [...] a conscientious objection to undertaking combatant service, having always been troubled with weakness of the bowels.

His brother said he had:

> [...] a conscientious objection to combat service and did not want to fight [...] soldiering [...] he had always detested and [he] had always had an objection to a soldier's life. It was morally wrong to blow a man's head off, and doubly wrong if he happened to be a Christian, even if he were a German.

Both applications were refused and later served, despite the fact that they were members of New Connexion.

Robert Lewsey seemed to over-egg the pudding. He believed in:

Unconditional acception [sic] of the Christ given precept, 'thou should not kill' [...] belief in the universal fatherhood of God [...] recognition of the law that hatred breeds hatred [...] that Germany had been provoked into this war [... he] had read a great deal about the mailed fist of our enemy [... he] was not in entire sympathy with it.

For good measure he threw in 'being ordered about would make me lose my manhood'.

The application was refused. Robert Lewsey later won a conditional exemption on appeal, and undertook a non-combatant role.

It is not difficult to see that the following applicant was going to have difficulties with his application on the grounds of conscience. The *Halifax Courier* of March 1916 reported his beliefs:

Having an honest conscientious and deep rooted objection to taking any part whatever in military service on religious and moral convictions. I am a member of the Elland Wesleyan Church.

The exchange continued with a revelation that completely pulled the rug from underneath his argument:

'Is it quite correct to say that since the war commenced you enlisted in the army?'
'Yes.'
'Therefore you had no conscientious objection at the time?'
'It was an unstable moment; and enlistment was talked of by all my pals. Sermons at the Elland Wesleyan Church had also an effect.'
'How did you get him back from the army?'
Father, 'The lad was under age.'

It should be noted that the father, a pacifist, was present at the tribunal hearing. The application was refused and his son was made to re-enter the army.

Despite appearances in the newspapers, it must be emphasised that conscientious objectors represented a very small fraction of applications to tribunals. They were nevertheless at the centre of the argument about applying compulsory military service to a liberal non-militarist state such as Britain.

The greatest problem for the tribunals was dealing with applications claiming absolute exemption on conscience grounds – those who refused to do anything that helped the war effort in any shape or form, however remote. The Military Service Act had made no provision for this type of application. Conscientious objectors could be granted exemption on condition they undertook a non-combat role or if he could be engaged in work of 'national importance'. Faced with the absolutist applicant who accepted neither, the tribunals were often given little scope but to refuse the application.

George Garside, as reported in the *Halifax Courier* of 25 March 1916, was one such example:

'How long have you held these views?'
'Ever since I could form an opinion of my own.'

John Selwyn Rawson, the military representative, was suspicious that some conscientious objectors were being trained in how to appeal:

'Do you go to school to get coached in these conscientious views? I note all claims are filled up in the same way?'
'No one has trained me at any rate.'
'Would you object to doing any sort of military work?'
'That is part of the war and I ask for absolute exemption.'

Often the tribunal would seek to undermine this position by probing what the applicant already did:

'Don't your employers do anything connected with the war?'
'My employers don't tell me what they do.'
'But you know as a matter of fact whether you are on government work or not?'
'I have heard it.'
'You could have gone elsewhere if your conscience was so strict.'
'I have to get my living.'
'You place your pocket above your conscience?'

That was sufficient ammunition and the application was refused.

Carefully argued applications on the grounds of conscience were successful, particularly where they were well-supported. It is also true that the tribunals later settled into a more open approach to the various types of conscientious objection, once the guidelines had been refined. The *Halifax Courier* of 5 July 1916 reported on George Lincoln Hanson, a painter and paperhanger:

> In reply to several printed questions, now sent to conscientious applicants, applicant stated that he was a revolutionary socialist, believing in the brotherhood of man. He held all human life sacred and he believed the wilful destruction of human life to be murder under any circumstances. He objected to non-combatant service as it was part of the military machine [...] The specific object of the RAMC work was to save life, to be used again in the destruction of other life.

He was supported by two witnesses including William Richard Stoker of the No-Conscription Fellowship. The tribunal chairman said they had no wish to force him into non-combatant service. If he should get work of national importance they would be glad to deal with him in that way.

Reaction to conscientious objectors

To say that conscientious objectors were unpopular is an understatement. In some circles they were loathed. There is little doubt that they had to withstand a considerable degree of anger, torment and contempt. The local newspapers tended to give full coverage to anyone who took a dim view of them. Reactions from soldiers in the field were perhaps predictable as can be seen from this report in the *Halifax Guardian* of 1 April 1916:

> We have just been reading and having a chat about a few of the 'conscientious objectors' [...] wondering what our parents, our JPs, MPs and the girls we left behind think of those, whom we term as the slackers of the worst type. There are thousands in France tonight, like we few sitting here, [and they] are crying shame on them.

Soldiers were not the only ones applying a bit of shame. The *Halifax Courier* of 1 April 1916 printed letters from local schoolgirls:

> You just ought to see in the papers the different appeals brought before the Tribunal. You would fairly be astonished to think that they would be so frightened of serving the King and Country.

Subtle disapproval was everywhere. One ex-soldier, who had been discharged for medical reasons, was asked if he could do light clerical work for the army. He replied that he would, 'If I'm not shoved in with a conscientious objector.'

Humourous postcard depicting the contempt and ridicule frequently directed at conscientious objectors. Tony Allen Collection. www.worldwar1postcards. com

The applicants were not without some friends, even if the support was somewhat qualified. The *Halifax Courier* of 1 April 1916 reported:

> We the undersigned ministers of Congregational Churches in Halifax and District, while not necessarily identifying ourselves with the position of conscientious objectors, enter our protest

against the discourtesy with which they have been treated by Military Tribunals and the frequent ignoring of the exemptions provided by law in these cases.

The signatories to this included Rev'd Edward Kiek, who was no anti-war campaigner.

Rev'd John Edward Wolstenholme and Rev'd W. R. Smith were moved to write to the *Halifax Courier* on 3 June 1916 and refute the common insult that conscientious objectors were cowards. They began by carefully acknowledging the men who were already serving:

> We have done all our best to help and cheer those young men who have gone from our midst in response to the call of their country [...] but there are those who see things differently and who can on no consideration whatever take up the sword [...] The public have little or no patience with the conscientious objector. He is something of a nuisance and a shirker. A little serious thought would reveal that whatever these men are they are not cowards. There are few things in this world harder to do than to take a stand against a solid public opinion [...] In our public work we have been very careful not to increase the difficulties of those who are bearing the burdens of the State in the prosecution of the war and whom we believe to be sincere man. We rather plead for British justice and fair play for a class of man whose consciences forbid them to render military service but who would and could render other kinds of national service.

In an ideal world, these carefully chosen words may well have appealed to the middle ground, but two types of applicant hardened opinion against the conscientious objector. In the first instance there was the absolutist conscientious objector. Even some churchmen were unwilling to accept their position. Rev'd Johnstone Dodd, a local Primitive minister, reporting in the *Halifax Courier* of 6 May 1916, believed that:

> [...] many conscientious objectors had flouted public conscience and invited severe criticism. Evidently they would not fight the Germans but they would by word of mouth engage with

tribunals. They were not followers of Christ so far as the full doctrine of non-resistance was concerned. While he sympathised with the man who had conscience objections to combatant service he had very little with man who objected to any kind of service which might help their country at a time like this.

Kitchener himself had some appreciation of the conscience argument, but likewise could not bring himself to accept the absolutists. The *Halifax Courier* of 27 May 1916 reported his views:

> Our countrymen in the mass have really deep sympathy with the genuine conscientious objectors. They have long known members of the Society of Friends to be such and have respected their opinions. They find now when we are in the throes of war there are other conscientious objectors who go the length of refusing all manner of service even if it helps indirectly in furthering our arms.

Kitchener touched on the other problem. There were impressions in many quarters that some applicants were 'objectors who act on hastily formed opinions in the hope of escaping every form of national service whatsoever'.

For some, the tactic of posing as a conscientious objector must have been too obvious a ploy to ignore. Not only did it make the tribunals immeasurably more difficult, it also set public opinion against genuine conscientious objectors. Who were the genuine cases and who were the fakers?

Abraham Gibson applied to the Hebden Bridge tribunal on the grounds that he was indispensable to his employer's business. After lengthy discussions, Mr W. A. Simpson-Hinchliffe, the military representative, rejected the appeal, whereupon Gibson then entered an appeal on conscience grounds. Clearly, Simpson-Hinchliffe did not believe him and, rightly or wrongly, rejected the claim in no uncertain terms. The *Halifax Courier* of 11 March 1916 reported:

> 'I doubt your conscience. I don't think you have one. You are no more a conscientious objector than the man in the moon. You are not a Quaker?'

'No, but I attend church or chapel regularly. I have an objection to combatant service. I feel I could not take human life.'

'You are one of those 'won't go until you fetch me' brigade.'

No answer.

'This conscientious objection of yours is an insult to all religious bodies.'

It would appear that he did not appeal and must have been drafted into the army fairly soon afterwards, because he is reported in the *Halifax Courier* of 5 August 1916 as wounded, presumably in the Somme Campaign.

Essential work

The largest numbers of tribunal cases were related to everyday problems of employment. Not only did the tribunals have to decipher a complex and ever-changing system of classification that attempted to place men as 'essential to the national interest' or otherwise, they also had to deal with the pleas of applicants who claimed they were essential to the running of a specific business.

The example of Fred Heyworth in the *Halifax Courier* of 19 February 1916 is fairly typical of an appeal on business grounds. He asked for his exemption on the grounds that his toy business could not be run by his partner (his sister) who had the additional burden of looking after their mother. The arguments centred on whether it was possible to find someone else to release the sister so she could run the business instead. The tribunal also pointed out that a toy business could hardly be said to be 'in the national interest'. The case suggests that the tribunals sought to find alternative solutions to the applicant's problems, but at the same time, would ultimately take a 'hard luck' approach to any business that was not contributing to the 'national interest'. In this case they granted him a 'deferment' of about three months to make alternative arrangements, and to train up his sister.

The approach to what was meant by essential could be very variable. John Staveley Fawthrop claimed that he was the only butcher in Mill Bank, and it was necessary that the public should be supplied with a little meat. He would not admit that it was possible for the residents to get a supply of meat from other shops in the village. The tribunal did not agree with him and the application was refused.

Sometimes the application could be truly bizarre, as can be seen from this case in the *Halifax Courier* of 25 March 1916:

> Music hall artiste claiming to be the 'exhibitor of the most wonderful trained pigeons the world had ever seen' appealed in a written application. The pigeons [...] would not perform for anyone else. Thus, if he had to go the birds would resume the wild state, and all his efforts in training them would be lost.

The application was refused.

Local tribunals frequently found themselves at variance with what the government understood as 'in the national interest'. The tribunals consisted of local men, so were better placed to see how removing men from a firm's workforce into the army could affect the ability of the firm to continue its production. This was particularly pertinent when the firm was engaged in 'government work'.

Often firms put in multiple applications on behalf of the men. The *Halifax Courier* of 20 May 1916 reported that R. and J. Holroyd of Elland appealed on behalf of three men saying they were down to nine out of fourteen workers. If they could not hold on to the three, they would have to close down one of their mills. 'It was like getting butter out of a dog's throat to get [replacement] men.'

The military representatives operated independently alongside the tribunal members and received different sets of orders from the government as to which applicants should be challenged. Understandably, this could lead to tensions between them and the tribunal members.

The following case in the *Halifax Courier* of 25 March 1916 illustrates this. When the military representative heard that Abraham Whitworth of Bowers Mill (Barkisland) had succeeded in getting a five month deferment for several of his men, he exclaimed that he would appeal. It was all too much for Councillor Gee:

> Well if you are going to do that what are we here for? The Tribunal, the chairman and the whole lot are Tommy-rot. They are all Tommy noodles [...] (sarcastically) Let all the men go and stop the mill. The coalition government gave us to understand that they would not cripple industry, but here we have the Tribunals going to stop the mills.

Agriculture was regarded as essential work, so farm owners found themselves in a favoured position. Such was the confidence of one smallholder that he left the room whistling before the tribunal had even come to a decision. If some conscience applications pushed the boundaries then this was also true of farmers. James Berry was a cotton twiner but claimed he then tended to twelve cattle. The military representative (John Selwyn Rawson) doubted that he could do a day's work at the mill and then walk 3 miles to tend to the cattle. Other farmers appeared to have taken up their trade very recently and in some cases there was the suspicion that the father had deliberately broken up the farm and installed his sons as farmers in the separate holdings.

Job titles were everything. The government drew up a list of certified occupations that should be granted exemption. In theory this should have simplified the tribunals' decision-making process, but the complexities of interpretation and the constant amendments to the lists made for some tortuous sessions. Tribunals were plagued by arguments over issues such as: was 'assistant foreman dyer' the same as a 'foreman dyer'? As reported in the *Halifax Courier* of 27 May 1916, Lister Drake of S. Smith and Co was classified as a 'worsted drawing overlooker'. This placed him in a certified occupation and exempt from military service. Unfortunately, he no longer had anyone to overlook, so the tribunal had to decide if that meant he was no longer an overlooker and therefore no longer in a certified occupation. The tribunal opted for deferment pending clarification.

Economical with the truth

Some applicants were not above playing fast and loose with terminology, and it was often difficult to establish if genuine misinformation had been used or the applicant had simply been careless. Convictions for misrepresentation could theoretically lead to six months in prison.

The *Halifax Courier* of 22 April 1916 reported that J. Maude and Sons had previously put in a claim for four employees on the basis that they were doing essential work for the government. They were making blankets for War Office Orders and several military hospitals including The Lord Derby Hospital. After making enquiries, the military representative asked for the firm's certificate to be reassessed on the basis that The Lord Derby Hospital had no contract with them, and the

War Office Orders had been sub-contracted. The firm pleaded they had only said 'they were on government work' and had submitted blankets to the hospitals but had been unsuccessful. The firm stated that there had been 'no wilful-misrepresentation', but the tribunal declared there had been 'indiscretions'.

The *Halifax Courier* of 26 February 1916 reported that Harry Mellor claimed exemption on the personal grounds that his mother was an invalid and depended on his care and he had three brothers in the war. Investigations revealed that there were other people available to look after the mother. Two of his brothers were indeed in the war, but he had failed to disclose that they were in munitions.

Sam Schofield was brought to Halifax Borough Court on a charge of bribery. In a letter to the recruiting officer, reported in the *Halifax Courier* of 19 January 1916, he said:

> […] could you do me a favour. I want to be placed in non-combatant service as I am a conscientious objector. I attested on Dec 8 1916 on the understanding that I joined the RAMC and the attesting officer endorsed my papers accordingly […] my conscientious objection [was ruled] out of court as they said, having attested I could not be a conscientious objector […] now I put it to you, as I believe you will act fair and square, can I be placed in the RAMC […] I enclose […] a note, 10s, as a 'New Year's gift'.

The full penalty for bribery of this sort was a fine of £100, but the court considered that he did not really know what he was doing, and fined him £2 instead. As a final gesture, 'the chairman supposed that prisoner was entitled to have the 10s back'.

Appeals
Refusal at a tribunal was not the end of it. There was always recourse to appeal tribunals. Many applicants had to take this route, including Percival Whitley, son of the local MP J. H. Whitley. He was not an absolutist but the tribunal was told that 'His deep religious convictions […] would prevent him from undertaking combatant service'. He did not represent himself personally because he was away in France helping to run a very large YMCA hut (recreational centre) for the

troops at the Front. There was a strong appreciation of what he was doing for the troops but the tribunal questioned why it was not possible for ineligible men to do the work and release the applicant to join the RAMC. They were told that 'He objects to being in the army at all'. They refused his application and insisted he must do non-combatant work in the army. Percival Whitley went on to win an appeal against this decision and was able to continue his work with the YMCA. He was later transferred to the Salonika Front where he spent most of his war. His records indicate that he received the British War Medal but not the Victory Medal. The latter could not be granted to civilians. His rank is listed as 'Mr' so it seems he never did have to take the military oath. He went on to do notable civic work in Halifax, particularly in education, and was elected Mayor of Halifax in 1941. After World War Two, he actively promoted reconciliation with Germany and helped setup the Halifax-Aachen exchange link. Calderdale College was formerly named Percival Whitley College in his honour.

The other side of the wire
It is very rare to find reports told from the point of view of the applicant. In this respect a series of entries in William Henry Stott's diary have proved invaluable. He appealed on behalf of his only son, Will, who was the manager of their business. It seems that William Henry Stott had effectively retired from the business on account of his age:

11 December 1915 […] Our suspense for the last few days has been very great. Lord Derby's Scheme closed on Saturday and all persons of military age are proved to be attested before then, or else they cannot appeal to the Local Tribunal. It is a difficult problem, and has troubled us deeply, as it would be ruinous to our business if Will had to go to the front. He was obliged to attest, that of course makes him a soldier, so today I was terribly distressed when he had to go to Halifax, but he went & was passed by the Dr who found him fit.

6 March 1916 […] Another nerve straining day […] I went to appeal this afternoon at the local Tribunal for Will, he went with me. I think by the questions they asked us etc. our appeal will be favourable, but shall know tomorrow.

28 April 1916 […] had to go to the Barracks again, but we are somewhat more settled, as he will have to await his appeal.

9 May 1916 […] Another trial today. We had to make further appeal at the Elland Tribunal tonight, and we are all doubtful about the result. We await the decision with great trouble. What will become of the mill without his help? God alone knows.

11 September 1916 […] Another nerve trying ordeal tonight. Appeal tonight for Will at the Tribunal. Pleased to say he was put back until January 1st. This to us is a great relief.

16 October 1917 […] We then had to leave the room. They had made up their minds before we went in so they let us leave without a word in our own defence […] We heard the decision later on in the evening. His appeal was dismissed but not to be called-up before January 31. This is a serious blow for us. What I am going to do in the mill without my boy's management and skill I cannot tell.

6 November 1917 […] Will went for consultation with Dr Leech about heart trouble. He said he could not find heart 'murmur'.

There is a fascinating juxtaposition in his diary. On the one hand he is telling of the dreadful anxieties he feels if his son is conscripted, while on the other he fears for the situation at the front, and the acute shortage of manpower:

15 November 1917 […] We are wanting more men for the firing line in the commons yesterday.

28 November 1917 […] Another trying ordeal today. Halifax Town Hall to attend to the Central Tribunal […] We were mere puppets in their hands and in spite of our hard exceptional case and every spindle on government work [it] had not the slightest influence. This plainly shows that Tribunals as far as justice goes are a mere farce. We are all distressed at our result of yesterday. Ma was literally cut up and distressed all the night.

6 December 1917 […] so depressed about Will, but we shall do our best with all the help we can get […] to send such an exceptional man and to cripple our business there is no justice in the tribunals .

13 December 1917 […] living in the greatest trial of our lives […] clutch at straws […] duty to our only child.

15 December 1917 […] I should take a rest or I might break down.

20 December 1917 […] trying every loop hole […] to save not only our son but save our business.

23 December 1917 […] we all pray that this nightmare will soon be over.
7 January 1918 […] Dr. Campbell the physician from Bradford came today to examine Will. He found exactly what Dr. Hoyle had previously told us. His heart was weak and gave Dr. H. a certificate with all particulars [in] which he found valves of his heart faulty.

10 January 1918 […] Mr Shepherd our solicitor wired us today. He had presented our case before the tribunal and got it adjourned for investigation, this is more hopeful.

22 January 1918 […] Will had to attend for medical examination at Halifax fortified with all certificates. Dr Hoyle, Dr. Campbell of Bradford very carefully examined him and they were bound to find him, as the other doctors had stated, that his heart was in a weak and faulty state and he was rejected by the Board. We were glad in one sense but sorry in another he will have to be very careful for the future.

It is clear that the process could, as in this case, be very long drawn-out, involving a considerable degree of stress. It had taken from December 1915 to early 1918. It is also worth noting that some families were able to call on an army of professionals such as doctors and solicitors to support them. Not everyone had these advantages. The medical problems that gave Will the exemption that the family craved were not unfounded. He died at the young age of 35 some years later.

Conclusion

Of the European nations, the tribunal system was unique to Britain, and clearly involved a considerable investment of time and nervous energy on both sides of the table. When one compares it to the heady ideals that are often associated with voluntary enlistment, it is a salutary reminder that huge numbers of people saw the Great War as someone else's war. There were many shades of grey between the enthusiastic patriot who went to war with such gusto in 1914 and the absolutist conscientious objector who would rather suffer a harsh imprisonment than do anything remotely connected with war effort. More than anything else it underlines the existence of whole swathes of society in Halifax for whom it was a case of 'For Gawd's sake don't send me'. The *Halifax Courier* of 25 January 1919 printed some interesting statistics on the work of Halifax Tribunal. Out of the 18,971 cases heard, absolute exemption was granted to 136 applicants, and conditional exemption was granted to 1,838.

For the moment the country was marshalling its conscript army. In the immediate future its voluntary army had its first real test ahead of it, on the Somme. Hopes were high.

CHAPTER 9

1916
The Big Push

The newspapers were full of it. Kitchener's New Armies were on the move, now a million strong and eager to teach Fritz a lesson. The tone of the *Halifax Courier* had long been that once the real crisis of 1914 had been overcome the Allies would mobilise their superior resources and remorselessly push Germany back to her frontiers. The war was surely won.

It was true that Britain and her allies had little to show for their efforts in 1915. It was also true that the Western Front had become a puzzling stalemate. Soldiers were not meant to cower behind vast defensive trench systems and the Germans had proved surprisingly adept at not rolling over and letting the Allies through to Berlin. There had to be a way of breaking through and this was surely what the generals were about to do.

The difference now was that the Allies had greater numbers than the Germans. More importantly for the Halifax public, they were British numbers stiffened by a British feeling of innate superiority that once they started to take things seriously the show would soon be over. The plan was simple. Britain and France would mount a combined offensive in the West at the same time as their ally, Russia, in the East. Their chosen area was where the British and French armies met, straddling the River Somme. At 7.30 am on 1 July 1916, and following detailed preparations and a week-long artillery bombardment,

Kitchener's New Armies went 'over the top'. At last, it was to be Britain's first real test as a genuine continental military power, something she had never been before – or since.

The *Halifax Courier* relied on press agency features and it was these that the local communities in and around Halifax read. One such agency gushingly headlined: 'The Great Offensive' and 'We are Winning the War'. Of course, it had little way of knowing what was really happening. News from the battlefronts was strictly controlled and all that the agency staff had to work on were some very bland press releases. The Press Agency reports were feeding on expectation, and this expectation was that here was the beginning of the end for Germany. What happened in the next few months sent rippling waves of unease through British Society.

For the last fifty years or more, the opening day of the Battle of the Somme has become the distillation of everybody's idea of what the whole of the Great War was about: rows of soldiers sent mindlessly forward by chateau generals to walk sedately onto the machine-guns, and certain death. But the civilian population at the time did not understand it that way. Neither did they attach the kind of iconic significance to the Somme that has become such a given today. What local communities did come to understand was that they were now in a very bloody war where a lot of soldiers were going to get killed. Recriminations and myth-making came later, much later.

On 8 July, the *Halifax Courier* printed the upbeat message that everyone had been expecting:

> The 'push' is proceeding very much along the lines that had been anticipated. The Germans have recovered from the staggering surprise of a tremendous blow struck at a spot where, as we now know, they had not anticipated it.

With hindsight we now know this was all nonsense. The push had not gone according to plan. Along about three-quarters of the line the push had been stopped in its tracks. Casualties were appalling with many of the new army soldiers back at their start positions.

Units with Halifax connections that were involved on the first day were:

2nd Battalion (Regular) West Riding Regiment (in 4th Division)
4th Battalion (Territorial) West Riding Regiment (in 49th Division)
21st Battalion (Wool Textile Pioneers) West Yorkshire Regiment (in 4th Division)

On the morning of 1 July 1916, the 4th Battalion West Riding Regiment (49th Division) was in reserve behind 36th Division and facing the village of Thiepval. They were not directly involved in the initial assault. Further north, 2nd Battalion West Riding Regiment (4th Division) was involved in the assault between the villages of Beaumont Hamel and Serre, and was to suffer some casualties. The 2nd Battalion was not, by any means, made up exclusively of Halifax men, and also was not in the first wave of the attack. Similarly, the 21st Battalion West Yorkshire Regiment was a pioneer unit and used in a support capacity. Halifax men were, therefore, not involved in the extreme carnage and mayhem experienced in the first frontal assaults made by other less-fortunate units. They did not suffer the 'all eggs in one basket' traumas of places like Accrington, Bradford, Leeds, Sheffield and Barnsley, who woke up over the next few days to traumatically large numbers of local casualties. Halifax was spared this body blow. Over the succeeding few months, however, it was still going to be bad enough. Contrary to what is normally believed, the 'disasters' of the first day were not entirely kept from the British public. The *Halifax Courier* reported to its readership:

> Now that it is possible to write with some fullness the story of the Northern attack of Saturday, one almost shrinks from recording it, so terrible is the toll [...] advancing as though on parade [the infantry] lost heavily by concentrated machine gun fire [...] the devastation of modern warfare is terrible and no offensive is possible without the exastion [sic] of a dreadful toll.

What this report was doing was putting the blame for heavy casualties on warfare itself. It was stating what should have been obvious to anyone. If you practise war in large numbers, particularly against an efficient well-armed foe, lots of men are going to get killed.

We are going to win this war, we are even now winning it, but
the final triumph must needs cost a heavy price, and the nation
must brace itself to the inexorable penalty.

Here was the nub of the argument. Winning the war was going to be
hard and above all costly. The unspoken question was 'are we up for
this?', and the expected answer was, 'Yes, of course. Whatever it takes,
because the cause is just and the war is necessary.' Despite what much
of the British public feels today, this was what most contemporaries
thought at the time. Furthermore, they were not being duped. They
were told it was going to be costly and they were asked to accept it.
With certain exceptions they did. The trick would be to maintain this
for another two years and more.

In Halifax, the stream of wounded soldiers arriving at local stations
and destined for local hospitals was obvious to all. In 1914 and 1915
Halifax had witnessed its first large 'convoys of wounded', each
numbering around 100. At the time they had made a profound
impression. Like a gambler caught in a gigantic game of poker, the
stakes were now being raised.

Halifax Courier of 8 July 1916 reported:

The first batch of men wounded in the great British offensive,
arriving in Halifax on Thursday were accorded a rousing welcome
[…] led people to assemble in Horton Street and near the station
in great numbers […] the train steamed in. It was not an ambulance
train but just an ordinary corridor train. Still the 230 wounded men
were comfortably seated […] They were in Saturday's fighting and
had been taken from dressing station to field hospital, to the French
coast, had crossed the channel during the night, and had entrained
at Dover at noon […] stationmaster Cornwall and his men so
arranged things that there was a minimum of inconvenience. Major
Crossley Wright […] from St. Luke's […] Chief Inspector Gledhill
with the police ambulance men […] made light work of the
transference of the biggest batch yet to arrive here. Outside all
available motor ambulances and motors including a number of
delivery motors suitably readapted […] and huge char-a-bancs
associated in the public mind with delightful trips, swallowed up
the men so that in 25 minutes not one was left.

In later years, George Bentley (Little Khaki George) wrote down his memories of these processions:

> The wounded soldiers arrived by train at the Halifax Station and it was quite astonishing how the news that a convoy was due spread through the town. Ambulances, vans, lorries etc were pressed into service to carry the soldiers to St. Luke's. Crowds lined Horton Street, Wards End and on to Skircoat Road and Huddersfield Road to cheer them along. I imagine that the townsfolk went out of their way to look after the wounded 'Tommies' [...] there was a vacant plot of land just above the Palace Theatre [...] A decision was taken to erect a large wooden hut [YMCA] on this site to serve as a canteen for the wounded soldiers who were able to travel by tramcar from St. Luke's [...] I can clearly recall seeing them dressed in their blue uniforms with white shirts and red ties sitting on a low wall in front of the hut and chaffing [chatting to] passing girls, who I am sure took a delight in walking along the street, and for all I know there may have been some brief romances.

There were also candid descriptions of how brutal the fighting could be. The *Halifax Courier* of 12 August published extracts from the diary of an unnamed soldier and captioned it 'Wonderful Battlefield Experiences'. Quite what the newspaper meant by 'wonderful' is difficult to comprehend.

> Gas and poisonous shells sent over every day [...] Got a stomach full of gas one night and felt very bad. Cook and Bowman hit by a shell [...] Cook blown to bits, Bowman lost his leg and in a terrible condition but still alive. Hundreds of English and Germans lying in the wood unburied [...] everywhere was ablaze with bursting shrapnel. Every minute someone rolled over or shouted and crawled away [...] dead horses and men lay everywhere. Kits were strewn all over the place, a perfect melee of limbers, equipment and wounded and dead men.

In statistical terms, the Halifax public now had to get used to another unpleasant fact. For most of 1914 a local casualty had almost been a headline grabber. The practice of publishing photographs and obituaries of fallen servicemen on a regular basis was introduced by the *Halifax Courier* in mid-1915. With certain exceptions (such as the gas attacks on the 2nd Battalion West Riding Regiment in May 1915 and the 4th Battalion West Riding Regiment in December 1915), these had numbered about five or six a week. For the duration of the 1916 Somme Campaign (finally closed down in late November) the weekly numbers were regularly between twenty and forty-five. Each week represented what had been regarded as exceptional prior to mid-1916. Despite this grim cavalcade, the *Halifax Courier* continued to publish soldier accounts of the battle which reassuringly gave the impression that all was well and that the British Tommy was having little difficulty in outfighting Fritz. How far this was accepted by the readership is a matter of guesswork. They may have reflected soldier bravado, wishful thinking, or very selective editing on the part of the newspaper.

The *Halifax Courier* 8 July 1916 reported:

> When cornered the Hun soon gives up […] I don't think we will settle down for a long trench fight again, now that we are on the move […] The German losses are four to every one of ours. […] and there is no doubt about it, we are the masters of them now.

The Germans were not giving up. Kitchener's New Army was not into open country and it was certainly not killing the enemy at a rate of four to one. The Halifax public also had over two more years of killing fields to endure.

Malins' film: *The Battle of the Somme*

While the Battle of the Somme was still in progress, the British public were provided with a novel experience. For the first time they were shown extensive moving pictures of the battlefront they were so earnestly being urged to support. The British Topical Committee for War Films had been directed by the War Office to produce a film of the Big Push, which would help the public understand what it was they were supporting. It is often dubbed a propaganda film but is better understood as a morale-boosting film. It was shown around the country at local cinemas and is estimated to have been seen by 20,000,000 people in its first six weeks. Cinema had been regarded by some 'in

The Albert Theatre, Brighouse (on the left). Stephen Gee Collection.

ALBERT THEATRE.

TO-NIGHT (FRIDAY), 6-50 and 9 o'clock.

SATURDAY EVENING—

6-30, 8, AND 9-30.

THE BATTLE OF THE SOMME.

MATINEE TO-DAY at 2-30.

MATINEE—Saturday at 2-30. Adults, Full Price ; Children, Half-price.

Next Week—JULIUS CÆSAR.

the same light as […] roller skating or ping pong […] a passing craze', but had become 'an industry […] of a very large scale'. In September it was shown at the Central Picture House (Wards End) and the Theatre de Luxe (Northgate), both in Halifax. The Albert Theatre in Brighouse carried a banner advertisement in the *Brighouse Echo* and showed the film earlier in the month.

Prior to its arrival in Brighouse the paper previewed the film:

There is nothing theatrical about the film […] it is grim realism […] the audience is not spared the horrors of the war – wounded soldiers, corpses […] the pictures constitute an epic of self-effacement and valour […] and they are a spur to those left behind at home to still greater effort in the prosecution of the war [...] above all the film shows munition workers how monster guns absorb ammunition and proves to them that their labours have not been in vain.

The *Halifax Courier* was more philosophical:

The fine film, 'The Battle of the Somme,' has brought vividly before the public the immense value of the cinema as an educational and instructive factor [sic], and when a film of a great war can be produced with such success there is no end to its possibilities [...] already famous plays and famous books have been screened [...] but it is in the depicting and bringing before the public the everyday happenings of the world that the cinema will score in the future [...] there is always more pleasure in witnessing the portrayal of an unrehearsed scene than a spectacle which is all make-believe.

There was some controversy in the national papers over the morality of showing dead bodies, but otherwise the film was received well. The British Government was pleased with its reception and considered it had brought a greater understanding of the war to the public. If Halifax and Brighouse were greatly excited by the film you would not have

A classic still from the film depicting British soldiers 'Going over the Top' and advancing over barbed wire. Wiki Commons.

Theatre de Luxe, Northgate, Halifax, looking towards North Bridge. In September 1916 it was showing The Battle of the Somme. *In February 1917 it was showing Charlie Chaplin. John Reginald Halliday Christie, the notorious serial killer worked here as a projectionist in 1919. Stephen Gee Collection.*

thought so from the newspapers. Apart from the reviews there was little if any comment on size of audiences or public reaction. For a film considered such a success, it also comes as a surprise that neither cinema showed it for longer than three days.

The follow-up film, *Advance of the Tanks*, was shown in February 1917 at the Electric Theatre, but by then the interest value seems to have fallen off. Cinemas reverted to type and became places for escapist entertainment. It is possible that *The Battle of the Somme* owed its success to a combination of novelty value and timing. When it was shown, there was still a degree of optimism about the Big Push. By early 1917, the Halifax public would have had less cause to look enthusiastically on what was happening on the battlefield. By then too many soldiers had died and victory was still looking remote. In Halifax, the Theatre de Luxe, which had previously shown *The Battle of the Somme,* was showing Charlie Chaplin in *The Fireman.*

After viewing the film on 1 September, William Henry Stott recorded in his diary:

> Halifax tonight to the New Picture House to see the film now showing the <u>Battle of the Somme</u> showing sights of the battlefield, Base Hospital, some of the pictures were terrible to look at, the horrors of war are truly represented. I came away with a heavy heart.

If we were to take this as representative, and that has to be a big 'if', then the film had arguably backfired. William Henry Stott's focus was on the dead and wounded, and it was the unpleasant experience of coming face-to-face with the war's realities that appears to have been his lasting impression. His heavy heart does not suggest any boosting of morale.

Expansion of medical facilities

In 1914-19 there was, of course, no centrally controlled National Health Service, so it was the local communities that had to step up and deal with most of the wounded soldiers sent back to the UK for nursing and convalescent care. Government help and control increased as the war progressed, but essentially it was local facilities that would drive it.

In 1914 the Borough of Halifax was served by two major medical hospitals. The Royal Halifax Infirmary on Free School Lane was a voluntary hospital supported by public subscription. The second was the Halifax Union St Luke's Hospital on Dryclough Lane, Salterhebble, and was an offshoot of the Halifax Union Workhouse, which was governed by its guardians, who administered the Poor Law. It had been built fairly recently and officially opened in 1901.

On 22 August 1914, the *Halifax Courier* carried a brief report that the Queen thought '[…] it would be much appreciated if, so far as possible, sick soldiers and sailors could be sent to convalescent homes nearest their own localities.' Apparently, the medical directors were 'in entire sympathy […] and will do everything possible to carry it out'. It was early days. Later, administrative necessity was to prove all too much for this seemingly simple ideal and soldiers were sent in trainloads wherever it was convenient. Where records exist for the wounded brought to Halifax, it is rare to find local names amongst them.

Halifax had already witnessed its first large convoy of wounded men on 21 November 1914 (see Chapter Four, Realisations). The ambulance train that pulled into Halifax Station on that occasion was a Red Cross corridor train drawn by two locomotives with nine coaches. One of the coaches had twenty beds carrying fifteen of the worst cases. Twenty-four stretcher-bearers were waiting to transfer them to the ambulances. Ten ambulance carriages from around the districts and five tramcars were assembled to transfer the wounded to the two hospitals. Sixty of the patients were taken to the Halifax Royal Infirmary, and forty to St Luke's.

A second large ambulance train carrying 100 wounded soldiers came to Halifax on 18 May 1915 following some heavy fighting (which had included gas) near Ypres. Some of the cases that were described in some detail by the *Halifax Courier* tell us something of the medical services of the time. There was a surprising number of cases of rheumatism, which sat incongruously with the shrapnel wounds, but this was a serious problem in wet cold trenches and, as its presence here suggests, often required hospitalisation. There was also 'shock and debility' suggesting that medical attention was not as cold and unsympathetic to these psychological problems as some authors would have us believe.

It has sometimes been said that the general British public had no idea of the realities of war. There can, of course, be no substitute for war at first hand but the local newspapers did not hold back in their descriptions of the wounded: 'crushed breast', 'shrapnel wounds both legs', 'gas poisoning', 'bullet wound head' and 'amputated leg'. A combination of these descriptions and the actual sight of the wounded should have destroyed any lingering delusions about the romance of war.

Graphic stories printed in the *Halifax Courier* added to the mix:

The conduct of the Germans they agree is positively wicked [...] the town of Ypres is something awful, bodies of dead men, women, children, horses, cats and dogs lying about the streets making a sickening sight.

Halifax Union St Luke's Hospital

Arrangements with the Halifax Poor Law hospital at St Luke's had continued on an *ad hoc* basis for most of 1915. The number of wounded soldiers varied, but inpatient numbers seem to have been typically around forty. They were therefore still a minority of its patients. It soon became apparent that there was a need to increase capacity for wounded soldiers. Closer and more formal arrangements with the military were necessary to administer this. On 4 November 1915, the *Halifax Courier* announced that preparations were in hand for the hospital to become an official military hospital funded by the government. Poor Law patients numbering 295 were transferred to the Union Workhouse. On 14 December, as was normal practice with military hospitals, the civilian personnel who administered the hospital were commissioned with a military rank. Dr Woodyatt, whose children, it may be recalled, had fled the German bombardment in Scarborough the year previously, was appointed lieutenant-colonel and administrator. The registrar and two resident surgeons were appointed majors. All were designated members of the Royal Army Medical Corps (RAMC). In theory, the hospital now had 400 beds for military purposes, but as the war progressed this was expanded to accommodate over 700.

Although the War Office funded the maintenance and the medical/surgical care of the soldiers, this did not extend to what can be collectively called comforts. Money was needed for hair cutting, tobacco, cigarettes, newspapers, stamps and expenses for visiting family. As was noted previously, self-help was a marked characteristic

St Luke's War Hospital

Panoramic group photograph taken of the staff of St Luke's Military Hospital, October 1917. Stephen Gee Collection.

of these times, so it is not surprising to find that a fund committee with its attendant events and collections soon sprang up. Mrs J. H. Whitley, wife of the local MP, became its treasurer.

Christmas was a particularly important event in the hospital's calendar and the *Halifax Courier* Comforts Fund was able to assist

A section of the panoramic group photograph showing the principal staff of St Luke's Military Hospital. Dr Woodyatt, the administrator (commissioned as lieutenant-colonel RAMC) is immediately to the matron's left. Stephen Gee Collection.

towards providing wounded soldiers with their traditional feast at the end of 1916, 1917 and 1918. It was noted that 1917 was less sumptuous on account of the restrictions on food prevalent at that time.

In amongst the grim business there was still time for humour. The following story appeared in the *Halifax Courier* on 24 June 1916. A wounded Canadian stretcher case had been brought in apparently holding a cage with a canary in it:

> In the necessities of removal, soldier and canary had, momentarily [...] to be separated. On losing sight of its owner, the canary was manifestly discomforted, screeching loudly. Its owner had only, however, to call out, 'All right Dicky, I'm here', to instantly restore it to composure, and it chirped contentedly when replaced on the stretcher.

It would be nice to think this was a true story, but we may have to accept some poetic licence. Tunnelling units did, however, use canaries as miners' friends to test for noxious gasses, so perhaps some elements of the story were rooted in reality.

On 30 May 1919 'the military ceased occupation of St Luke's Hospital'. The Board of Guardians inspected the premises to assess what was needed to renovate the hospital after three-and-a-half years of intense military use. They noted that 'the hob-nailed boots of thousands of men have by daily contact, made a distinct impression on the floors', but generally were pleased that painting and decorating were all that were required. There had been no epidemic outbreaks. Incredibly it had even escaped the influenza pandemic of 1918, the only cases being the men who had been brought in already suffering from it.

Prior to the military taking over the hospital in November 1915, it had tended to 133 patients. Since then there had been ninety-four convoys and 15,137 cases to handle. The total number of deaths at the hospital had been eighty-seven, including the influenza victims brought in.

During their stay in St Luke's Military Hospital the wounded soldiers passed their time in a variety of ways. For some it was an opportunity to sketch, and a charming record of this exists in the Central Library.

Some of the nursing staff at St Luke's Military Hospital. Stephen Gee Collection.

The Royal Halifax Infirmary

This was a subscription-supported public hospital. It received many wounded soldiers but it remained under civilian control and continued to take civilian patients.

The auxiliary hospitals

Numerous additional hospitals sprang up, particularly in response to the need for convalescent facilities. At first they were fairly modest

Drawings done by soldiers whilst in St Luke's Military Hospital.
(Left) Humorous comment on the licensing laws by Lance Corporal MacKenzie of the Seaforth Highlanders. D. Holland Collection.
(Right) Satirical comment on the Kaiser by J. McAvie, 4th Battalion King's Shropshire Light Infantry. D. Holland Collection.

affairs, but as the numbers of wounded increased, government pressure led to the creation of many auxiliary hospitals. They were a mixture of government sponsorship and local initiative. However, much depended on the self-help principle because they were run almost entirely by volunteers and owed their existence to local benefactors who loaned premises. The British propensity for forming committees was much in evidence. In the Halifax district the two earliest were at Mill House, Triangle, and Glenwood House, Southowram. They provided some limited care assistance in the first twelve months of the war.

John Selwyn Rawson was the first to act in October 1914 by providing twelve beds in the upper floors of his Mill House factory. The medical training of his son, Fred, may have had something to do with this move. In common with the familiar pattern, it was run by committee, staffed by volunteers and supported by voluntary donations. Its first case was a casualty from the Battle of Mons, Corporal W.

Staff and patients at the Halifax Royal Infirmary. Stephen Gee Collection.

Nichols of the Royal Engineers. He had been a dispatch rider when 'he was hurled a dozen yards (by exploding shrapnel) alighting on his head and smashing his front teeth and receiving internal injury'. However the premises were not quite ready and Corporal Nichols was accommodated in Rawson's own house at Haugh End. Given this philanthropic act and his family's long standing military connections, it is not particularly difficult to understand the root of John Selwyn Rawson's dislike of conscientious objectors, and his very public outburst against the No-Conscription Fellowship in early 1916.

In May 1915, Mrs Edith Marchetti, the wife of Marc Ernesto Ulysse Marchetti (later MD at John Crossley and Sons), created facilities for the care of six soldiers at Glenwood House, Southowram. This appears to have been a private house owned by the Crossley family. It was used to provide further convalescent care for soldiers who had received treatment at the Halifax Barracks hospital.

Centre Vale (Todmorden)
In the week following the outbreak of war, the local Todmorden Voluntary Aid Detachment (VAD) received instructions to prepare a temporary hospital. On 2 November 1914, after some searching, Todmorden Town Council granted the use of Centre Vale. Sister Murray was installed as matron (later replaced by Sister Sutcliffe). She was salary paid, but most of the staff were unpaid volunteers. The hospital was maintained by public funding.

The first wounded arrived on 17 November (the same time Halifax was receiving its first large convoy of wounded). Many local residents lined the route with 'great interest' and 'rousing cheers'. The first batch of nine was walking wounded, followed by the more severely wounded. As with Halifax, the effect on the locals was something of a wake-up call.

> Many of them were severely wounded and looked haggard and were evidently in great pain. It was a moving experience for those unaccustomed to such sights.

Before closing on 28 February 1919 it had dealt with about 1,000 patients.

Spring Hall Mansion and Shaw Lodge Annexe (South Halifax)
By the beginning of 1916 the size of the British Army was reaching continental proportions, and was being prepared for a major offensive on the Somme in the summer. The numbers of wounded were expected to increase and it was clear that the military authorities needed to expand convalescent facilities. Compared with other towns of comparable size, Halifax had no major convalescent hospitals. It offered only a small number of beds at Mill House and Glenwood House, and much further west up the Calder Valley at Todmorden there was also Centre Vale. General Kenny, the deputy director-general of the Medical Services Headquarters at York, approached Dr William Shaw with a view to using Spring Hall Mansion. This building had originally been a home of the Holdsworth family but the house had stood empty since the death of its last occupant, James Booth JP, in 1907. At the time it was owned by the Midland Railway Company, which was prepared to loan it free of charge.

The set-up at Spring Hall was modelled on similar schemes in other towns. A committee was formed and contributions towards furnishings and equipment, with a fund of £2,000 for soldier comforts, were invited. All preparations, administration and medical care (Drs Alan Howie Muir, William Shaw and Thomas Taylor Smith) were undertaken by volunteers, with the exception of the cook, kitchen maid and laundress. In February 1916, the facility was opened and designated an 'auxiliary hospital B' with provision for fifty beds. This was not going to be enough.

Staff of Spring Hall Auxiliary Hospital. Holdsworth Family.

On 14 April 1917, the *Halifax Courier* carried a letter from Dr William Shaw appealing for funds to help run an extension to the existing beds at Spring Hall:

> [...] it is a privilege that we, who stay at home, should show our gratitude to the men who have fought our battles for us and been wounded, by giving them every comfort during their convalescence [...] funds are urgently required.

He explained that 'Six weeks ago military authorities asked us to find more accommodation for the wounded expected from General Haig's advance.' This was presumably a reference to the heavy casualties anticipated in the forthcoming offensives around Arras in April/May. In response, Clement Holdsworth lent Shaw Lodge for conversion into sixteen wards. This increased the overall bed capacity considerably to 220, making Spring Hall and the Shaw Lodge Annexe the 'largest convalescent home in Northern Command'. It was re-designated as a 'class A convalescent hospital'. It still had Passchendaele (1917) and the killing fields of 1918 to look forward to before its work was done.

'Spring Hall Convalescent and Auxiliary Hospital' from Halifax in Old Picture Postcards *(Source: European Library, Zaltbommel, Netherlands) by Dr John A. Hargreaves.*

By the end of February 1919, the number of convalescent soldiers using the Spring Hall facilities had fallen to uneconomical levels. It was therefore closed, with the few remaining soldiers being transferred to St Luke's Military Hospital. It had handled a total of 3,619 soldiers, almost entirely through voluntary help.

Boothroyde and Longroyde Houses (Brighouse)

Boothroyde House was loaned by William Smith JP for as long as it was needed. Headed by Dr Bogdan E. J. Edwards, it opened as an auxiliary hospital on 11 February 1916, and was staffed by twenty-three nurses. Initially, it had provision for forty beds but it was hoped this would reach 100. Longroyde was opened on 2 November 1916. Both hospitals closed in May 1919 and between them had treated 1,975 patients.

William Henry Smith School, formerly Boothroyde House: Copyright Humphrey Bolton and licensed for reuse under Creative Commons Licence 1202367_c7cdcc06.

Staff and patients at Priestley Green Auxiliary Hospital (Holroyd House) June 1917. Stephen Gee Collection

Priestley Green Auxiliary Hospital (Norwood Green Area)

Holroyd House at Priestley Green was made available by Sir Algernon Firth. It opened in April 1916 and was supervised by Lady Firth. It closed in December 1918 after handling 900 patients.

Castle Hall (Cragg Vale)

Miss Ethel Maude Rigby offered part of her house at Castle Hall, Cragg Vale. Preparations were complete by October 1916 and it was receiving patients the following month.

Staff and patients at Castle Hall, Cragg Vale. Sam Hellowell, History of Cragg Vale.

The Plains (Elland)

By the end of October 1916 when the Battle of the Somme was reaching its final stages, the *Halifax Courier* announced:

> [T]hough Elland has largely subscribed to the various funds for war relief purposes, the public men of that place are working strenuously for the accomplishment of another important scheme, namely the provision of a couple of military auxiliary hospitals.

The Plains Auxiliary Hospital, Elland. Stephen Gee Collection.

One of the hospitals was set up through the loan of Plains House, Park Road, which had become available following the death of Isaac Dewhirst in April 1915. The other was a building called the Brooksbank School on Westgate, a former dissenting school occupied after 1911 by the Ambulance Association for the training of its students. This was not the site nor the building occupied by the current Brooksbank School Sports College, although it was its spiritual ancestor.

The prime movers were local dignitaries Dr George Hoyle and Councillor Lumb. As with the other auxiliary hospitals, they were prepared and run by voluntary staff, with a committee to raise support funds. The official opening of the Plains Auxiliary Hospital was on 6 December 1916, with provision for thirty-two beds, and that of the Brooksbank Auxiliary Hospital on 21 March 1917, with provision for thirty beds.

Crow Wood V.A.D. Hospital, Sowerby Bridge

Crow Wood Mansion, Sowerby Bridge, was offered on loan by William Paterson Eglin, and was accepted at a public meeting on 8 March 1917. Its establishment received advice from the staff of The Plains (Elland) and Spring Hall Mansion (Halifax), both of which had been in

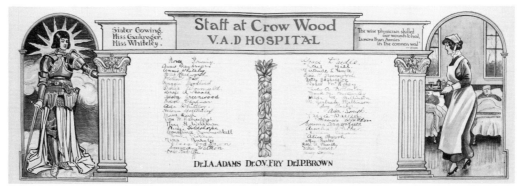

Inside page of Arthur Siddal's souvenir booklet of Crow Wood V.A.D. Hospital showing signatures of its staff. Artwork by J. J. Mulroy. Calderdale Libraries Service.

operation since 1916. Frank Clay was appointed chairman of the committee, Mrs A. Sutcliffe was appointed to the comforts fund, and the facility was officially opened on 5 April 1917. It had provision for fifty-three beds and received its first patient on 27 April 1917. When it ceased as an auxiliary hospital in March 1920, it had dealt with 764 soldiers. By then the property had been bought by Sowerby Bridge Council. The building was demolished soon afterwards and the land converted into Crow Wood Memorial Park.

A very fine illustrated autograph book of the hospital (designed by J. J. Mulroy and presented by Arthur Siddall), complete with signed details of many of the soldiers, was handed over to Sowerby Bridge Council and can be seen in the Calderdale Central Library.

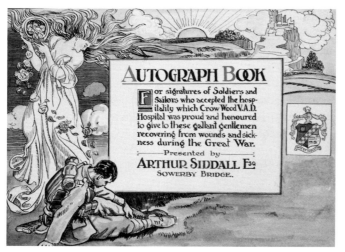

Covering page of the souvenir autograph book of the Crow Wood V.A.D. Hospital. Designed by J. J. Mulroy and presented by Arthur Siddall. Calderdale Libraries Service.

CHAPTER 10

1915–18
A Woman's Place

Suffragists and suffragettes

Before the outbreak of war in 1914, British society was not at peace with itself. It was actually a time of great unrest and militancy. Both trade union disputes and suffragette activity were never far from the newspapers. Suffragettes had already made themselves felt in the Halifax area through the activities of Laura Willson and Lavena Saltonstall. Both had defied the law and both had spent time in prison. Halifax born Laura Willson (née Buckley) had married local businessman and socialist sympathiser George Willson. She had been influenced by the radical thinking of the Halifax Independent Labour Party and it was through their meetings that she first heard Christabel Pankhurst speak, thereafter becoming increasingly drawn to the militant wing of the women's suffrage movement. She first gained her notoriety during the Halifax tram-workers' strike of 1906, and later in the Hebden Bridge fustian workers' strike of 1907. It was here that Laura Willson was arrested for allegedly urging crowds 'If you cannot get justice by fair means get it by foul' and 'take the law into your own hands; the police are few and you are many'. Denying the accusations, she conducted her own case, protesting strongly that she was not allowed a woman solicitor. Unable to prove the accusations, the court bound her over to keep the peace. She refused to pay the surety and opted for a fourteen-day prison sentence instead.

Lavena Saltonstall was equally fiery, and uncompromising in her beliefs. She had moved to Halifax from Hebden Bridge and very soon became part of the same circle as Laura Willson. Unlike Laura she was a very poor speaker but her wry writing style served her well through the columns of the local newspapers. She later came to believe that the way to make progress was not through militancy but by education, and turned to the Halifax Workers' Education Association (WEA).

Suffragettes were not popular. Following a militant protest outside the Houses of Parliament, Laura Willson and Lavena Saltonstall were both arrested and later imprisoned for a second time. William Henry Stott recorded in his diary on 7 March 1907:

The country is very much upset with the suffragette movement, that is a number of unsexed women are speaking and kicking up a lot of bother wanting the vote. To give every woman the vote would be ridiculous.

These women had been the headline grabbers, but there were other non-militant groups lobbying for women suffrage, such as the Halifax Women's Suffrage Society. At one of their meetings in the summer of 1914 its chairwoman pointed out:

[...] that they strongly repudiated all illegal and immoral methods of propaganda. They regretted very much that certain misguided advocates of women's suffrage had seen fit to damage the cause and their own reputation by methods which for a single moment they could not support [...] to refuse the franchise, however [...] because of the excesses of a small minority was altogether illogical.

On the outbreak of war, unity of national purpose in support of the war spread even to the suffragette movement. They called a truce. The *Halifax Courier* of 12 June 1915 reported the annual meeting of the Halifax branch of the National Union of Women's Suffrage Societies where they declared that 'An interesting programme had been arranged at the last session, but owing to war it was deemed advisable to abandon all meetings of a controversial nature.' For the moment energies were being channelled elsewhere. The report continued:

Suffragists and suffragettes have great reason to be proud of their several associations [...] magnificent lead [...] in the way of preventing and relieving distress, financing and equipping women's workrooms, financing and equipping day nurseries [...] tending sick women and children and [...] nursing back to health or soothing the shattered manhood of Europe.

There may have been a truce, but militant suffragettes were on the whole qualified in their support of the war solidarity that gripped many others. The desire to make peace rather than see things through to the bitter end was never far below the surface. Lavena Saltonstall's voice was one of the few instances of closet dissent that managed to get newspaper space. On 8 August 1914, when all about her were grimly turning their faces to the war with some degree of vigour, she wrote to the *Halifax Courier* from her WEA course in Oxford:

We students of the Oxford Summer School are realising very acutely the horrors of this war, because men with whom we have studied and fraternised for the last four or five years are being hauled up to take their part in the defence of England, and incidentally to fight with other men who year by year have come over from Europe to share our studies and recreations [...] there seems to be an added horror in the fact that the rabble here in Oxford are screaming themselves hoarse with vindictiveness against those whom we have known and liked in past years [...]

Socialism, pacifism and the suffragette movement were never far from each other. One of the great frustrations of the practitioners of these ideologies was the impotence they felt in the face of the country's war unity. Lavena Saltonstall was nothing if not pragmatic. She recognised what other suffragettes recognised: women would be needed in the struggle ahead. She noted, with a wry wit:

[...] while the men here are mobilising to blow each other to pieces, the women are being asked to mobilise to piece them together again.

Of course, there was to be more than piecing men together. The future held opportunities for women to assert their importance in ways that would have been unthinkable before the war. What follows in this chapter has to be viewed through the prism that gender stereotyping at that time was the norm. Women were not full citizens, and were generally thought to be inherently incapable of many types of work. They were deemed to be limited by their mental attributes as well as their physical abilities. Even today, changes in gender stereotyping have still not fully run their course, but in Edwardian Britain it was one of life's cultural certainties.

Mobilisation of women

A report in the *Halifax Courier* of 1 May 1915 gives us a candid snapshot of attitudes to women workers just at the point where their status was about to change. It was the time of the Shell Scandal and Lloyd George was advocating greater industrial involvement in the war. The employment of women was on his agenda.

On 30 April 1915, a meeting for women was held at Halifax Town Hall to consider the appeal from the Board of Trade for women to do war work, in order to replace the 19 per cent of men who had left industry to join the army. One of the interesting aspects of this report was how the question of female employment was all subjugated to men's needs. Employment clearly did not equate to equality.

Speaking from the platform to a largely female audience, Miss Julia Thornton, who was the government 'senior organising officer for women's work', outlined what kind of work women could do. The government wanted women of leisure and those who had lost employment (due to short time) 'to show their patriotism and capacity for work in a practical way'. They did not want those who were in domestic service or those who were married with families. Miss Thornton was there to tell them that 'they would not be required in the heavy engineering but they could fill fuses, sort and store them'. With hindsight it all looked a little tentative in its ambitions.

> Among probable posts for women she mentioned shop assistants, bank and insurance clerks, tram conducting (she would leave driving to men), many openings on the railway such as ticket collecting [...] carriage cleaning, chauffeurs for motor vans and the textile trades. There was also a need for nurses.

Women cleaning railway carriages in Sowerby Bridge Station. Stephen Gee Collection.

None of this seemed to predict the kind of seismic shift towards an understanding of what women were capable of doing. In fact, women were later to be employed in all sorts of capacities that went far beyond 'light housework'.

Miss Julia Thornton also seemed a little defensive about how this might all be received –

> [...] employers were most conservative and would not take women but [she hoped] ladies would use their persuasive powers.

Exactly what persuasive powers these ladies were going to employ was not explained. Local MP J. H. Whitley, had a practical suggestion. He thought 'that women might approach labour exchanges in much the same way that the male recruits had done for the Pals' battalions, by going together in groups of supportive friends'. All very military.

In the audience, one woman asked if women would receive equal pay. The reply from the platform was that, 'Women were sufficiently alive to know that if they accepted lower rates they would be unfaithful to the men who had gone to the front.' Not exactly the point of the question and related to men's employment wellbeing rather than that of women's.

The mayor, however, heartily welcomed the plan and said he could vouch for the work that women did. It was almost like recommending that a child was capable of doing an errand without supervision.

Another questioner dared to raise the subject of hierarchy – 'Could they be employed as overlookers?' The platform replied that it saw no reason why women should not superintend women. So, not quite ready for that one yet.

Sir George Fisher-Smith summarised. He believed it was:

> [...] a woman's first duty to look after some good man [...] those who had not got a man to take care of should assist the men who were fighting for their lives.

So it was men's needs first. If women were unable to fulfil this important requirement, then the least they could do was help the men at the front by enlisting as workers. It is easy to find gentle humour in these attitudes from the comfort of the twenty-first century, but every age has its mind-set. From 1915 the gender mind-set was about to change. The suffragists had laid out the arguments. Now it was time for the field-tests.

The women were not found wanting. Despite the genteel approach of the government's 'senior organising officer for women's work', it was to be women from all walks of life who came forward. Wages were attractive, so many included those in domestic service and women with families. The jobs undertaken went far beyond the original guidelines.

In the *Halifax Guardian Almanacks* issued for 1915-17, there is a wonderful series of illustrations depicting the many occupations newly taken on by women. They included acetylene welding, turning copper bands on high explosives, grinding machine operators, drawing the retorts in gas works, coke sorters, horse grooming, ploughing, feeding pigs, acting as shepherds, postwomen, ambulance women, window cleaners, railway porters, barbers, policewomen and, yes, even tram-drivers.

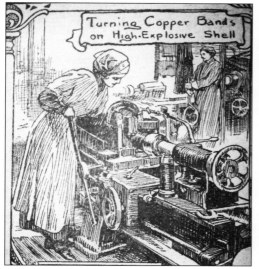 

Halifax Guardian Almanacks 1915-17.

Women in the workplace

The experiences of firms employing women have been described in more detail elsewhere, but some of them bear repeating. The various munitions workshops overcame the lack of skilled workers through dilution in which the employment of unskilled women played a big part. The workforce of W. H. Asquith Ltd. rose from 373 to 1,310, of which 610 were women. If we assume, as was likely, that no women were employed before the war, then two thirds of the extra workforce were women. Men employees were still, overall, in a slight majority.

It seems to be something of a myth that munitions factories were filled almost exclusively with women. Halifax may not have been typical for the country as a whole, but none of the cases that has come to light had a workforce where women were in the majority. Even at the Greetland Explosives Factory, which was purpose-built for the war, the *History of the Ministry of Munitions* quotes a figure of only 24 per cent women employees. The history also reported that 'the women proving quite satisfactory on the lighter kinds of work', which indicated some degree of ambivalence over women's capabilities. Asquith's employed them to handle the huge 9.2 inch shells, yet Francis Berry of Sowerby Bridge employed only 15 per cent where the heavy work 'was rather too much for them'.

One largely forgotten story is that of the welfare work done by suffragette Laura Willson. She had thrown herself wholeheartedly into assisting the welfare conditions at her husband's factory, organising, amongst other things, crèche facilities for women workers' children. Her scheme appears to have been adopted as a model by other factories. For this, she received the MBE. Not bad for an ex-jailbird who had had 'cocked a snook' at the establishment only eleven years previously.

Women's football

One sign of growing emancipation was the formation of womens' football teams. There does not appear to be any evidence of a womens' football league system in the Halifax area, as was the case in other parts of the North, but the *Halifax Courier* of 20 October 1917 reported a match between the munitions girls of Asquith's and the wounded soldiers at Cragg Vale auxiliary hospital:

> The sympathies of the crowd lay, of course, with the girls. The referee winked at all their transgressions of the rules, but did not allow the soldiers much latitude [...] they had to retire beaten by the girls by a score of 6 goals to 4. A few of the girls proved themselves to be very agile and they were evidently proud of their victory.

Conclusion

The position of women in society would never quite be the same again. Many lost their jobs with the returning servicemen, although some firms attempted to find other work for them. Nevertheless, the mould had been broken. Women were to be given a partial franchise in 1917 (those over 30 who met certain property requirements) and were able to use it in the December 1918 election. Some historians have claimed that the Act of Parliament was part of a natural progression started before the war, and highlighted by the suffragists' arguments and the militant activities of the suffragettes. It is difficult to believe, however, that the wholesale employment of women and their demonstrable worth did not play a part in the process.

CHAPTER 11

1917
When Will This End?

Slogging it out

If ever there was one year that symbolised the wretchedness of the Great War, then this was it. Even the pessimists had expected the war to last no longer than 1917. Behind them lay the slaughter of 1916 on the Somme and at Verdun, and victory still seemed a long way off. Politicians took stock. Did they really think the war was worth continuing? Peace had been tentatively suggested by the Germans at the beginning of 1917, but the sticking point was Germany's insistence on retaining all of its conquered possessions, which would have included Belgium and Northern France. To the new and ruthless leaders of Britain and France, David Lloyd George and Georges Clemenceau, this was unacceptable. The alternative was to continue to the bitter end, and this indeed was what they decided to do.

The German strategy, on the other hand, was to put down roots on the Western Front and concentrate on defeating Russia. These roots came in the form of the Hindenburg Line, a carefully and elaborately constructed system of defensive fortifications. It consisted of at least three separate defence lines, each with a deeply dug trench system protected by areas of barbed wire up to several hundred yards deep, and interspersed with concrete bunkers. Concealed machine-gun posts were everywhere. Having constructed this fortress wall, the German Army retired behind it at the beginning of 1917. Over the next two years, the military problem for the Anglo-French armies was how to break through it. There was only one way in and that was head-on. It was going to be a slogging match.

Round one: Arras

In terms of Halifax casualties, the relatively unknown battles of Arras in the spring of 1917 were to be even worse than the battles of the Somme. The offensive involved the newly arrived Reserve 4th Battalion West Riding Regiment, which had so proudly paraded around the Halifax districts in aid of recruitment in 1915. Now it was two years on, and the battalion was tasked with assisting the assault on the village of Bullecourt (April 10-11). It is one of the myths of the Great War that most, if not all, British generals were incompetent, but the action at Bullecourt was one of those that encouraged that belief. The plan of attack was flawed and its execution poor. On this occasion it is probably fair to apply Siegfried Sassoon's famous poetic description:

'Good morning, good morning,' the general said,
When we met him last week on our way to the line.
Now the soldiers he smiled at are most of 'em dead,
And we're cursing his staff for incompetent swine.
'He's a cheery old card,' muttered Harry to Jack
As they slogged up to Arras with rifle and pack.

The brutal truth was that the empire forces at Bullecourt, which included members of the Reserve 4th Battalion West Riding Regiment, achieved very little. Even though the battalion was not involved in the murderous frontal assaults, local casualties were bad enough. The *Halifax Courier* published a gallery of fallen soldiers whose numbers matched the worst that had been seen since the Somme battles of 1916.

The casualties were being noticed. William Henry Stott was moved to say in his diary:

9 May 1917 [...] We are distressed today to hear of many Elland lads of the Dukes [West Riding Regiment] have been killed. It is terrible. Everybody is sick at heart with this sorrow.

11 May 1917 [...] A family at the bottom of our street have

Halifax Courier *5 May 1917.*

THREE ELLAND BROTHERS.

In the centre, Pte. E. G. Dyson, West Ridings, aged 23; on the right, Gnr. L. Dyson, West Ridings, aged 26: both of 101, Huddersfield-road, Elland. Both were killed on May 5, the former dying in the arms of the third brother (on the left), Pte. W. Dyson, R.A.M.C. Two other brothers are also serving.

Brothers E. G. Dyson (centre) and L. Dyson (right), both killed on the same day in April. Halifax Courier 5 May 1917.

received news of two of their sons killed in action. They have three more with the Colours. This is terrible.

In a letter dated 22 April Private Fred Arthur Barrett, of Sowerby Bridge, commented on how life had changed for the battalion:

> Since we landed here in January we have had a rough time of it, with rain and snow every day until a week ago [...] We have been very busy since we came out here. They used to say to us when we came home on leave from the home camps "Aren't you out yet! Haven't you been to France yet?" Even some of our own townspeople would hardly look at us [...] because of our long stay in England. But just let a few of those critics come out here and they would alter their tale. When we did get out they soon found us something to do, as you will know by the number of local lads that have been wounded and gone under. Yes, we had it very hard [...] Shells and bullets are flying all around, and we never know whose turn it is next, but we keep plodding on.

On 3 May they were ordered to attack a second time. This time the battalion was involved more directly in the assault, but 'was hung up by the thick wire entanglements which were insufficiently cut'. The results were depressingly predictable. On 26 May, the *Halifax Courier* published the highest number of casualties of the war yet seen in a single week.

Halifax Courier 26 May 1917.

An unnamed Royal Field Artillery gunner wrote to the *Halifax Courier* offering his insight into what was happening:

> You know the offensive is only in its infancy yet. Just as the child, when learning to walk stops and falls now and again, so may we. But as the child keeps on trying, by and by he could walk, and then run [...] But you need not be over elated at success, nor unduly depressed at reverse (this is the year when the Huns will be defeated), and if I had my way, they would be thoroughly defeated before any peace papers are signed. You at home, I tell you, cannot realise the awfulness of it all, and the inhuman things that have been done by the enemy out here.

Here there was no recrimination, no blame culture, just the simple acknowledgement that the British Army, with its newly recruited soldiers, was still learning its trade, and mistakes were being made. The gunner may have been unduly optimistic in his assessment of when the Germans would be defeated, but he was still sure why it was necessary. The German Army was still far from beaten, the Hindenburg Line was still a formidable obstacle, and the allies were still dreaming of a way through to 'the open fields beyond'.

One of the casualties at Arras was John Staveley Fawthrop, who had appealed for exemption early in 1916 claiming he was the only butcher in Mill Bank and therefore essential (see Chapter 8). He was killed on 27 April, and his body was never found. His name is on the Arras memorial.

Round two: Passchendaele (Third Ypres)
The Arras offensive had primarily been a French affair, and had ended badly for them. They likewise had no real answer to breaking the Hindenburg Line and suffered huge casualties. Ominously their army began to experience serious problems with mutinies. In the East, Russia had also had enough, collapsed into revolution, and deposed its Tsar. There were hopes that the new Russian provisional government might still continue to fight alongside the Allies, but basically she was a spent force. It was a dangerous time for the Allies.

The main weight of military responsibility now fell on the British. The Somme and Arras offensives had been instigated to fall in line with

French strategy. But here at last, in the summer of 1917, Sir Douglas Haig, the British commander-in-chief on the Western Front, had the freedom to choose his own field of battle. He had his eyes on an offensive in Flanders. With hindsight it was an unfortunate choice.

There were genuinely sound strategic reasons for choosing Belgian Flanders. A breakthrough would have forced the Germans to pull back from the Belgian coast, and allowed the British to eliminate the U-boat bases there. The British Army was also becoming more proficient in its infantry and artillery tactics, battle-hardened by the Somme and Arras. Part of the plan, code named 'Operation Hush', was to stage an amphibious landing on the Belgian coast. This was to be supported by inland units and included the 4th Battalion West Riding Regiment, which had spent the high summer months near the coast in training and preparation. The operation was supposed to link up with the advancing British Army pushing out from around Ypres.

The main thrust from Ypres began well, with a spectacular if somewhat localised success at Messines. Thereafter, the line did move forward in fits and starts, but the over-riding memories of this offensive were of rain, mud and paltry territorial gains. The worst rain for thirty years and the badly drained Flanders battlefield did their worst. Sir Douglas Haig's plan for a sweep into Belgium became yet another slogging match. This time it was a slogging match in a swamp.

By late September, when it was apparent that the main thrust from Ypres was not matching the strategic design, the 4th Battalion West Riding Regiment was marched from the coast to take its part in the swampy bloodbath that had developed in front of the village of Passchendaele. It was joined for a while by the 2nd Battalion West Riding Regiment. Both played a part in the battle of Poelcappelle as the British Army edged towards Passchendaele. Both suffered.

William Stott's thoughts reflected what he read in the newspapers, and these give us a reasonable picture of how the war was probably being perceived in Halifax. Typical comments were:

20 August 1917 […] More sharp fighting, British advance.
22 August 1917 […] Very heavy fighting going on at […] Ypres [and] gained a lot of ground.
8 November 1917 […] Our push on the West is slow but sure.

The reality of the 'slow but sure push' was rather different. Captain P. G. Bales in his history of the 4th Battalion West Riding Regiment, described one small incident as it approached the Ravebeke, one of many Belgian streams in the area:

> In normal times this stream would have been a very slight obstacle, but the devastating fire of the British artillery in the recent heavy rains had converted its course into a formidable morass. Lieutenant H. S. Wilkinson […] went forward […] to try to get in touch with the men of the 146th Infantry Brigade […] Near the Ravebeke, a bullet lodged in his steel helmet, fortunately without wounding him. As he could find nowhere with a means of crossing, he waded through the stream, the water coming above his waist. He then advanced […] across awful mud and with machine-gun bullets whistling all round. It was in this crossing […] and the advance to Peter Pan [a German block house] that the battalion suffered its heaviest casualties that day.

Like many others, William Henry Stott still clung to the idea, which had been there since 1916, that a breakthrough was just around the corner and a German defeat would then swiftly follow.

> 12 October 1917 […] Great battle in preparation for the last ridge. Then we shall have them in open country.

There was to be no open country. It was all a mirage. The British finally took the Passchendaele ridge, and on 10 November that was where they stopped. As with the offensives of the previous years, it had promised much and delivered little.

Considering the battle's later notoriety, the Halifax newspaper coverage of this major battle was surprisingly muted. Mud and the appalling fighting conditions hardly figured. It seems that, by now, there was some greater restraint over what the local newspapers published about fighting conditions. Gone was the multitude of frank and graphic soldier accounts of the battlefield that had characterised the years 1914 to 1916. Then they had often been referred to as 'thrilling accounts'. What were the possible reasons for the change? The most obvious candidate was pressure from the government, but as was noted before, it may have been the policy of the editors themselves. They may have sensed that the best line of support for the war was to gloss over what had become a grim and bloody business of attrition.

The following example taken from the *Halifax Courier* of 13 October 1917 was probably the exception, but even this seemed more of a weary good humoured grumble than anything else:

> Let me try and give you a pen picture. [We] arrive in a little town, which once was a prosperous town behind the line, now a heap of stones […] Our soldiers get into a trench which, through previous rains, is nearly knee deep in water […] Some may reach their destination, wet to the knees, perhaps with no clean socks to put on, and to their discomfort find there are no dugouts worth mentioning […] Some go to another part […] This place too is a heap of stones. The first alarm is "Gas!". You put down things you are carrying, get your gas helmet on, and "carry on". You hear a shell coming your way; you listen, and as it explodes on your right or left you "carry on" again. Attaining your destination, you hear that so-and-so and private so-and-so, members of your platoon, have got killed on their way […] Then your dugout! Well, really, one does not expect a chintz-covered bedroom. You go on hands and knees through a little hole into a place measuring 2 yards by 2 yards. Seven live there. Oh the comfort and the joy of it.

It may simply have been that the public no longer wanted to hear too much. They had plenty of evidence in the local newspapers that there was a butcher's bill to pay in the weekly cavalcade of dead, missing and wounded. Arras had been Halifax's worst passage of the war, but the steady carnage of Third Ypres continued to remind people that the meat grinder continued to turn relentlessly every day. Between July and late November 1917, approximately 1,000 more of Halifax's sons were destined to be added to the district's post-war memorials.

Cambrai: A ray of hope
The Reserve 4th Battalion West Riding Regiment had not spent its time at Third Ypres. It had a relatively quiet time holding the line further

east. It had not been slogging through the mud of Passchendaele, so it was a natural choice to be allocated a late and unexpected operation. The 1917 Battle of Cambrai completely bucked the trend of an otherwise depressing year. The concept of the tank had been under development since 1915. The tanks were tested on the Somme in September 1916 and found to be largely useless but with interesting potential. At Bullecourt in May 1917, where the West Riding battalions had suffered so much, the misuse of tanks had been the fundamental flaw in the plan. At Third Ypres, late in 1917, they had sunk in the mud. The Germans did not rate them. The Cambrai plan introduced some new tactics that were to prove to be the template for what became the pattern of all modern land warfare. Amongst many other innovations, the plan deployed tanks *en masse* to spearhead the attack, and punch a way through the Hindenburg Line.

On 20 November 1917, the Reserve 4th Battalion West Riding Regiment, along with other units of the 62nd Division, emerged from Havrincourt Wood behind its tanks and burst almost effortlessly through two lines of the Hindenburg Line. Everard Wyrall, in his *Story of the 62nd West Riding Division* takes up the account:

> […] thus when night had fallen on 20 November, all three infantry brigades had won through to their allotted objectives and had achieved what, at that period, must be regarded as a remarkable performance, having advanced 4½ miles from their original front, over-running two powerful German systems of defence and gaining possession of two villages.

First-hand accounts of advancing infantry and tank crews are full of giddy excitement at the undreamed of penetration into enemy defences, all the more remarkable for the hitherto formidable reputation of the Hindenburg Line. The British Army had spent long bloody months and years attempting to break through into the 'green fields beyond', and here it was brushing it aside with nonchalant ease. In a single day's operation the Reserve 4th Battalion West Riding Regiment had advanced the same distance that had been 'achieved' at Passchendaele in the whole four-month campaign.

William Henry Stott Diary: 'These monstrous engines of war have played a prominent part in this last battle.' Stephen Gee Collection.

At home, 'joy bells' were rung by some churches in celebration of what they regarded as the first good news in a very long time. Halifax and the *Courier* were not so sure. The paper's editorial of 24 November 1917 was more cautious than enthusiastic:

> [F]or the first time in the war, joy bells were rung in London, yesterday [...] London's example will set the provinces thinking. Indeed, they have been discussing the topic during the last day or two, and doubtless many peals went up from scattered areas in support of St Paul's. But the joy bells were not heard throughout the land [...] Germany, which is over fond of joy bells has made herself ridiculous on that account more than once [...] British caution will probably guard against that. In Halifax, for instance, serious consideration was given to the idea of ringing the belts but it was decided to "wait and see" how Sir Julian Byng's [Commander at Cambrai] movement developed.

Was the breakthrough at Cambrai the beginning of what had been expected for the past eighteen months? Not quite. The British Army was unable to exploit its breakthrough, reverted to the customary crawl and fell back into the usual slogging match. The German Army counter-attacked about a week later, regaining much of the ground it had lost. Cambrai, in the final analysis, was a draw. From the military perspective the year ended almost as it had started, with everyone, more or less, in the same positions where they had started.

Corporal George Douglas Goose of the Reserve 4th Battalion West Riding Regiment was one who did not make it. He was killed on 22 November in the battle. He had probably experienced the thrill of the first day's 'giddy' advance, and then got caught up in the familiar slogging match. He enlisted on 5 December 1915, probably in the York Café as part of Lord Derby's scheme. On his attestation papers was the signature of the recruiting officer Richard Wycliffe Flanagan.

U-boats and food shortages
In mid-1916 the German failure to mount a successful challenge on the British Grand Fleet at Jutland led the commander of the German High Seas Fleet, Reinhard Scheer, to press for a return to an aggressive U-boat campaign. His arguments prevailed and on 31 January 1917, Germany announced that its U-boats would engage in unrestricted submarine warfare. Any ships entering the warzone around Britain, regardless of type or nationality, would be sunk without warning. Scheer predicted that six weeks of this would be enough to bring Britain to the point of starvation and defeat. He recognised the risk that it might bring America into the war on the side of the Allies, but calculated that she would be unable to mobilise her vast reserves of manpower before Germany had eliminated Britain from the war. Germany would then overrun France. It was a potential war-winning strategy.

From the very beginning things began to bite. William Henry Stott noted in his diary on 7 February 1917: 'Enemy Submarines are just now playing havoc [...] This is getting very serious. It will take some stopping,' and on 10 February he was making the clear connection that 'this is assuming a terrible aspect as regards us getting food etc, etc'.

An adequate supply of food for Britain's population had been a concern of the government for some time and, more out of caution than alarm, it had created a minister for food control in December 1916 (initially Lord Davenport, being succeeded by Lord Rhondda from June 1917). From February 1917, ship losses began escalating to alarming levels. In April they had reached nearly three times the pre-campaign monthly totals. It appeared that Germany's strategic gamble was paying off.

The approach of the government seemed to follow the same lines that had occurred with recruitment. It wished to avoid too much state control and relied on voluntary co-operation, loosely regulated by food orders from the Ministry of Food. As with military recruitment, the control of the supply and demand of food was still largely to be in the hands of local administration. Voluntary food vigilance committees sprang up in local communities, for the purpose of reporting abuses such as hoarding or profiteering, and to monitor problems with prices and distribution of food.

By July 1917, shopping was becoming a battleground. The Halifax Food Vigilance Committee sought a meeting with the Halifax Corporation Finance Committee over its concerns regarding the fair distribution of food. What it advocated took its inspiration from the left-wing Workers National Committee manifesto on food. They believed that the government should buy or commandeer all imported and home-grown foodstuffs, and place them on the market 'at prices that would give the full benefit of government action to the consumers', a clear nod to national price control. Bread was singled out as a special case requiring a fixed government purchase price, with 'any loss involved [...] to be charged to the cost of the war'. In other words, government subsidies.

There was a feeling that the wealthy could always ride out any shortages because of their spending power. The relatively poor who, after all, constituted the vast majority of the nation, would always lose out, as had been the case during that summer when there had been a shortage of sugar and potatoes. The sore point was that sacrifices were being made unequally, with unfair distribution of food, rising prices, and a resentment that some sectors were profiteering while others went without. Niggles and tensions abounded. The *Halifax Courier* of 7 July 1917 described one report of the Food Vigilance Committee:

One of their members had stood in a shop [...] for 15 minutes [...] watching the crowd struggle for sugar with the distracted assistants hardly knowing what they were doing or saying [...] Sometimes the assistants said they were not allowed to make sales based on conditions [...] and then arbitrarily imposed conditions [...] Sometimes, an assistant said the customer could only have 4 oz of sugar, other times she said 8 oz [...] All of this unfair and shady business should be stopped.

As the year dragged on into late autumn, food issues began to seriously intrude into what had already been a bad year. William Henry Stott's diary for 1917 records that these were grim times that severely challenged everyone's morale. On 14 November 1917, he wrote gloomily that 'If you go to Halifax or Huddersfield all is altered [...] People have lost the good old spirit.'

William Henry Stott Diary, 9 November 1917. Stephen Gee Collection.

The government eventually bowed to the inevitable. Statutory food orders were issued to local authorities, who were made responsible for their enforcement through the formation of local food control committees. The *Halifax Courier* of 8 December 1917 had a glimpse of how its committee operated:

> [...] their work is of a character which is more likely to cause abuse than praise from those who have no idea of the immensity of the task [...] their duties are to see that the many, and sometime vague, orders are properly interpreted and put into operation. The work is divided into sections each in charge of a sub-section [...] One committee deals with sugar, another with meat, one with transport, a fourth of an economy campaign and so on.

The threat of absolute starvation had passed with the introduction of the convoy system, and U-boat sinkings were brought under some control. Nevertheless, the problem remained that many foodstuffs such as sugar, butter, meat and margarine continued to be in short supply. This was to get worse before the situation stabilised. The food control committees had to handle what was, for Britain and Halifax, becoming a highly charged political situation. People who go hungry also become difficult.

Things came to a head just before Christmas 1917, the point where perhaps the government might have lost some control of the war. This was epitomised by the 'scandal of the food queues'.

On December 15 the *Halifax Courier* was reporting 'unprecedented scenes':

> The early morning [tram] cars carried a large number of persons from the outskirts of the town and these assembled in the vicinity of the butter shops about 5.30 [am]. From that hour onward the crowd increased [...] Some idea of the dimension of the crowd might be gauged from the length of one queue [...] this extended from Northgate, in thick grouping along Crossley Street (here the line was serpentine in character and the crowd denser in formation) to Wesley Court [...] women are making themselves ill by long standing in the public thoroughfares.

John Lee noted in *Todmorden and the Great War* that:

[...] articles were frequently unobtainable and when it was known that a trader had received a supply, news quickly spread [...] had to be marshalled into queues, the police and special constables being occasionally called upon to maintain order.

On Friday and Saturday of 21/22 December:

From noon until late at night [...] a queue five or six deep extended [...] For a period of nine hours the queue rarely numbered less than four or five hundred people [...] When the shop closed [...] there was still a large number unserved.

An advertisement in the *Halifax Courier* of 8 December had a whiff of revolution about it; a foretaste of what might have happened had the crisis deepened, and control of events had slipped away from the government. Alderman Morley and John Law JP spoke at a meeting held at the Electric Theatre on Commercial Street:

Workers! Come and protest against the present Queue System and disappointing Food Supply.

A week later, W. H. Asquith, one of the major munition works in Halifax, gave the Food Control Committee notice that, unless the present system was remedied, the firm would cease work in protest. It was not 'Russia' yet, but it is difficult to ignore the emerging political edge to the rhetoric.

The government did act. The Ministry of Food dispatched an order giving local food control committees the power to conserve the supply of margarine and butter and to make arrangements for equitable distribution. The Halifax Food Control Committee appointed a sub-committee consisting of wholesalers, retailers, a nominee of the Co-operative Society, and one of the Economic Stores. This sub-committee immediately announced a 'fat card' scheme, similar to one already in use for sugar. Households had to register with specific retailers, who supplied them with a card allowing them to purchase butter or margarine from them only. The retailers had to register at the food office and make weekly returns of stock. Crucially, the sub-committee had powers to ensure 'equitable distribution of supplies'.

These were the key elements that were missing before. The system was not for all foods, and neither was it yet a full ration scheme, but it was getting close. Significantly, control was still in local rather than government hands. More importantly, it ended the 'food queue scandal'. Asquith's did not strike.

Bit by bit a full national programme of rationing was introduced in 1918. This began in January with sugar, followed in April by meat, butter, cheese, and margarine. By July the programme covered most of the essential foodstuffs, and ration cards became another fact of everyday shopping. The system was to extend for some time after the Armistice.

Allotments

An integral part of Britain's food story was the campaign to increase home grown produce to ease the strain on imports. Clearly there was plenty of land that could be turned to food cultivation. Towards the end of 1916, the government turned its attention to how they could encourage people to do this.

The *Halifax Courier* editorial of 25 November 1916 noted:

Suddenly the Food 'Dictator' comes and people are stirred into thoughts of using the land [...] a feeling that, if it is necessary to prepare for a long war with men and munitions, there must be the same foresight in respect of food.

It was all part of the creeping process of state control to win the war. Liberal Britain, with its values placed on individual freedom and localised control, was having its legs cut off. The Small Holdings and Allotments Act of 1908 was already on the statute books, making it obligatory for local authorities to provide rental allotments where there was a demand. By and large this had been something of a dead letter and authorities often cited a lack of demand as their reason for inactivity. Halifax had no allotment plots except one at Pellon used for poultry. The *Halifax Courier* continued:

A conference of some 200 representatives from Urban District Councils in the West Riding met in Leeds on Thursday [...] each council should take steps to provide a sufficiency of allotments [...] a definite movement in land cultivation is probable.

By December 1916, local authorities were given the powers to acquire any land they deemed suitable, and the movement began to gather real momentum. By the beginning of 1917 the subject of allotments, allotment associations and the need to grow food had become a regular feature in the local newspapers.

Meetings sprang up everywhere. Typical of this was the one held at Lightcliffe National School, reported by the *Halifax Courier* of 20 January 1917, where a lecturer from Leeds University attended to give advice on gardening in wartime.

> There had been a good deal of talk about allotment gardening, and it had become a cant phrase, but now the time had arrived for serious activity […] Before the war a great many people had taken up gardening as a hobby, but now the food supply was a vital necessity, and the rose-grower must turn his attention to more serious attainments […] It was acknowledged that England did not grow enough food for the people […] Steps must be taken to reduce our dependence in some measure, and by means of allotments some assistance would result […] The present was the time to get the land in condition by digging, and each one might still help to win the war in the garden […] Every man should take a plot as near his home as possible.

On 28 February 1917, William Henry Stott wrote in his diary that 'Every town & village are going in for allotments to grow potatoes or some other kind of vegetable'.

How far all this went towards easing the food problem is difficult to tell. The main problem, the U-boat menace, was eventually overcome by the introduction of the convoy system, and Britain did not starve, although it was necessary to introduce rationing in 1918.

Dual munition explosions shock Halifax

The year ended on a note that seemed to sum it all up:

> Herman van Dyk Diary, Saturday 22 December 1917 […] there was an explosion at 5.30 am at Hipperholme, which shook the

house and certainly awoke this town. This afternoon at 2.00 pm two distinct reports of an explosion at the works below The Rocks [a Halifax location] gave us another shock.

William Henry Stott Diary, March 1917. Stephen Gee Collection.

By a remarkable coincidence the district's two picric acid factories suffered explosions on the same day, just three days before Christmas Day. Were workers simply tired and getting careless? Was it anything to do with drink?

It was only after the war that details were published in the local newspapers. The early morning explosion at 5.30 am in Hipperholme was at Brookes Ltd, where there were five casualties. Two were killed instantly, and the other three died later in the Royal Halifax Infirmary. The *Halifax Courier* of 4 January 1919 reported:

> Great consternation was caused in the district, people running into the streets terrified [...] windows were broken wholesale at many of the houses. The damage, however, was nothing compared to that at Low Moor or even at Copley.

The five men were working where the waste sulphuric acid was concentrated and recycled back into making picric acid for shell explosive. Picric acid becomes highly unstable when it is allowed to dry out and it was possible that some had percolated out of the main process. The works manager, Mr Chambers, was satisfied with all the personnel employed at the factory. The coroner's verdict was that Brookes Ltd had all the necessary safety measures in place, and a verdict of accidental death was recorded. He made special mention of Herbert Smith of Hipperholme, who had been woken by the blast, hurriedly dressed, and ran to assist at the incident. He heard groaning from the top end of the tank shed where he found John Cowburn 'standing in an acid tank and holding on to an electric wire'. Smith got him out and dressed his injuries, but John Cowburn died in hospital later. For his actions, Herbert Smith was later awarded the OBE.

Later in the day there were two more explosions at 1.45 pm and 1.47 pm. These took place in the Copley Chemical Works, which housed some of the processes associated with the National Explosives Factory at Greetland, located further down the valley:

> Two drying stoves [small detached buildings at the Sowerby Bridge end of the works] were blown completely away and two others were damaged [...] a large volume of smoke was seen encircling this. At the top was a large mass of flame [...] houses were violently shaken, many of them badly damaged and fearing there may be further explosions, many of them [residents] fled to the woods for safety.

The stoves of the Copley plant were used for spreading picric acid over glass for drying. The explosion set fire to the neighbouring stove, where Mrs Haigh was cleaning. She ran out with her clothes on fire. Although she was rescued, she died from the effects of the burns about three weeks later. The coroner could find no fault with the practices of the factory and recorded a verdict of accidental death. The following month, in January 1918, the Ministry of Munitions transferred the making of picric acid from the Copley Works to HMEF Greetland, further down the valley.

The *Halifax Courier* continued with the tragic story of another victim who was a local resident. At the time of the explosion, Mrs Elinda Elsie Pearson of 72 St Stephen's Street, Copley, was in her house with her three children Joseph (6), Annis (4) and Jack (2). She took the youngest in her arms and grabbed the hand of Annis. The eldest child followed her as she began to flee the house and, like many of the other frightened residents, headed towards the woods. As she was leaving, the second explosion took place, causing bricks and stones to fly through the air. One brick flew at the group, breaking the baby's arm, striking Elinda Pearson on the breast, and instantly killed four-year-old Annis with a blow to the head. Despite the fatality to one child and injuries to another and herself, Elinda continued to walk the considerable distance through the woods and struggled to West Vale. There she caught the tram to the Royal Halifax Infirmary. From the comfort of the twenty-first century, with its ubiquitous phones and emergency ambulance services, the whole event seems surreal.

There was however, a further twist. Elinda Pearson was also very heavily pregnant. The following month she gave birth to her daughter Nellie. Many years later, in 1993, Nellie was able to retell her story to the *Halifax Courier*.

The year's end

This was a miserable time for Halifax. There had been over three years of war with little to show for the countless enlisted men, the massive effort at home and the proud hopes on the battlefield. If the army was bogged down on the Western Front, then the people of Halifax were sinking into their own mire. Food was short and prices rising. Casualty lists filled the *Halifax Courier*. War weariness was everywhere.

J. J. Mulroy Cartoon. Halifax Courier *1 December 1917*.

A cheery little item appeared in the *Halifax Courier* and was placed by Pohlmann's Pianos. Incredibly, its message was to go out and buy a piano to brighten things up. It seems advertisements were capable of capitalising on anything.

William Henry Stott sounded as though he was getting close to the end of his tether as well. He had already gloomily observed that whisky was going to be £1 (£150) a bottle by Christmas. On 5 December 1917 he wrote what was probably at the back of everyone's mind:

> Things are getting from bad to worse. Everybody is weary of this dreadful carnage, but we cannot give out. If we do we have Germany a menace to civilisation, but how it will all end. God knows. I cannot fathom it.

With Russia out of the war, and the Germans transferring their divisions from east to west, there was one way it might end, and it was not the outcome for which the people of Halifax had entered the war. Nineteen-eighteen was going to be a testing time.

CHAPTER 12

1918
Last Man Standing

By 1918, the war had gone on too long for everyone. All the European nations with a major commitment to the war were already in a state of complete collapse, experiencing partial collapse or showing dangerous signs of collapse. Who could go the extra mile and be the last man standing? With hindsight it is too easy to think that Britain was in some way immune to all this. The reality was that sheer exhaustion was making itself felt everywhere. On the battlefield the British Army had a manpower crisis and, at home, food shortages and strikes were testing the nation's resolve.

Tank week
Tanks were highly topical following their dramatic exploits at the Battle of Cambrai only a few months previously. Some had been put on display by the government in Trafalgar Square and had created such a degree of interest that they decided to commission seven of them to tour the towns and cities of Britain, as travelling displays to encourage investment for National War Bonds and War Saving Certificates. The plan's originators were not disappointed. The seven tanks attracted £250 million investment (£22 billion in today's values). Halifax alone raised £2.3 million (£345 million).

The tank that came to Halifax in the week of 16 March 1918 was named *Egbert*. This practice of naming tanks might seem curious now,

Illustration by J. J. Mulroy depicting Tank Week. Halifax Courier *16 March 1918.*

but at the time they were seen as some sort of small armoured dreadnought battleship that was capable of travelling over land – hence the name of the first official body setup to develop them, the Landship Committee. Brighouse and Hebden Bridge also had their tank weeks.

In common with all the presentation tanks used, they were real tanks with real operational histories. *Egbert* was E26, tank no 2348 of 6 Section, 14 Company, E Battalion, commanded by Second Lieutenant Staniforth. *Egbert*'s career, however, was not perhaps as illustrious as it might have been. It had been dispatched to active service as part of the battles of Third Ypres (which had ended in the infamous Passchendaele). Assembling at its starting point on 26 September 1917, it received a direct hit and played no further part in the battle. After salvage repairs it was shipped back to Britain to begin its new role as a presentation tank.

It arrived at Shaw Syke goods station and began with a demonstration on Shay Field, where 30,000 people gathered to watch. This was an open field at the time but in later years was converted into a football stadium for the Halifax Town Football Club. After the tank's demonstration, it trundled up Hunger Hill along to George Square in the town centre, where the serious business of raising investment began.

It should be remembered that tanks were machines of some size, so its journey from goods station to town centre must have been something of a spectacle. It is possible to get a sense of the drama of the occasion from George Bentley's (Little Khaki George) recollections:

> [...] to show off its capabilities it was driven first across the Shay which at that time was an open area of tipped ashes [...] and up the quite steep embankment to Skircoat Road at the top. I believe it had no difficulty in achieving this climb and proof that this happened was shown by the two deep tracks which remained visible for a number of years.

According to the *Halifax Courier*, a 'vast crowd' attended the official opening at noon. The mayor read out a stirring earthy message from the 2nd Battalion West Riding Regiment:

> If you are only half as keen to get this little stunt over as are we [...] then you will flock to the Tank as Fritz flocks from it. Bring your money in sacks, in handkerchiefs and any old thing for the Tank will take it all [...] Just now we are all well and smiling but if you don't roll up with your cash we'll jolly soon shan't be. Put your money on us and we will not let you down.

After the war many towns and cities around Britain, including Halifax, were to have their own display tank proudly mounted for all to see. Tank no 208 was donated to Halifax and displayed at Rock Hollow Park, Ogden. Sadly, their interest value evaporated almost as soon as they were in place. The Halifax tank and all the others around the country (with the exception of one) disappeared under the scrap merchant's hammer. They belonged to a passage of time that people perhaps wanted to forget.

Egbert on George Square. Stephen Gee Collection.

An article in the *Hartlepool Daily Mail* of July 2013 tells the sad fate of *Egbert* himself. He was donated to Hartlepool at the end of the war, to commemorate Hartlepool's outstanding fundraising achievement. In 1937 he was no longer wanted. One councillor described him as 'a relic of barbarism'. By a vote of twenty to twelve the decision was taken to scrap him. Three years later, German forces, which this 'relic of barbarism' had helped to resist back in 1917/18, returned to France and Belgium. This time France was crushed in a matter of weeks and the British Army was pushed into the sea. Much of the German success would be attributed to the use of tanks.

Kaiserschlacht (the 'Kaiser's Battle')
There was little at the beginning of 1918 to cheer the British public. National food rationing was introduced by degrees and there were still shortages in the shops. More than anything else there was the feeling that there seemed no prospect of an end to the war. Russia was, to all intents and purposes, out of the war, and there was an expectation that extra German forces would be massing for an attack in the West, something the enemy had not been able to do since early 1916.

William Henry Stott had also had a bad winter. Not only did he have the food shortages and the war situation to contend with, he was also battling wearily to keep his son from conscription. His diary chronicled the mood of Halifax:

> 20 February 1918 […] All the papers now point to a heavy battle in the near future. The enemy are going to make one final effort to break through. The people are getting weary of waiting for the victory promised them now for a long time.

> 1 March 1918 […] Meat cards are now issued it looks like having cards for all kinds of foodstuffs etc, we are just beginning to realise what war is […] Depressed all day.

> 7 March 1918 […] Shall we never be out of all our troubles?

> 17 March 1918 […] We saw a convoy of wounded soldiers coming into St Luke's Hospital. A most depressing sight.

With unintentional irony, William Henry Stott was slightly upbeat on 21 March, the very day the German offensive in the West began. He wrote:

> Beautiful day for the beginning of Spring. Let us hope this is the forerunner of better weather. All the allotments are now busy, digging and got ready for another crop. Much more land everywhere is being cultivated.

While Halifax was still gazing at the wonder of tanks, the dam broke. It was Germany's gamble to win in the West before the American troops arrived in sufficient numbers to make an impression.

> 23 March 1918 […] The great offensive started in the West. The enemy on a 50 mile front has made massed attacks in some cases have broken through, but at fearful cost of lives.

The note about 'fearful cost of lives' reflected the attempt of newspapers to find the silver lining. For once the newspapers were not spinning an untruth. German casualties were high, but at this stage all that really mattered was that Germany had seized the initiative and was rolling forward relentlessly.

24 March 1918 […] The paper today brought us the sad news of the break of our line in the West. The enemy by an overwhelming mass of 4 to 1 broke through, and we had to fall back, which we did in good order.

27 March 1918 […] British have had to fall back 15 miles […] The position is critical.

29 March 1918 […] The situation in the West is still very serious, the enemies onrush is somewhat checked […] The Germans are using a new long range [gun of] 70 miles and have been shelling Paris this last few days. Today above all others, <u>Good Friday</u>, the day our Saviour was crucified they shelled a church during mass and killed over 60 worshippers and an equal number of injured. This is what the world must expect from Kulture.

This sudden change from the static slaughter of the last few years to a moving battlefront, with the added menace of an enemy threatening to break through to the Channel Ports, actually had a galvanising effect on the British public. The industrial unrest at home subsided, and people were more motivated to work harder in the factories. Unbeknown to them the Germans had shot their bolt and the battlefront was stabilising again.

For a while it had been tough and many British positions had been overwhelmed in the first few days with many casualties and prisoners. One young man would not be returning home. He was Ernest Hodgson Nicholl who had joined the army under age, been brought back by his parents and later applied unsuccessfully for exemption on grounds of conscience. He was killed on the first day of the German offensive while serving with the heavy artillery.

In the early days of April, William Henry Stott remained downbeat, but for the first time in months his entries had a sense that the worst may be over. He noted that there was a 'lull after the heavy losses they have sustained. I hope we give them the same dose next attack.'

Nevertheless, he still had time to bemoan life at home:

4 April 1918 […] Living gets from bad to worse. You cannot buy anything, ration cards are the order, every public house has cards hung in the window (no beer today). Tobacco bad to get.

Nevertheless, Stott managed some fighting talk:

> The German people are now beginning to realise that they are economically beaten and that they will for the future be a boycotted nation, are beginning to wail. This will go on and the time is drawing near when they are about to find themselves beaten and crushed.

But they were far from beaten and crushed. Germany threw a new offensive at the British, this time in Flanders (Battle of the Lys). It was just as threatening as the last, and was nearer to the Channel Ports.

> 11 April 1918 [...] Heavy fighting now going on in Flanders. The enemy are using all their strength to break through. We are all now looking very grave. The new Manpower Bill has come [...] all men called-up to 50 years of age.

The last entry signifies that conscription was now becoming a barrel-scraping exercise.

> 12 April 1918 [...] Severe fighting still continues. Hour of crisis in Flanders battle. Grave message from Haig. Our backs to the wall order to the Army. Positions must be held to the last man. There must be no retirement. The safety of our homes and the freedom of mankind depend upon the conduct of each one of us at this critical moment [...] These are grave words.

> 13 April 1918 [...] an air raid on Paris with loss of lives and many injured, one of the hospitals was shelled. This is most brutal. Oh God is there no recompense for such cruelty?

The three-week battle ended in much the same way. After initial successes, the German Army outran its supplies and was halted by dogged British defence. Although the British public did not know it at the time, the worst was now over.

Another butcher's bill
The story of the Great War often concentrates on The Somme and

Halifax Courier *27 April 1918.*

Passchendaele, where it is commonly assumed that most of the slaughter took place. The year 1918 is often forgotten, but the casualties were even worse than 1916 or 1917. If we can talk in terms of 'black days', then the blackest single day of all for Halifax was 27 April 1918, when the *Halifax Courier* carried sixty-four notifications of dead or missing servicemen. It exceeded anything from The Somme, Arras or Passchendaele (Third Ypres).

Somewhere in 1918 everything would begin to change. Somewhere, the optimistic hopes of a German defeat, first voiced in 1916 on the back of The Big Push, would finally begin to look real.

The watershed

In May 1918, it certainly did not look that way. The Germans launched yet another offensive, and yet again the allied armies were alarmingly broken through. This time the offensive was directed more at the French, on the Chemin des Dames, and its objective looked ominously like Paris.

The *Halifax Courier* of 6 June 1918 observed:

> Since March we have been continually on the defensive, meeting the force of unprecedented blows.

Germany's apparent success was papering over the cracks of a failing strategy. The fundamental weakness of her position was that her time was running out. After initial alarm, the French were able to halt this German offensive. While still in a position to do so, the Germans attempted a negotiated peace. They offered concessions in the West, including withdrawal from Belgium, in exchange for holding their gains in the East. This had its appeal to the many that yearned for peace, but few people were fooled. James Parker MP, a self-confessed peacemonger in any other circumstances, believed there was only one satisfactory outcome to this war. He wrote in the *Halifax Courier* of 1 June 1918:

> You read the words 'German peace offensive' in the daily press […] As the night follows day… any German peace proposals […] are but so much dust to blind the eyes of the civilian populations of the Allied nations. They are put forward to weaken and divide the allies in their purpose. They are an appeal to the selfish and the weaklings among us, an appeal to the war weariness of the Allied peoples, in the hope that the Huns may remain in possession of all their ill-gotten gains […] These proposals were only to come to the Allied nations in the West on the condition that things remain as they are in the East. All the Russian invaded territory was to be held with no doubt Austria or German princes on the throne of Poland Finland and the Baltic provinces of Russia […] The mailed fist of the Kaiser […] would be twice as strong as it was in August, 1914 […] We shall always have to stand on guard against another attack […] your children will have a worse hell to face than that which their fathers […] have gone through during the last four years.

Elsewhere in the *Courier* its editorial dwelt on another aspect of the war, which, in its way, was proving just as important to the outcome of the war:

The news of the fighting is none too good, but there is a much improved outlook for foodstuffs [...] A great step is being taken towards making the island self-supporting. Compared with 1916 we have over 4 million additional acres available, and wheat, barley and oats will occupy more ground than ever in our history, while the potato acreage is the greatest since 1872 [...] Each of the hundreds of thousands of small areas (there are 800,000 more allotments than in 1916) represents a ton of foodstuffs. We also have the assurance of the food ministry that the bread supply is assured until the next harvest [...] The acting Food Minister [...] holds out the expectation that before long the quantities of food will be so sufficient as to enable the rations to be increased [...] The growing effectiveness against the U-boat has had the primary influence upon the improved position in foodstuffs.

Britain had therefore won its 'food war' even if it still had to contend with rationing, shortages and high prices. All things are relative; this was not starvation, and there were no riots on the streets. This was not true elsewhere. William Henry Stott wrote in his diary:

20th June 1918 [...] Austria seems at the last ebb. The populace are rioting for bread, & their friend the Kaiser, will not help them. He has simply made a catspaw of them.

21st June 1918 [...] 50,000 Demonstrators demand Peace and bread in Vienna.

The cracks were appearing. In what we might see as a dress rehearsal for Germany's experience only a few months later, Austrian resolve was crumbling. Her civilians had had enough, and their soldiers at the front were losing their determination to continue. The local newspapers had, in the past, been plagued by false dawns. However, the *Halifax Courier* felt moved on 22 June 1918 to offer what, it believed, was genuine optimism:

Statesmen's 'reviews' in the past have not proved very accurate in the light of subsequent events, but Mr Bonar Law's speech [...] had, at least, the virtues of sanity and balance [...] Mr Law did not cloak the dangers of the past or belittle the perils still before is. The Germans scored victories [... they had] expected securing one or more objectives – Paris, the Channel Ports, or the disorganisation of the Allied armies. [They have] failed absolutely in each particular [...] and the next three months are likely to be 'the supreme power of that struggle' [...] It would seem that he [Bonar Law] thought the final stages of the struggle at hand [...] He spoke emphatically of the disastrous campaign in which the enemy would find themselves involved if they failed in their present effort. America is the deciding factor [...] her rivulet of troops to Europe has become 'a great river' [...] submarine menace has failed [...] our Higher Commands face the future, not only with hope, but with confidence.

The mood was infectious. William Henry Stott wrote:

6 July 1918 [...] My reading of the papers, portends to the finishing of the war. The Germans know now they have defeat facing them. It may not be immediately, but the end, thank God, is fast approaching.

The summer influenza epidemic of 1918
Another entry in William Henry Stott's diary reminds us that another menace affected 1918:

29 June 1918 [...] Influenza very bad just now in Elland, in fact all over the N. of England.

The influenza pandemic of 1918-19 was one of the largest outbreaks of infectious disease in recorded history. In some respects the use of the word 'influenza' is unhelpful, because of its present day association with any feeling of being unwell accompanied by weakness and a high temperature. A more accurate understanding of what happened in 1918-19 is better served by the use of the word 'plague'. Its destructive effect went beyond the respiratory tract, although the most common cause of death was through respiratory complications such as pneumonia. Some historians have considered its impact to be even worse than the Black Death of the fourteenth century. The adjective 'Spanish', which is frequently used to identify it, is also unhelpful, as its origins have nothing to do with Spain.

The 1918 pandemic was a worldwide phenomenon killing an estimated 50 to 100 million people, due to the virus's ease of transmission. In Britain there were three major epidemics. The first one occurred in June/July 1918. A more serious one occurred the following autumn, peaking around the time of the cessation of hostilities. The epidemic returned again to peak in March 1919. It is not easy to pinpoint exactly when this new virus began to infect people in Britain. Early reports may not have distinguished it from normal influenza. First reports began appearing in America from March onwards. Some believe it was the American soldiers, arriving in Europe during the spring of 1918, who brought the virus with them. Late in April, the *Halifax Courier* reported that the newspaper magnate Lord Northcliffe had been recovering from a bout of influenza that had lasted nine weeks. The protracted period of his illness suggests this was normal influenza, but we cannot discount that this may have been one of the early cases.

By 29 June 1918, the *Halifax Courier* was reporting that "a new form of influenza" was reaching epidemic proportions in other parts of the country, particularly Lancashire. Even in nearby Huddersfield schools were being closed:

It is severe but not of long duration. People are stricken with it suddenly and it seems to work in 'colonies', for it is no unusual thing for a greater part of a room full of workers to be affected together.

This was describing some of the features of this new type of influenza quite accurately. It was virulent, severe, but of short duration. The *Courier* report went on to say that Halifax itself was not suffering badly, yet in the same issue it appears that both Elland and Sowerby Bridge were already having to deal with health problems reaching epidemic proportions.

The new epidemic of influenza has made its appearance locally on Thursday, only one teacher in the boys' department at Bolton Brow Council School put in an appearance, and over 20 scholars in the same school are reported to be down.

On 6 July the *Halifax Courier* reported that in Todmorden:

> [...] the Medical Officer of Health and the Schools' Medical Officer held a consultation, as the result of which it was decided to close the whole of the elementary schools in the borough until August 6.

Coroners were beginning to report details of how the deaths were occurring. The *Halifax Courier* of 6 July 1918 reported:

> Thomas Gannon (9) [...] died under painfully sudden circumstances. He retired to bed on Tuesday about 10 pm in his usual health, but the following morning he complained of headache and pains in his body. A doctor was sent for, but he died before he arrived [...] a post mortem examination of the body [...] found it healthy, with no marks of violence. There was marked congestion of blood vessels over the brain.

The doctors were clearly struggling, as can be seen by the death of a 13-year-old girl reported in the *Halifax Courier* of 13 July 1918:

> Doris Hallowell [...] complained of feeling unwell and went to bed. There was nothing in the symptoms she exhibited during the day to cause any anxiety. Next morning [...] she seemed very ill, and [the mother] went for a doctor. The family, she explained only came to Halifax on the Friday. Thus there had been no time to arrange for a panel doctor [...] She successively visited the surgeries of [...] four [doctors], to receive the reply in each case that they were busy. Finally, about 9 o'clock, she got a doctor [...] But it was 1 o'clock when he put in an appearance. Deceased had then been dead two hours [...] The coroner, addressing the jury, observed [...] Doctors [...] were now so hard worked, that they had a difficulty in getting round to their own patients.

On 13 July, Elland also closed its elementary schools and two of its secondary schools, but the *Halifax Courier* was able to report more optimistically on 20 July that:

The influenza epidemic is not yet stamped out, but it has waned again during this week. The best indication of that is the greatly reduced demand on doctors and chemists.

For the moment, the epidemic had run its course, but a second more catastrophic epidemic was to later return in the autumn, probably exacerbated by large numbers of soldiers being moved about prior to demobilisation. This will be dealt with in the next chapter.

The sands run out

Some have speculated that the summer influenza pandemic may have affected the Central Powers more than the Allies, not because it killed greater numbers, but because the Central Powers were nearer the end of their tethers. The collapse of Austria has already been mentioned, and this occurred just at the point when the epidemic was reaching its peak. In the case of Germany, it is more usual to attribute the decline in its morale to the stark realisation that the war was lost, after its failure to gain a decisive victory in the first half of 1918. Either way, the German Army lost much of its dogged determination to keep fighting from July onwards.

The German's final offensive was against the French over the River Aisne on 15 July. This petered out much more rapidly than the previous offensives and was immediately followed by a French counteroffensive (Second Battle of the Marne), marking the point where the Allies regained the initiative from the Germans. The Reserve 4th Battalion West Riding Regiment was involved in this famous turning point as it was part of the 62nd Division which, along with the 51st Division, was hurriedly transferred to this sector. The history of the 62nd division pointed out that they were:

> [...] amidst the cornfields of the Marne Valley [...] on this occasion the troops would be Territorials [...] worthy successors of the old regular army, many of whom lay buried beneath the very ground over which [they] were to once more drive the Germans back.

On 8 August a combined Australian, Canadian and British force dramatically burst through the German lines facing Amiens. That it was reminiscent of the Battle of Cambrai in 1917 was no coincidence. The idea of deploying massed tanks, along with other tactical developments, was used again. This time the Allies were more able to exploit the breakthrough, advancing a considerable distance beyond the start line. The British Army had come a long way, both in experience and tactical development, since huge sections of its volunteer army had walked into the machine-guns on the infamous first day of the Battle of the Somme in July 1916. Ludendorff, by now the virtual military dictator of Germany, famously described this as the 'Black day of the German Army'. He was particularly disturbed by the number of German soldiers who were now giving themselves up into captivity.

If the second Battle of the Marne was the turning point, then the Battle of Amiens signalled that the British Army now had the tactical means to break through any defensive system which the Germans cared to build. The years of trench stalemate were now, thankfully, behind them. There was still much fighting to be done, and casualty lists continued to fill a lot of space in the *Halifax Courier*, but there was no denying the new mood of optimism prevailing on the Home Front.

'Don't you think we had better turn back Father. It seems to be coming on very rough.' William Henry Stott Diary, 11 August 1918. Stephen Gee Collection.

For William Henry Stott it had become one-way traffic:

19th August 1918 […] French have made a good advance on a 9 mile front. We also are gradually pushing our line back. It looks like the last lap.

25th August 1918 […] The news from the front is splendid […] The military victory is being accelerated at a speed beyond the most sanguine hopes of 6 weeks ago.

29th August 1918 […] American troops still pouring in at Liverpool.

One hope remained for the Germans: they might hold the Allies at the Hindenburg Line, and perhaps force a temporary halt before winter set in. This was not to be. Sensing victory was possible this year, the British, French and the Americans successfully assaulted this formidable obstacle, and went on to complete several other operations 'in the green fields beyond'. The German Army was now in headlong retreat.

The Germans had continued with peace overtures during this period. With each additional passage of time, their bargaining position became less favourable. By late October the game was up and all that remained was to negotiate an armistice on virtually any terms. It was effectively unconditional surrender. This was what the Allies, the British public and the people and newspapers of Halifax had cried out for, even in the depressing days of the trench stalemate. Their purpose had been to destroy German militarism, but not the German nation, so it was not thought necessary to pursue the war deep into Germany. The German Army salvaged one concession and this was to have significant consequences for the future peace and security of Europe: it was not required to surrender. Instead, it was allowed to return to Germany carrying its weapons, thus helping to create the myth that the German Army was never actually defeated, but was forced to call a halt because it was 'stabbed in the back'.

For Halifax, the final two months were another peak on the casualty graph. Nearly all of the Halifax battalions who have featured in this account were involved in breaking the Hindenburg Line. Nothing compared to some of the previous casualty peaks, but the announcements of soldiers dead, wounded and missing remained a regular feature across the *Halifax Courier* pages during this campaign. The breaking of the much vaunted Hindenburg Line meant that, for Germany, it was all over. On a dank cold November morning, a delegation from the German Army met with a delegation from the Allies at a railway siding in the Forest of Compiegne and reluctantly acceded to the Allies' punitive armistice terms. Both sides had finally agreed to stop fighting.

Armistice

'Victory' had finally arrived.

It was over four years since 4 August 1914, when James Parker had spoken of his revulsion at what he saw as 'blood lust' on the streets of London. In his time he had gone from a man of peace, who had voted against increases in armaments, to someone who had embraced the need to go to war. He had been a tireless advocate of recruitment, robustly supporting the need to crush German militarism. Now that victory had at last been achieved, his mood was far from one of celebration. He wrote in the *Halifax Courier* of 16 November 1918:

> In this the hour of triumph of our cause […] the justice of which I have never for one moment doubted […] I feel tired and weary. I don't want to cheer nor shout […] I could pray rather than cheer, and weep rather than laugh.

The feelings of some local men at the Front, printed in the *Halifax Courier*, were also ambivalent about the victory.

> We had expected it, felt sure of it, but as there was a tiny gram of uncertainty about it, we just heaved a sigh of relief, shouted, capered, and shook hands with one another […] There was not that great excitement and upheaval that people at home would expect. This does not mean that we received the great news with indifference. We all felt too deeply for words. I even think there was some depression among us. We had whistled up our courage day by day as we dodged from cover to cover, and kept cheerful in mud holes and under trying conditions. Now that the need for this is over, we feel something has gone.

Halifax itself was more prepared to celebrate, but likewise joy was mixed with restraint. The *Halifax Guardian* of 16 November 1918 reported:

> Flags were hoisted. They appeared to spring from nowhere [...] people who had not smiled for months positively beamed [...] where the people came from nobody knows. They must have trudged in from the surrounding villages and towns in their thousands, because earlier in the day the tram employees took the law into their own hands and ceased work [...] as the darkness fell, the crowds seemed to get denser. Commercial Street was filled with a throng of happy irresponsible young people. Soldiers in Khaki, Jack Tars in blue, arm in arm with munition girls in silks and satins [...] It speaks well for the town as a whole that the people were in the main quite sober. True, one or two gazed on the red wine and some amusing scenes were witnessed. One gallant Tommy insisted on kissing a policemen and then doing the goose step up the street [...]

But overall it was not a moment that called for wild rejoicings:

> A feature of the rejoicings has been the absence of wild and lawless riotings, such as marked the end of the Boer war.

In Elland it was similar:

> [...] although there was satisfaction expressed on every hand, there was no rowdy jubilation at Elland when the news became noised abroad [...] three heavy explosions were arranged and these, reverberating through the valley, roused enquiries. Almost immediately flags began to fly, the official news having been made through the Post Office [...]

There was of course the memory of the sacrifices. In Hipperholme, 'The news was received with subdued exhilaration because of the losses sustained in the district.' In Todmorden, it was all too much for someone:

> The sudden death took place of Mrs Martha Ann Exelby [...] Her husband [...] found her ill. She died before a doctor could be got. She was excited over the signing of the Armistice as her soldier son had written saying he would soon be home for good.

In Hebden Bridge the bunting was out, and a band played patriotic airs in front of the Council Offices. Elsewhere there were touches of bitterness and vindictiveness. In Spring Hall Auxiliary Hospital grounds, they burnt an effigy of the kaiser. In Brighouse there were memories of the U-boats:

> If retribution had to be made for inhuman orders, surely the man who gave the instructions to 'sink without truce' must be brought before the tribunal and pay the just penalty.

The end of the war was not the end of everything. All the belligerents, including the victors, were damaged goods, in some cases very badly damaged. Who knew what normality was anymore? For some there were ideals. Woodrow Wilson, the American president who had helped broker the Armistice, hoped for a better world. Lloyd George hoped for a better Britain, 'fit for heroes'. The pacifists hoped for a world without war. None of them were to come even close.

CHAPTER 13

1918–19
The Remains of the Day

It is impossible to separate 1919 from the previous four years. For the moment the Armistice had stopped the bloodletting, but it had not removed the antagonisms that had brought the nations into armed conflict in the first place. Indeed, there were now more problems to deal with. It was already apparent how difficult it was going to be to affect a closure.

1914 belonged to a bygone age. Now, it was necessary to take stock, attempt to complete unfinished business and plan for some sort of reconstruction.

The Treaty of Versailles

Nothing exemplified the lack of closure more than the peace treaty. Some say it was too harsh, some say it was too lenient, while others believe the future problems of Europe lay with a lack of enforcement of its terms. Whichever interpretation is favoured, it is evident that when the nations came to sign the peace treaty, there was a conspicuous lack of reconciliation from all sides. On the eve of the signing, the *Halifax Courier* editorial of 28 June 1919 was both critical of Germany and pessimistic about the future:

> [T]here is no doubt about spirits in which Germany approaches that meeting. In her official agreement to sign, she said she

252 HALIFAX IN THE GREAT WAR

yielded only 'to overwhelming force' and talked a lot of cant about retaining her honour [...] There has been nothing of [...] the repentant, nothing of honesty or sincerity in the German bow to fate. Instead, we have had the scuttling of the German ships at Scapa [...] The burning of the French flags captured in '70 [...] due to be returned [...] and the disquieting news that war against Poland is being actively prepared for [...] In Germany itself the decision to sign has been the signal for demonstrations, riots and many other tokens of bad will [...] The peace is, indeed, being obtained under the most disagreeable of conditions, and that fact is the more distressing when we look into the future and wonder how the peace will be observed [...] The general fear in 1919 is that the Germans will not stand by their promises [...] They are signing the treaty quite dishonestly and reserving to themselves a mental right to evade their signed obligations if they can [...] German dishonour is rooted deeply and German signatures will be as valueless as those on the Belgian 'scrap of paper', unless ample safeguards are taken to collect debts, punishments, and preserve the peace.

If those sentiments were universal, it is little wonder that the peace was, as Marshal Foch predicted, 'nothing more than a twenty-year armistice'.

Repatriated prisoners-of-war

Some things demanded immediate attention. There were tens of thousands of prisoners-of-war who had been forced to live out a grim and unforgiving existence. They needed repatriating as quickly as possible.

As early as June 1916, alarming reports had reached the British public that prisoners-of-war in German camps were receiving treatment well below the requirements of The Geneva Convention. Brutality and starvation were rife. This had led to the establishment of various help organisations, which endeavoured to get food parcels delivered to ease the situation. The Germans themselves had been feeling the effects of the British naval blockade and had progressively become more and more short of even essential foodstuffs. This was something the German population bitterly resented, and prisoners-of-war may have felt the backlash from it.

Late in 1918, the prisoners poured back into their communities with a multitude of 'horror stories'. Although we have to take into account both newspaper bias and the degree of bitterness felt towards the Germans generally, the evidence suggests that many prisoners did indeed suffer brutal mistreatment, and in some cases starvation. John Lewis-Stempel's account in *The War Behind the Wire* paints a very negative picture:

> Who today knows that the death rate in the Kaiser's prisoner-of-war camps – from brutality, starvation and disease – was sometimes higher than that on the Western Front?

Tommy (writing home from prison camp): "Dear Maria, – everything 'ere is lovely, comfortable quarters, best of food, a regular 'ome from 'ome. Bill, who was of a different opinion, was shot yesterday." Halifax Courier 1 May 1915

Both the *Halifax Courier* and the *Halifax Guardian* published extensive reports, usually under emotive headings such as 'Cruelty of the Hun'. They had both organised the supply of comfort parcels to prisoners-of-war, so there was a natural tendency to emphasise how important the parcels had been. There was little newspaper mileage in

CRUELTY OF THE HUN.

More Prisoners' Revelations.

MEN BULLIED, BEATEN AND UNDERFED.

Headline. Halifax Courier *14 December 1918.*

reporting stories where treatment had been adequate, and parcels less of a 'life saver'.

Nevertheless, this is how the Halifax papers reported the repatriation of their soldiers from the German prisoner-of-war camps. The *Halifax Courier* of 7 December 1918 reported:

> For days we have been passing through perhaps the most thrilling of all our experiences – receiving calls from returning prisoners who, many of them say, owe their lives to the subscribers of the Courier Comforts Fund […] some had got no parcels, but all the same they said they knew we had done our share of the work faithfully: it was the brutal, abominable Germans who waylaid the goods en route, and often times took them for themselves. The men taken in the big German offensive in the spring were most unlucky – with very few exceptions, the enemy allowed them neither parcels nor letters, and lots were told too, they could not write home.

The *Halifax Courier* took particular pride in reminding everyone that:

> We feel especially thankful to have been among the very first in Britain to begin this work for the benefit of local lads – aye, 25 months before the general organisations of the country got going.

The stories flowed:

Private Joss Pearson, Reserve 4th East Lancs. Captured March 21. At Ors about three British prisoners died daily, Huns said from pneumonia (our men thought starvation).

Private J King 1st West Yorks. Captured March 21 [...] had starvation diet. Boots stolen, wooden shoes given in place.

Private C. Whitehead, 2nd W. Yorks., Taken April 24 at Villers-Bretonneux [...] First two camps filthy, and first two days no food. Later, four man to a loaf [...] Sgt in wood dump very cruel. On Armistice, marched 60 miles in four days; given third of loaf and two spoons of jam to set off. Several died en route.

Private J. Eastwood, 4th Yorkshires [...] Caught May 27 on Aisne, eight weeks on road working, next to an iron mine [...] seven days a week. Guards, who used rifle butts freely, have been reported. Knows of lad [who] literally starved to death. Was struck by bully 12 days since: right arm bad still.

The fort at Lille, often referred to as 'The Black Hole of Lille', was a notorious prison camp and gets a mention in this next story:

Private J. H. Harrison [...] taken April 11 [1918] and with 390 was housed in small room at Lille Fort: allowed five minutes out a day for food; all six weeks without wash. Lavatories in same compartment: two small windows only ventilation. Three Britishers died, others left frightfully weak [...] Sgt-major at Lille invited Britishers for boiled potatoes given by Belgians, but as they ran up he struck out with a whip. Always addressed British as 'swine'. British were thrashed for accepting Belgian food; he has seen Belgian women felled by gun butt for this generosity. German doctors were butchers [...] Two days before Armistice, was shown map, and told way to frontier [...] German officer had said, 'you will have your Christmas dinner in England this time. We never believed it would prove true'.

Private G. Hudson [...] Tells a startling story [...] A guard at Steinen, known as 'Ginger' struck a Scottish Tommy with his gun butt for taking and eating blackberries: then he jabbed him half a dozen times with the bayonet, and concluded his shameful ferocity by firing twice at him. Brother prisoners buried the lad.

In the *Halifax Guardian* of 14 December 1918:

Private Morris Astwood of Friendly. First the Germans stripped him of his possessions, and he was then taken to Hallowin and for six weeks was engaged carrying shells for the enemy. They were 9.5 shells, which it took two persons to lift onto their shoulders [...] moved on to [...] road mending and cleaning up billets for the enemy. Six weeks later they were moved [...] worked on a shell dump from 6 am to 4 pm without a break for any refreshment [...] carried out every day, including Sundays [...] Two lots of parcels and biscuits sent by the Red Cross Society were received [...] after the Germans had opened them, and taken out what they required [...] Four of them died owing to kicks and bayonet thrusts, mostly inflicted by Sgt by the name of Holbach [...] When they had worked until exhausted and fell to the ground, a bayonet was thrust into them to force them up [...] [after the Armistice] they were told to get ready from moving. They were a sorry spectacle – scarcely any clothing – no trousers, and many wearing the proverbial fig-leaf, a woman's skirt wrapped round them.

Not all prisoners were servicemen. Wilson Cockroft went with his family to manage a factory in Silesia in 1913 and was caught up in the changing events. The factory he managed was closed due to a shortage of coal. The *Halifax Courier* of 30 November 1918 continued:

[O]n November 6, 1914 [...] sent to Gorlitz [...] and here they were placed in the workhouse. On all occasions when they had to proceed to the station, crowds assembled and threats, insults, and full vulgarities were openly used against them by the Germans.

Eventually they reached Spandau and were marched to Ruhaleben [sic] [...] Here they were herded together like cattle [...] The whole arrangement was vile, and with the scanty food

supplied (substituted coffee, sour bread, and vegetable soup) […]
Mr Cockroft also asserts that the Huns in the neighbourhood
actually petitioned for the prisoners of war to be starved on two
days per week.

One report described treatment at the hands of the Turks in the Middle
East theatre:

> Cpl. Joe Wilde, 34699, South Wales Borderers […] is the first
> local prisoner of war to return from captivity with the Turks […]
> they were stripped of clothing, boots and equipment and forced
> to march barefoot. Over 350 miles had to be marched […] the
> suffering was intense. For food they were given four small black
> biscuits […] supplemented with a small portion of boiled wheat
> made up the days rations. Fresh water was unobtainable [… later]
> under the control of the Germans they were employed […]
> constructing a railway. The treatment afforded them here was
> based on the rule – no work, no food. The food, however, was
> slightly better […] For offences against discipline they were
> flogged, put on bread and water diet, and given the laborious
> task of chopping tree trunks.

Not all experiences were bad. Private Arnold Emsley, 2nd West
Yorkshire Regiment, was captured on 12 August 1916, and had a more
positive story to tell in the *Halifax Courier* of 21 December 1918:

> The first six months in captivity, he says, were terrible, his fare
> being a small piece of bread and cabbage water daily. But better
> days were in store […] Taken […] to Schneidemhull in [sic]
> Posen, where he was put to fishing on a large lake. The German
> people there had not much food themselves, but what they had
> they frequently shared with him […] He got every single parcel
> and letter addressed to him. The German people with whom he
> stayed were particularly kind, and the old woman of the house
> cried when he was leaving.

The *Halifax Courier* organised a reception for many of the prisoners-
of-war at the Drill Hall, Prescott Street. Rev'd Henry Ironmonger,

minister at Highroad Well Congregational Church, reported in the *Halifax
Courier* of 18 January 1919:

> What a dinner it was too. No
> German fare this time, not even
> bully-beef and biscuits! Not even
> maconochie [stew]. How the men
> laughed when I recalled their late
> menu [...] [now it was] oxtail soup,
> boiled cod and parsley sauce, roast
> beef and roast pork! There was plum
> pudding with as much sweetening as
> would make a housewife sick to
> think of [...] drinks for all palates,
> coffee, cigars, cigarettes [...]

*Certificate of Gratitude to the Halifax
Courier and its Comforts Fund. West
Yorkshire Archives (Calderdale).*

The autumn influenza pandemic

As if the end of the war did not create
enough problems, a second influenza
epidemic took hold around Britain in the autumn. The *Halifax Courier*
of 10 October 1918 remarked on an unusual feature of the influenza:
it was 'most deadly among persons between 25 and 45 years of age.'
Influenza usually affected the very old and very young, whose
resistance to disease was more limited than a mature adult. Medical
experts have since established that the virus seemed to trigger the
immune system into an overreaction that overwhelmed the body.
People in the prime of their life, with healthy, vigorous immune
systems, were therefore more likely to die from the effects of the virus.
As news on the battlefields was becoming more positive by the day,
the epidemic, on the other hand, was growing more serious. The
Halifax Courier editorial of 2 November took stock:

> Grave concern is being aroused throughout the country [...] by
> the persistence and danger of the influenza epidemic. In this
> district there is greater freedom from its ravages than in many
> places [...] but there is every reason for care; during the week,
> cases have become more numerous [...] The actual influenza is

very like other visitations, but the secondary infections are of a more acute character than usual [...] pneumonia [...] which is drastic and rapid in its action. There is the official assurance that the food rations are not considered a direct cause of the spread of the disease. That is satisfactory, but it is mere common sense to say that the restricted diet and "war strain" (in all its forms of anxiety and overwork) must contribute to a lower vitality [...] in which influenza flourishes [...]

Positive measures were taken by schools:

It is estimated that about 600 schoolchildren in Halifax are suffering from the "flu" [...] In the case of [...] schools, the scholars will assemble as usual, but instead of going into the school buildings they will be given exercise in the open air [...]

Of course, clinical details and statistics hide the personal tragedies, as the epidemic tightened its grip in and around Halifax. In the same edition of the *Halifax Courier*, human stories were beginning to appear:

[T]he most depressing case recorded locally being from Primrose Street, Claremount, where Mr and Mrs Ashworth and three children have all died. Two children were buried last Saturday, the father and mother were buried on Wednesday, and the youngest child, aged four months died on Thursday [...]

Depression and insomnia could be a complication in 'recovered' patients, as is witnessed by this coroner's enquiry.

Mabel Gertrude Dargue (22) [...] had suffered from influenza in June or July last [...] but had no troubles or worries. [The father said] She was a little downcast on Sunday [...] She did not come home that evening [...] The next morning they received a letter addressed to her [...] sister, Alice, as follows:

'to my darling Alice, who I hope will forgive
me. Everything is yours.
-Your loving Mabel.'

[…] About noon on Thursday they were informed that her body had been found in the canal.

The coroner passed a verdict of suicide by drowning whilst in a depressed condition from influenza.

Some famous names were appearing among the reported cases. At the national level there was David Lloyd George, and locally there was James Parker MP, as well as three of the Elland candidates nominated to contest the forthcoming general election. The *Halifax Guardian* of 7 December 1918 reported:

> Mr Trevelyan was the first to arrive. It was noticed that his right arm was in a black sling, the unfortunate result of septic poisoning. But in these days of "flu", no Parliamentary candidate is immune. Mr Harry Dawson […] has not completely recovered from his recent and fashionable attack, while Lieutenant Ramsden […] has not been as well as he might have been. Here the three nominees met on common ground, with common commiseration.

All deaths were tragic, but there was poignancy about soldier deaths. Having survived the war, and in some cases having distinguished themselves, it seemed grossly unjust for influenza to take them. The *Halifax Courier of* 8 March 1919 reported:

> The death took place on Tuesday morning of Mr Horace Sykes (27) DCM […] who has been the victim of complications following influenza […] Having gone through the trials of war for over four years, it is especially sad that his life should be so early sacrificed. He had only been back in civilian employment a week […] Joining the [Reserve] 4th W. R. Regiment in November, 1914 […] was transferred to the First 4th, with whom he went to France in April, 1915 […] In December, 1915, he was awarded the DCM.

And from the *Halifax Courier* of 11 January 1919 there was:

> Pte. John Martin, WRR […] Capt. R.H.W. Oliver writes that he contracted influenza and died on March 6 [1918] […] 'Private

Martin's case […] was a particularly hard one, for he had served his country for 11 years, had taken part in most of the fighting and had survived three wounds. Such a man deserved to live the rest of his life in peace. I assure you of the deep sympathy of his comrades.'

Examination of even a small sample of soldier obituaries in the *Halifax Courier*, such as those between November 1918 and January 1919, reveal that the deaths occurred in many different locations. Soldiers stationed in India seemed badly hit, and one case was even found on a Royal Navy ship at sea.

The worst two months of the second epidemic were November and December 1918, but by January 1919, there were optimistic reports in the *Halifax Courier of* 11 January 1919 that the worst was over. Even the gravediggers were able to ease up:

During the period of the influenza epidemic, gravediggers had to work long hours each day, sometimes well into the night. Happily, there has been a slackening in this respect and one hopes that normality has been reached.

The report noted, perhaps unsurprisingly, that there had been a larger number of burials in 1918. The peak months had corresponded, as might be expected, with July, November and December.

Deaths continued into 1919, and a third period in March reached epidemic proportions. Thereafter, the disease died out leaving a death toll worldwide that had exceeded the total war dead of all countries.

1918 'Coupon election'
Within three days of the Armistice it was announced that parliament would dissolve on 25 November 1918, and a general election would be held on 14 December. This was to have many features, which made it one of the most remarkable elections of the twentieth century.

There had not been a general election since the Liberal victory of 1910. The Liberal government, which had taken the decision to go to war in 1914, was not the most suited, ideologically, to lead Britain through the conflict. In 1916 Asquith had been forced to form a 'coalition' government, which included both Conservatives and members from the rising Labour party. At the end of 1916, Asquith himself was replaced as leader by fellow Liberal David Lloyd George. There is little doubt that Lloyd George's drive and determination to pursue total war was a major factor in the triumph of Britain over Germany.

Once victory had been achieved, Lloyd George was determined to represent Britain at the peace conference at Versailles. In order to facilitate this, he conducted the general election as leader of the already existing coalition government. It was a case of 'let me finish the job'. In collaboration with the leader of the Conservative party, he issued a 'coupon' to selected Liberal and Conservative candidates. Anyone voting for candidates with a coupon, whether Conservative or Liberal, did so in the knowledge that they were voting for Lloyd George to continue as prime minister. It was expected that candidates who had the coupon were, politically, in a very strong position at the general election.

This made for an elaborate mix of options for the electorate. Not only did they have the coalition government candidates, they also had the option of the official Liberals under the still existing leader of the party, Herbert Asquith, and also the rising Labour party, which was expected to increase its membership in parliament. This turned the election into a three-horse race. The unpredictability of the situation was heightened by the extended franchise to women aged 30 and above (with certain qualifications) and men aged 21 and above. The size of the electorate had leapt from 7,700,000 to 21,400,000.

The final factor that made this general election so fascinating was that the country had just emerged from the most traumatic passage of time in its history. Normal divisions along party lines were therefore severely compromised by issues that had emerged from the past four years of bitter warfare. It was difficult to ignore the depth of feeling there was to make Germany pay for the war, and to make German leaders, particularly the kaiser, accountable for their 'crimes'. In order to be taken seriously as a candidate it was almost obligatory to include these two aims in your manifesto.

The candidates who lined up in the three local parliamentary constituencies of Halifax, Elland and Sowerby added to the drama of an already extraordinary general election.

The Halifax division (constituency)
The two nominated electoral candidates were:

John Henry Whitley (coalition Liberal)
Arthur McManus (Socialist)

The notable absentee was James Parker, the widely respected and hard-working member, who had represented the Independent Labour Party in Halifax since 1906. Following a re-organisation of parliamentary seats for the 1918 general election, Halifax was allowed to return only one member, instead of two. James Parker declined to run against John Henry Whitley and instead ran as a Labour coalition candidate for the Cannock division of Staffordshire, where he was successful.

The colourful wild card was Arthur McManus. He ran as a Socialist, but this tells us only part of the story. He had a background as a member of the Clyde Workers Committee (of 'Red Clydeside' fame), and had experienced both imprisonment and deportation as an agitator. He later became the first chairman of the British Communist Party. One of his election meetings in Victoria Hall was supported by Sylvia Pankhurst, who has been described by some as 'more left wing than Lenin'.

(Left) Arthur McManus. (Right) John Henry Whitley. Library of Congress Prints and Photographs Division Washington, D.C.

McManus must have thought Halifax was fertile ground, but he commanded little support from the local newspapers. The *Halifax Courier* was quick to point out that the Trades and Labour Council was not responsible for his candidature, and if elected 'he would refuse to act as a member of the Parliamentary Labour Party'. The *Halifax Courier* of 7 December1918 then turned to ridicule his philosophy:

> He states quite frankly that he is a revolutionary socialist, but, lest that title should alarm us, he says that his revolution will be a bloodless one – rather a novelty in revolutions! Take the very latest one accomplished, Russia. From what we can gather, the bloodshed there has been somewhat extensive […] He seems to assume that those he terms the workers have a monopoly of all the virtues, and that all others are models of iniquity. He is particularly nasty about the class he lumps as 'capitalists' […] If you own your house, through your own thrift, if you own War Bonds […] if you have a bank balance […] you are a 'capitalist' […] If our comrade could find his ideal Bolshevik constitution, i.e. government by the mob, you would be straightway dispossessed of 'capital' […] Mr McManus was asked at one of his meetings whether he was in favour of making Germany pay for the damage done on the war […] He was perfectly indifferent about it. It did not matter if not a penny was paid. Everybody cannot get to hear this curious candidate. That is a pity, because the more you do hear him, the worse 'second' he will be in the contest […] I cannot imagine Halifax sending a man of such ideas to 'represent' the town in Parliament.

The paper was right. Arthur McManus was crushed by a majority of 18,100 and lost his deposit. Nevertheless, there were 4,036 voters who found his message attractive. On the face of it, approximately one in six of the voting population of Halifax were prepared to return a revolutionary member. William Richard Stoker, as one of McManus's nominees, must have been one of them.

Elland division (constituency)
This was a more complicated contest with four nominated candidates. Charles Trevelyan, the controversial minister who had resigned from

the government when war was declared, had been its popular MP since 1899. Following his resignation he had become a founder member of the Union of Democratic Control, an organisation that became increasingly pacifist in its outlook. The local Liberal Party deselected him, but he refused to stand down as MP and in 1918 returned to run as an Independent Labour Party candidate.

The four electoral candidates were Lieutenant G. T. Ramsden (coalition Conservative), Harry Dawson (Liberal), Dennis Hardaker (Labour) and Charles P. Trevelyan (Independent Labour).

Candidates in the Elland Division. Brighouse Echo *18 December 1918.*

An interesting situation arose because it seems that Trevelyan, who had long since fallen out with the local Liberal group, was not entirely welcome with the local Labour party either. The *Brighouse Echo* of 6 December 1918 reported:

A piquant situation has arisen in the Elland division by reason of the presence of two candidates, each addressing his appeal especially to the adherents of the Labour Party. Alderman Dennis Hardaker was some weeks ago adopted as the official candidate of the Elland division Labour Party. Mr Charles Trevelyan [...] standing as an independent candidate [...] announced his intention, a fortnight ago, of joining the Independent Labour Party.

With perhaps a touch of 'do you know who I am', Trevelyan advocated that it was in the best interests of the Labour Party if a compromise could be arranged with Alderman Hardaker. Trevelyan's 'compromise' consisted of the singular suggestion that Alderman Hardaker should stand down, and was backed up with 'for four years I [Trevelyan] have been in intimate contact with the Labour Party leaders'. Trevelyan continued to argue his case, often in public and rather tortuously, despite the fact that he had declined to 'submit his name and let the Labour Party locally say who should be their candidate', and in the face of the local Labour Party's own assertion that 'they were amazed at the suggestion that Mr Trevelyan should take the place of Alderman Hardaker, who was the officially selected candidate'.

Lieutenant G. T. Ramsden had all the electoral advantages. He was a coupon candidate, had been a serving officer and supported the clear vote catcher 'Make Germany pay'. Harry Dawson was the candidate of choice for local Liberals, but he was not a supporter of Lloyd George, and therefore did not receive the 'coupon'. The result may well have been heavily influenced by split votes, but Lieutenant G. T. Ramsden was elected by a moderate majority.

Lieutenant G. T. Ramsden (coalition Conservative)	8,917
H. Dawson (Liberal)	7,028
D. Hardaker (Labour)	5,923
C. P. Trevelyan (Independent Labour)	1,286

Trevelyan suffered humiliation, and appears to have had few friends left in the area. *The Brighouse Echo* of 13 December 1918 dismissively referred to his supporters as 'a little handful of pacifists' and 'those who have approved of his attitude during the war'. The *Halifax Courier* of 4 January 1919 sardonically commented that:

Mr Trevelyan [...] styled himself 'Independent Labour'. The majority of the electorate gave him quite another name to that by which he had labelled himself.

According to the *Oxford Dictionary of National Biography,* this was a particularly low point in Trevelyan's long and chequered political career.

Sowerby division (constituency)
The three candidates were:

John Sharp Higham (coalition Liberal)
Major Robert Hewitt Barker (Discharged Soldiers and Sailors)
John William Ogden (Labour).

Higham was the sitting member (since 1904) and possessed the coupon, although he preferred not to campaign under its banner.

The interesting wild card in this division was Robert Hewitt Barker, who represented the National Association of Discharged Soldiers and Sailors, which had no particular political allegiance, except to represent the interests of discharged servicemen. In later years it was to unite with other groups and become the British Legion. Barker's service career, no doubt, stood him in good stead. In 1914 he was a Territorial who was immediately called-up to serve with the 6th Battalion Lancashire Fusiliers in Egypt, Gallipoli and the Western Front. The *Halifax Guardian* of 14 December 1918 seemed to warm to him, reporting on 'the most enthusiastic political meeting held in Hebden Bridge for a long time'. As might be expected, he had a strong message in support of the returning servicemen:

> Major Barker had come forward to champion the soldiers' cause, and see that they had different treatment to what they had had in previous wars [...] in the past, selling laces and matches, pushing barrel organs, often with a monkey to attract. We did not want the soldier to be again the object of charity, and certainly we did not want to see them come again under the Poor Law. We wanted to see the crippled man well provided for, and the discharged men who were sound in health and limb, get plenty of work on good terms. We also wanted to see the widows and children get a good living.

He also struck at Higham's association with Liberal leader Asquith:

> What had Mr Higham done for the soldiers and sailors? They heard nothing until the election was broached and then Mr Higham got very busy saying what a bloodthirsty man he was so far as the Germans were concerned. Up to then he had supported Mr Asquith in his 'wait and see' policy and the boys who went out in the early stages of the war got the benefit of it,

thousands falling at Gallipoli because the government had neglected to supply them with sufficient ammunition.

Barker's views on Germany were clear and direct. These well targeted words may well have caught the mood of the moment:

> They were not out for vengeance, but the soldiers wanted to make the Germans pay every penny that the war had cost this country. If the Germans could have landed on these shores they would have made us pay until we starved. Then why should we not retaliate in the same way, for they deserved no mercy because of their terrible crimes. It was said the Germans were getting contrite, but his experience of the dirty Hun was that he would follow his Kaiser tomorrow if he thought there was a reasonable chance of landing an Army in England [...] He had no love for any German. The best way to speak to him was with a bayonet [...] Politics and social measures must take a backseat until we had settled the war, got our terms, and made it impossible for the Germans to ever again show their teeth.

The irony and sadness of these words lies in their bleak anticipation of the future. The 'land fit for heroes' ideal came to nothing and Britain did allow too many of its ex-servicemen to end up selling matches on the streets. As to 'his experience of the dirty Hun was that he would follow his Kaiser tomorrow', it may have been uncharitable, but it was chillingly prophetic.

It seems that Barker may have gained some political advantage from a speech made at Blackpool by his Labour opponent, Ogden, concerning the forthcoming peace conference. Ogden believed that:

> [E]very avenue of peace should be explored [...] for making a clean and reasonable peace [...] He hoped no nation in this war would make the mistake that Germany did in 1870 with France, when in making peace they imposed terms that were a disgrace to the conquerors, and laid the foundations of a future war.

It allowed Barker to refer to Ogden as 'an avowed pacifist'. After hearing the result, the local Labour group believed that 'with [...] a straight fight on purely social and political issues they will ultimately succeed'.

It seems that Barker was an outstanding and popular candidate, but it is possible that the Liberal J. S Higham lost votes to the Labour candidate, who himself fell short because of his perceived 'soft' stance on the peace conference. This may have allowed Barker in. In the event, he was the only NADSS candidate out of twenty-six national contenders to take a seat in the House of Commons, winning with a small majority of 981. Over the succeeding years, it must have been a great disappointment to him how badly many of the soldiers were treated.

R. H. Barker (soldiers)	8,287
J. W. Ogden (Labour)	7,306
J. S. Higham (Liberal)	6,778

Demobilisation

Having created a vast army complex involving not only front line soldiers but also its many associated support services, it was clearly going to be a challenge for the government to return its citizen soldiers back to normal life. The *Halifax Courier* editorial of 23 November 1918 said:

The War Office announces the military situation does not admit of the commencement of the mobilisation yet. The only exceptions are on 'compassionate grounds' and in a limited number of special cases [...] required for re-constructed industrial conditions preparatory to demobilisation.

As well as the logistical problems of transporting the sheer number of men, consideration had to be given to 'who went first', and the problems of flooding the home market with hundreds of thousands of men in need of employment. This was further complicated by the release of 300,000 workers no longer needed for the munitions works. Additionally, it had to be pointed out that the current situation was an armistice and not a full cessation of hostilities. Some men still had to be retained for military duties, which included the army of occupation and troops for operations in Russia. The latter campaign was extremely unpopular because most men felt that the job they had been called on to do was now complete and did not involve additional foreign adventures that were not related to the defeat of Germany. There were complaints about the reasons for retaining some men. One man had been 'employed for five months looking after the tame jackdaw of the Captain', while another was employed 'making rattles for officers to rattle at football matches.'

By January, a degree of restlessness was beginning to creep in. The editorial in the *Halifax Courier* of 11 January 1919 commented on the darkening mood:

> In several of the home camps and embarkation ports in France [...] there has been a good deal of trouble during the last week in association with demobilisation. Happily, there has been no serious disturbance, but, by breaking camp, declining to follow the usual routine, demonstrating with processions and deputations, and in similar unmilitary ways, the soldiers have made their dissatisfaction clear to all [...] The complaints are varied, and one gathers that they are directed mainly at the red tape and slowness. It is after all, a civilian army, and thousands of men feel that their work is done. They have filled [in their] forms – and nothing happens. Nothing can be said against the authority's arguments that a large army is needed until peace is signed, [and] that 'pivotal' and 'key' men [...] must have the first release, that older men with business and family obligations have a greater claim than the youngster [...]

The disturbances did seem to have had the desired effect. The *Halifax Courier* of 18 January 1919 reported an improvement:

> [T]he protest from the military camps last week, while regrettable in many ways, did apparently bear fruit. The first result was to draw a precise statement from the authorities of their plan of campaign: this cleared the air [...] The second result seems to have been a speeding up in the execution of the plan [...] The statistics tell the story. Last week the discharge is numbered about 5,000 a day; this week's daily total has been 19,000 or 20,000 and the Department sees its way to deal with

nearly 50,000 a day [...] They have naturally retained, as long as they could, the men they thought essential to themselves and thus put Sprag (sic) in the wheel of 'pivotal' and 'key' releases [...] It is also clear that the length of service and wound stripes [are] to count for more. The moral pressure in the ranks has probably brought that about. These things count for more in the minds of the average soldier than the economic claim.

There were frequent complaints that the actual procedure for demobilisation was unnecessarily complicated, time-consuming, and tedious. A returning soldier from the 4th Battalion West Riding Regiment gave the *Halifax Courier* of 11 January 1919 a detailed account of the final stages. It involved a journey to Dublin, followed by a steamer to Holyhead and then on to his 'dispersal point' at Ripon:

At noon we arrived at Ripon and marched to North Camp [...] We were placed in huts to wait, and removed our equipment and had a good meat dinner. At 4 p.m. our party was paraded and we entered the demobilisation machine. First, our papers were checked in one hut [...] The next room visited provided the much coveted ticket [...] This is called an Identity and Protection Certificate [...] Three rings for the post office stamp, when one proceeds there on the months leave to draw weekly pay [...] a railway warrant entitling one to journey to one's home free of charge [...] A few more entries are made on the ticket [...] an advance of £2 [...] a receipt form for 'one overcoat, the property of H.M. Government' entitling [him] to £1 on [its] return to any railway station [...] A smart youth [...] takes your ticket off you, scribbles [...] on the back, denoting whether you go north or south by railway. There is a good deal of red tape, but as matters stand the system is efficient, though it might be made more so if all the signing and scrutinising [of] papers could take place in one room. We had one saturnine gentleman with us who groused all the way from Dublin. He started the same at Ripon and immediately was led in front of a noticeboard and made to read the following:

'Don't grouse you are going home – we are stopping. You are not the only one who is fed up. You'll get home all right – just wait and see. We'll do the rest.'

They then walked out as civilians.

Peace day celebrations

For some time there had been a resolve to mark the official end of the war with organised celebrations. Committees from Halifax and all the surrounding districts had set about organising their own particular mix of events. The official Peace Day date was set for 19 July 1919. Although this day was the climax of the celebrations, events took place on many other days around that date. The *Halifax Courier* of 26 July 1919 reported:

Halifax honoured peace [on] Saturday. One of the outstanding features was the complete spontaneity of people's expressions of loyalty [...] Every class added in some shape or form to the celebrations. The day was given over entirely to rejoicing and nothing marred the pleasure of the occasion [...] the customary rather sombre appearance of the town had been thoroughly transformed. At first it was thought the centre of the borough would out rival all others [...] but with the notable exception of the triumphal arch in Princess Street [...] this was not the case.

It seems that the neighbourhood street parties stole the show:

Little communities [...] had entered into competition with their neighbours [...] Every street, lane and court in town [...] had 'dressed' [with] a similar aggregation of flags and bannerettes, streamers and festoons [...] The most profusely dressed thoroughfares were those numerous streets [...] dwellings rather than shops [...] Quite the prettiest ensemble was seen at Cromwell Street [...] The event of the day [...] was the burning of the ex-Kaiser [...] A sprinkling of paraffin gave him a start and his gradual dismemberment was greeted with loud cheers and laughter. He was filled with crackers, and as his legs fell off,

The Triumphal Arch set up in Princess Street, Halifax for Peace Day, 19 July 1919. Stephen Gee Collection.

Peace Day in an unknown Elland Street 19 July 1919. Stephen Gee Collection.

and were burned through, these went off with a series of explosions, which highly amused the children. The climax of the ceremony was reached when his heavy, two-faced head […] fell down on the setts with a thud.

Larger displays of pyrotechnics took place on Savile Park and Beacon Hill:

The Moor [Savile Park] was crowded with sightseers. There must have been about fifteen thousand present. Suddenly a succession of loud reports rang out, and people had a picture of shells bursting at 1000 feet from the ground – a fine imitation of a phase of anti-aircraft warfare […] The Moor [Savile Park] was revisited by thousands about 9 o'clock […] A magnificent display of night fireworks […]

Naval flares […] were lighted on Beacon Hill [… and] had been arranged for by the Government to form a necessary link in a chain of such illuminations which extended right through the country […] In the earlier part of the evening hundreds of young people had proceeded to the summit be present at the lighting of the flares […]

Even the toffee manufacturers got in on the act:

The chief event in the morning was the distribution of the prettily designed souvenir tins of toffee to the scholars attending the elementary schools and secondary schools in Halifax. 14,000 of these tins, each of which contain half a pound of toffee, had been obtained.

Commemoration

As Halifax was a garrison town it had already undertaken the creation of a memorial in West View Park, Highroad Well, to the soldiers of the Boer War. As their soldiers went to war in 1914, the concept of memorialisation was therefore already in the minds of its citizens.

As early as 1915 there had been references in the newspapers to what the district might do to commemorate the soldiers of the current war. One early possibility was published in 1916, and suggested the use of the Bull Green site, which was the subject of redevelopment at the time.

Memorial to the Boer War, West View Park, Highroad Well. Author's collection.

Proposed memorial to the soldiers of the Great War in Bull Green. Halifax Courier 14 October 1916.

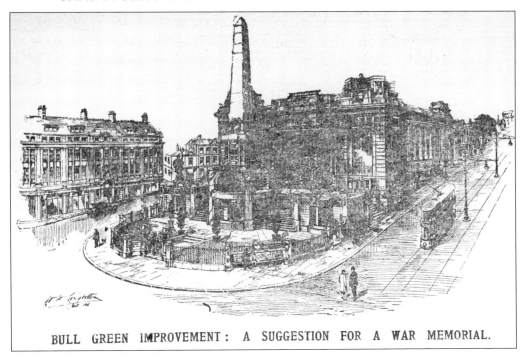

BULL GREEN IMPROVEMENT : A SUGGESTION FOR A WAR MEMORIAL.

By 1917, there was another candidate, Wainhouse Tower, the well-known local folly. This certainly would have dominated the landscape and would have been one of the country's most conspicuous memorials. Joseph Walsh, a significant Halifax architect, of Walsh and Nicholas, wrote to *the Halifax Courier* of 27 October 1917 saying that:

> I have prepared a plan of the site and surroundings [...] if the matter is worthy of further consideration it should be submitted to the very best experts in the country.

The editor of a local art journal believed:

> There is no more noble way of expressing veneration for the dead than by erecting a stately architectural monument.

An integral part of the plan was to create a recreational garden area around it. Some reservations were expressed that Wainhouse Tower would have been a second-hand memorial, and its association with the status of a folly would detract from its dignity.

The idea resurfaced again in a slightly different form in 1918. This time the proposal came from Charles Edward Fox, another notable Halifax architect. The garden idea had become a little more ambitious with proposals to construct a horizontal promenade, with a wall to its rear bearing panels containing bronze plaques with the names of the fallen soldiers. 'The district would then be in possession of a memorial which would be absolutely unique in the country.' It certainly would have been.

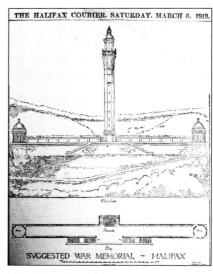

Charles Edward Fox proposal to convert Wainhouse Tower into the Halifax Memorial, Halifax Courier 8 March 1919.

It was nothing if not grandiose, but when the Halifax War Memorial Committee met in April 1919 to consider all the submitted schemes, Wainhouse Tower did not make it to the final six. Under consideration were:

Homes with a central memorial
A public art gallery
A soldiers' garden
A statue or obelisk on Beacon Hill
A triumphal arch, circus at Ward's End
A winter garden and lounge attached to the YMCA

The Halifax memorial was not a 'catch all' for every community or organisation in the Halifax area. The outlying towns and villages of the wider district of Halifax had their own decisions to make, and most schools, firms and churches added their own. There was even an occupational memorial to the butchers of the Halifax borough market. The approach was variable. Most listed the fallen only, but others included the wounded, and a minority included all who had served. Some were boards within buildings, while others were stone monuments of various designs. Some used local craftsmen (Norwood Green) and in some other cases incorporated distinctive local designs (Norland). In Lightcliffe the whole of the Stray (open parkland) was the memorial, and incorporated a stone monument with no names.

For the Halifax memorial, the corporation opted for a replica of the Whitehall Cenotaph, and located this in Belle Vue Park. Designed by H. Scott Davies, it was unveiled by Sir George Fisher-Smith on 15 October 1922. It weighed 130 tons. Many years later, in 1988, it was moved to a new location in Duffy's Park, next to the Halifax Parish Church (later renamed the Halifax Minster).

Royal Antediluvian Order of Buffaloes laying their wreaths at the Halifax Cenotaph in Belle Vue Park. Stephen Gee Collection.

The Halifax Cenotaph at Belle Vue Park. Stephen Gee Collection.

The last word

Ecclesiastical Table Talk was a regular feature in the *Halifax Courier*. As its name suggests, it aired views mainly on religious matters. Most religious denominations broadly supported the war. On 20 January 1917, the column printed an extract of a story from the *Manchester Guardian,* in which the writer had overheard a hospital visitor asking a wounded soldier if he was longing to get back to the front. The soldier's reply was candid:

> If I have to go back, I shall go, and if I go, I'll try and do my duty, but if you ask me if I want to go back, and see my mates blown to pieces, and run a good chance of being blown to pieces myself, I can only say I do not.

For *Ecclesiastical Table Talk* this bore out 'what the writer of this column has heard again and again from wounded soldiers':

> Our soldiers are well instructed as to the principles England stands for [...] it is a profanation to suppose they are fighting with a desire for gain or lust of power, or to destroy Germany as

a nation. It is not to capture German trade or to gain material possessions, but for international righteousness, liberty, and security.

The *Courier* writer might well have added that it was not just the soldiers who were fighting for these beliefs. Despite what many current writers, dramatists and film makers would have us believe, Halifax's Great War had been a good war. This does not mean, of course, that war itself is a good thing. Most people would accept that war is a tragic, wasteful, and in many respects an obscene way of settling differences. The Great War does, however, need to be placed alongside the more frequently accepted World War Two, as a war that had to be fought. The pity is that for its countless dead, for its maimed and traumatised, it is not always remembered that way.

Index